Mediation in Context

of related interest

Advocacy, Counselling and Mediation in Casework
Processes in Empowerment
Edited by Yvonne Joan Craig
Foreword by Daphne Statham
ISBN 1 85302 564 X pb

Advocacy Skills for Health and Social Care Professionals
Neil Bateman
ISBN 1 85302 865 7

Ethical Practice and the Abuse of Power in Social Responsibility
Helen Payne
ISBN 1 85302 743 X pb

Arts Approaches to Conflict
Edited by Marian Liebmann
ISBN 1 85302 293 4 pb

Family Support
Direction from Diversity
John Canavan, Pat Dolan and John Pinkerton
ISBN 1 85302 850 9 pb

Domestic Violence
Guidelines for Research-Informed Practice
Edited by John P. Vincent and Ernest N. Jouriles
ISBN 1 85302 854 1

Making an Impact
Children and Domestic Violence
A Reader
Marianne Hester, Chris Pearson and Nicola Harwin
ISBN 1 85302 844 4 pb

Mediation in Context

Edited by Marian Liebmann

Jessica Kingsley Publishers
London and Philadelphia

First published in the United Kingdom in 2000 by
Jessica Kingsley Publishers Ltd,
116 Pentonville Road, London
N1 9JB, England
and
325 Chestnut Street,
Philadelphia PA 19106, USA.

www.jkp.com

© Copyright 2000 Jessica Kingsley Publishers

Library of Congress Cataloging in Publication Data
Mediation in context / edited by Marian Liebmann.
   p.   cm.
Includes bibliographical references and index.
ISBN 1 85302 618 2 (pbk : alk paper)
1. Mediation--Great Britain. 2. Conflict management–Great Britain. I.
Liebmann, Marian, 1942–
HM1126.M44 2000
303.6'9–dc21   00-039120

British Library Cataloguing in Publication Data
A CIP catalogue record for this book is available from the British Library

ISBN 1 85302 618 2 pb

Printed and Bound in Great Britain by
Athenaeum Press, Gateshead, Tyne and Wear

Contents

List of figures

List of tables

List of boxes

Introduction

Marian Liebmann

The rise of mediation

Although mediation is a traditional non-confrontational method of resolving conflict and practised widely in Asia and Africa, the West has used largely adversarial means of achieving resolution during the last few hundred years. The recognition that courts often do not resolve conflicts, especially where a continuing relationship is involved, has led to a recent interest in mediation and a burgeoning of mediation services.

This book has arisen from the need of professionals in a variety of fields to know more about mediation and how it operates in the different contexts where it is practised. There is still very little literature on mediation in the UK, despite the advanced state of much practice. This book is written from the UK perspective but most of the material will also be relevant elsewhere. Many of the ideas and practices grew from contact with American and Australian mediation services, were amended to suit UK circumstances, and in turn are now being adopted and adapted by several European countries.

Such is the speed of current developments in mediation that it is impossible to write a book that is up to date. Already several chapters have been revised at least once. It is hoped that readers will bear this in mind. Nevertheless the main basis of knowledge and information of each chapter will still hold good, as practice has developed to quite a firm standard in most areas.

This introductory chapter contains some basic definitions and an outline of the benefits and limitations of mediation, and the conflict resolution principles lying behind mediation. The chapter goes on to look at mediation and justice, the processes of mediation and an overview of the chapters in the book. The chapter finishes with comments on recent trends: working across the board; standards and accreditation; equal opportunities and anti-discriminatory practice.

Some definitions

It may be helpful to include some definitions here, although some of them may be modified slightly by their different contexts (Mediation UK 1995).

- *Negotiation* is a general term for the process of disputants working out an agreement between themselves.

- *Mediation* is a process by which an impartial third party helps two (or more) disputants work out how to resolve a conflict. The disputants, not the mediators, decide the terms of any agreement reached. Mediation usually focuses on future rather than past behaviour.

- *Arbitration* is a process in which an impartial third party (after hearing from both sides) makes a final, usually binding, decision. The discussion and decision, while structured, may not be as regulated by formal procedures and rules of evidence as is courtroom procedure.

- *Litigation* is the process of settling a dispute in court according to legal statutes, with advocates presenting evidence on behalf of the parties. Litigation is an adversarial process, in which a judge (or jury) adjudicates in favour of one party after hearing both sides.

These processes can be seen to range from the least interventionist (negotiation) to the most interventionist (litigation). At either end are two other forms of dealing with conflict: 'avoidance' and 'aggression' (Moore 1986) (Figure I.1).

Figure I.1 Dispute resolution methods

Thus mediation is the least interventionist of the dispute resolution methods which involve a third party, and the intervention by the third party is limited, as the decision making remains with the parties themselves.

Benefits of mediation

- It encourages disputing parties to focus on the problem rather than on each other. Instead of taking up positions, parties are encouraged to look at their needs and interests in a particular situation. Mediators help to identify common ground between the disputants and help them look for the way forward.
- It gives both parties an opportunity to tell their side of the story.
- It provides a setting in which both parties can listen to and hear the other party's story.
- People are more likely to change their actions if they hear how their behaviour is affecting the other person.
- People are more likely to keep to a solution they have been involved in reaching than one imposed by an outside person.
- A solution imposed by a court generally makes one party a winner and the other party a loser. Mediators help parties look for a 'win–win' solution.
- People are able to reach agreements which can take their particular situation into account.
- Mediators encourage people to identify what they really want from the situation.
- Mediation is a confidential process – this enables people to speak without the fear that their words will be taken down and used in evidence against them. The Court of Appeal decided that admissions or conciliatory gestures made during mediation are not admissible if the mediation is unsuccessful and comes to court, except in the rare case where someone indicates that he has caused, or was likely the cause of, severe harm to a child (*Re D (minors)* Court of Appeal, 11 February 1993. TLR 12 February).
- Mediation is more likely to get to the root of the problem.
- Disputes have many strands or aspects to them. Courts can only deal with matters of law, which means in many cases they cannot deal with the whole picture.
- Although mediation looks at the past, its focus is on the future – how do the parties want the situation to be from now on? This is important where there is a continuing relationship.

The general public seems to find the legal system unsatisfactory for similar reasons to those mentioned above. A survey carried out by the National Consumer Council (Taylor Nelson AGB 1995) showed that about three-quarters of those who had experienced a serious dispute agreed that the present legal system was too slow, too complicated, too easy to twist if you knew the rules, needed bringing up to date, and was off-putting for ordinary people.

All those who had experienced a dispute were then given three alternative ways in which the case could be resolved and asked which they preferred. Only 8 per cent preferred 'a full trial in court'; 23 per cent opted for 'sitting round a table with an independent expert who makes the decision'. The largest majority, 53 per cent, chose 'sitting round a table with an independent expert who helps you to reach an agreement between yourselves'. Those with recent experience of going to court made similar choices. Clearly the idea of mediation appeals to a growing number of people.

Limitations of mediation

It is important to know when mediation is appropriate and when it is not. There are several indications which may help to determine this (Acland 1995; Liebmann 1994). Mediation can help when:

- the law is not clear;
- both parties want to keep on good terms with each other;
- it is in both parties' interests to sort things out;
- both parties are tired of the dispute;
- there is good will on both sides.

Mediation is not appropriate if:

- either party is unwilling;
- either party is incapable of taking part or keeping to an agreement;
- it is not really in one party's interest to settle;
- there are threats or fear of violence and police action may be indicated;
- the dispute needs a public judgement.

Conflict resolution principles

Implicit in mediation work is a set of ideas and values, which emphasise such concepts as:

- listening to others, for feelings as well as facts;
- co-operation with others, valuing their contributions;
- looking for common ground rather than differences;

- affirmation of self and others as a necessary basis for resolving conflict;
- speaking for oneself rather than accusing others;
- separating the problem from the people;
- trying to understand other people's points of view;
- using a creative problem-solving approach to work on conflicts;
- looking at what people want for the future rather than allocating blame for the past;
- looking at all the options before selecting one to try;
- looking for a 'win–win' solution, where everyone's interests are satisfied, rather than the adversarial 'win–lose' approach where one person wins and the other person loses (Cornelius and Faire 1989; Liebmann 1994, 1996).

Mediation and justice

Mediation agreements do not have any special legal status and are not legally binding (although they can subsequently be made binding if both parties wish). Mediation agreements are made and kept because it is in the interest of both parties to do so. One of the advantages of mediation is that agreements can be made without recourse to the law. Occasionally parties will make a formal contract to mediate before starting the process, but usually an informal agreement to do so is regarded as sufficient.

Given the advantages of informality, speed and ability to take both parties' interests into account, it makes sense for mediation to replace legal solutions where possible. There is some evidence (Faulkes 1991) that this is slightly more possible at the beginning of a dispute, when neighbours may still have a reasonable relationship with each other, and also at the end, when the dispute has 'run its course' and both sides are heartily sick of it and can see no good in continuing, especially if court costs are escalating out of hand.

The increasing costs of civil litigation and the length of time taken to deal with cases led to the Woolf Inquiry on 'Access to Justice'. The interim and final reports were published in 1995 and 1996, in which Lord Woolf highlighted the benefits of alternative dispute resolution (ADR) and mediation (see Chapter 1 for more details).

Nevertheless, there are some dangers in overenthusiastic use of mediation. There is a fear that mediation will result in the least powerful party agreeing to the demands of the other party, because they 'fear the worst' outside the mediation setting. There is also anecdotal evidence from the USA that mediation can be in danger of being used as 'cheap justice'. Another danger is that of disguising responsibility (e.g. noise disputes where the real culprit is poor soundproofing) and of ignoring rights (Grosskurth 1996). Poorer citizens may be diverted to mediation because it is cheaper on the public purse, while citizens who can afford a lawyer have the choice whether to go to mediation or to go to law. There is also the point that compulsory mediation can result in parties just 'going through the motions' when they have been directed to mediation, rather than choosing it voluntarily. Sometimes parties directed to mediation are willing – but unable to abide by decisions made, due to mental health or learning difficulties. Most mediators feel that mediation has to be a voluntary process, with meaningful participation, to stand a chance of working properly. There is still a great need for public education so that people can choose mediation appropriately.

Some community justice centres in Australia and the USA have found a useful compromise formula. The court may direct neighbours to attend a compulsory information session given by the mediation service, after which the parties may choose whether to go for mediation or to come back to the law court. In this way mediation is described by the people who will undertake it, while also giving parties the chance to ask questions and to check out the mediation service for themselves. This approach was included in the Family Law Act 1996 and is one of the options in a current discussion paper from the Lord Chancellor's Department (LCD) on ADR (ADR Policy Branch, LCD 1999). However, there are doubts arising as to whether this is the most effective way to encourage the use of mediation (see also Chapter 1, 'New developments in civil justice').

This situation may not arise in some sectors, such as community mediation, as very few disputes would go to court. However, it is still necessary to guard against 'compulsory mediation' in the form of pressure from other authorities, while welcoming the offer of mediation before other harsher measures are tried.

Processes of mediation

Mediation can be practised in several ways, using different processes. What they all have in common is that they have a number of stages, and that the mediator is impartial and does not make a judgement. Particular processes all have their champions, but there are also questions of context.

In employment and commercial mediation, it is customary for all parties to meet briefly at the start of the process to share opening statements. Then the parties separate to different rooms in the same building, while the mediator 'shuttles' between them, carrying messages and offers. This separation helps to keep commercial and industrial confidentiality. When the parties have agreed all the substantive issues, they are brought together to finalise the details and sign the agreement.

In community mediation, by contrast, the process usually starts with visits by the mediators to the disputing parties separately in their own homes. This may be vital in gaining an understanding of neighbour disputes. The mediation can then proceed with a face-to-face meeting or with 'shuttle mediation', depending on whether the parties are willing to meet.

Family mediation has a tradition of working directly (i.e. face to face) with the parties, but where there is the possibility of domestic violence, individual screening interviews are now practised by National Family Mediation (NFM) affiliated services. Victim–offender mediation also proceeds carefully, with safety in mind. Good separate preparation of the parties is regarded as the foundation of the final joint meeting.

Environmental mediation usually includes designing a process to fit the particular situation, using a mixture of differently sized meetings to accomplish the decision-making process. School-based peer mediation is nearly always face to face.

Mediators in all sectors are trained, but some sectors have a tradition of using volunteers (community mediation; elder mediation; peer mediation; some victim–offender mediation); others have sessionally paid workers (family mediation; medical mediation; some victim–offender mediation), while some mediators are salaried or freelance professionals (Advisory, Conciliation and Arbitration Service, ACAS; workplace mediation; commercial mediation; environmental mediation). This situation is fluid and may change as mediation develops.

The decision whether to use volunteer or paid mediators is sometimes based on the obvious factor of cost. But it may also be based on the philosophy of the service. Some mediation services believe in a grass-roots, community-based philosophy, in which mediation is a skill to be passed on to as many people as possible. Such a service would use volunteer mediators as a matter of principle. Other mediation services concentrate on service delivery. Such a service might use paid mediators because in some areas this would probably provide a more reliable service. (This does not imply that volunteer mediators are less competent than paid ones – but in some areas they are hard to recruit.)

Similarly, there are differences between sectors concerning clients' payment for mediation. Community mediation, victim–offender mediation, school mediation and medical mediation are generally free of charge. This is partly because many of its clients are not in a position to pay, but also because mediation is often an alternative to free statutory services, such as environmental health, so any charge would be a barrier to the use of mediation. This is not the case where the alternative is a court case, as in divorce proceedings. Most family mediation services charge on a sliding scale and those eligible for legal aid can claim a free service. Where the alternative is a lengthy and expensive court case, as in commercial mediation, mediators charge professional fees, which still represent considerable savings for their clients.

Overview of chapters

Chapter 1 gives a history and overview of mediation in the UK, to set the scene for the subsequent chapters which describe mediation in different contexts. These chapters are designed to show the reader how the mediation process works in a particular context, so the mediation process is described in each one in much greater detail than in this chapter. To someone reading this book from beginning to end, this may seem repetitive, but it is useful for anyone using a particular chapter as a starting point for further research. The chapters have different styles, reflecting both the context and the author's perspective.

The book covers the main fields where mediation is currently practised, but new fields are developing all the time, so any omission will be for the next volume. Where there is more than one chapter covering a particular sector, the chapters are concerned with different aspects of the same context – for instance, peer mediation in primary and secondary schools.

Each chapter includes one or more case studies. In some chapters, these are presented separately to illustrate the whole process, while in others case studies (or different stages of one case) are included to illustrate different stages or points being made. Some chapters also include cases found unsuitable for mediation, with the reasons. Case studies are in italic script to help the reader identify them easily.

At the end of the book is a list of national mediation organisations in the UK and a Further Reading list for those who want to explore particular sectors or aspects of mediation in more detail.

Working across the board

Although each kind of mediation is presented in this book as operating separately, there is an increasing tendency for services to undertake more than one kind of mediation. Chapter 7 on community mediation in the USA points the way, with its expansion from community mediation to include agricultural mediation, victim–offender mediation, schools mediation, mental health mediation and equal opportunities mediation.

In the UK, many experienced community mediation services branch out to take on school peer mediation and victim–offender mediation. A few have also taken on family mediation, while one or two family mediation services have applied for funds to expand into community mediation. Thus many UK mediation services are now on their way to becoming 'multi-mediation centres'.

Similarly, mediators and mediation staff have begun to work across the board, so that there are several who now work in community and in family mediation, or in schools and in victim–offender mediation, or in community and medical mediation, and so on. At the moment this may mean undertaking more than one training, though in some situations they can do a basic mediation training and then further specialist training in the areas of mediation where they choose to work.

There are several national mediation organisations, mostly catering for a particular kind of mediation; and some sectors have several national organisations involved in mediation. The picture will be clarified in Chapter 1. Some of the larger national organisations also have a regional structure, so that mediators and services can meet each other locally and join together for such purposes as conferences and further training.

The questions of transferability of skills and organisational co-operation are already under discussion at a national level. The new Joint Mediation Forum (involving most of the national mediation organisations) has begun to meet, to discuss the possibility of positive collaboration, including the development of joint standards. Some mediation organisations would like to see an overarching body for all mediation, while others feel this is not appropriate for them.

Looking further afield, mediation in the UK has always had links with the USA and Australia, but is now developing more links with Europe. Family and commercial mediation are well known in Europe, and there are European forums for mediation in schools and for victim–offender mediation. Community mediation is more established in the UK than in the rest of Europe, but there is increasing interest now in several countries. The European Conference in Peacemaking and Conflict Resolution (ECPCR) has been meeting biennially since 1992.

Equal opportunities and anti-discriminatory practice

Although it is not the focus of this book, and some chapters may not mention it, equal opportunities and anti-discriminatory practice are of great concern to mediation services, especially those providing a public service. The aim is to provide equal access to mediation for all members of the community. This involves recruitment policies for administrative staff and mediators, accessibility of buildings, provision of interpreters, translation of leaflets, awareness of bias and stereotyping, learning how to handle racism from mediation clients, and much more. Britain is now a multicultural society and this needs to be acknowledged in every service provided.

There is an extra point of concern for mediation: those who fear that mediation will take away people's rights or rubber-stamp an unacceptable 'status quo' need to be reassured that mediators are aware of these dangers and sensitive to clients' rights, as well as their needs and culture.

Conclusion

This is a very exciting time for mediation, especially in the UK. The dissatisfaction with litigation and the good experiences from mediation so far have combined to push mediation from the margins to the mainstream of many organisations and processes. The chapters in this book will give a flavour of mediation and how it works in the main contexts where it is practised at the moment. This may only be the start – many more kinds of mediation are already being tried out and may become established practice within a short time. Whatever the context, the principles remain the same, so are transferable to new fields, given thoughtfulness and creativity.

Acknowledgements

Some parts of this chapter have already appeared in *Community and Neighbour Mediation* (ed. M. Liebmann), 1998, London: Cavendish.

I would also like to acknowledge the help of the following in reading this chapter: Tony Billinghurst, Mark Bitel, Sue Bowers, Mike Coldham and Marion Wells.

References

Acland, A. (1995) *Resolving Disputes Without Going to Court.* London: Century.

ADR Policy Branch, Lord Chancellor's Department (1999) *Alternative Dispute Resolution: A Discussion Paper.* London: LCD.

Cornelius, C. and Faire, S. (1989) *Everyone Can Win.* Sydney: Simon and Schuster.

Faulkes, W. (1991) 'Community mediation as a crime prevention strategy.' Plenary address, Forum for Initiatives in Reparation and Mediation Annual Conference, 2 July.

Grosskurth, A. (1996) 'Mediation: forming a view.' In R. Smith (ed.) *Achieving Civil Justice: Appropriate Dispute Resolution for the 1990s.* London: Legal Action Group.

Liebmann, M. (1994) *Neighbours' Quarrels.* London: Channel Four Television.

Liebmann, M. (1996) *Arts Approaches to Conflict.* London: Jessica Kingsley Publishers.

Mediation UK (1995) *Training Manual in Community Mediation Skills.* Bristol: Mediation UK.

Moore, C. (1986) *The Mediation Process: Practical Strategies for Resolving Conflict.* San Francisco: Jossey-Bass.

Taylor Nelson AGB (1995) *Civil Law and the Public.* London: National Consumer Council.

Lord Woolf (1995) *Access to Justice: Interim Report to the Lord Chancellor on the Civil Justice System in England and Wales.* London: HMSO.

Lord Woolf (1996) *Access to Justice: Final Report to the Lord Chancellor on the Civil Justice System in England and Wales.* London: HMSO.

1

History and Overview
of Mediation in the UK
Marian Liebmann

Introduction

Although mediation still feels relatively new in the UK, there were several initiatives
as early as the 1970s. In those first days of mediation in the UK, the few pioneers
developed links across their different fields to prevent isolation. Developments have
gone ahead more quickly in some fields than others. However, small changes in
funding, government policy, the law and climate of opinion can make a big
difference, leading to rapid expansion in different sectors. This chapter attempts to
chart the history and development of the most well-known sectors, and provide an
overview of mediation activity in the UK. The sectors are described in the order in
which they started in the UK.

Industrial/employment mediation

In the employment field, the development of conciliation/mediation services was
associated with laws designed to safeguard individual employment rights. There
were several Acts of Parliament over the years 1963 to 1974 (Contracts of
Employment Act 1963, amended in 1972; Redundancy Payments Act 1965;
Industrial Relations Act 1971; Trade Union and Labour Relations Act 1974),
leading to the provision of five services: collective conciliation, individual conciliation, arbitration, advisory work and longer term inquiries. These were all under
way by the early 1970s.

However, there were worries, especially from trade unions, that these services
might be affected by government incomes policy, and doubts also arose concerning
the independence of the services from government influence or even control (ACAS
undated).

The new (Labour) government which took office in February 1974 introduced
the Trade Union and Labour Relations Act 1974, and then set up an independent
Conciliation and Arbitration Service, which started on 2 September 1974, with a
London headquarters and offices in Scotland, Wales and six English regional centres.

In January 1975 the title was changed to the Advisory, Conciliation and Arbitration Service (ACAS) and on 1 January 1976 ACAS became a statutory body under the Employment Protection Act 1975. Its independence was enshrined in Schedule 1 (paragraph 11) of this Act:

> The functions of the Service and of its officers and servants shall be performed on behalf of the Crown, but the Service shall not be subject to directions of any kind from any Minister of the Crown as to the matter in which it is to exercise any of its functions under any enactment.

Although ACAS is best known (especially in its early days) for resolving high-profile industrial disputes, it also does considerable work 'behind the scenes', preventing disputes from escalating, promoting good industrial relations, dealing with individual cases of employee and employer disputes (ACAS 1996a). Its mission is 'to improve the performance and effectiveness of organisations by providing an independent and impartial service to prevent and resolve disputes and to build harmonious relationships at work'. To achieve this, ACAS seeks to:

- prevent and resolve employment disputes;
- conciliate in actual or potential complaints to industrial tribunals;
- provide information and advice;
- promote good practice (ACAS 1996b).

It is worth noting that ACAS uses the terms 'conciliation' and 'mediation' in a slightly different way from most other organisations. 'Conciliation' is used for the process which is elsewhere known as mediation, that is, a voluntary process in which a conciliator tries to facilitate two disputing parties to work out their own agreement. 'Mediation' is used for a process similar to arbitration, where the mediator hears the evidence and arguments of both sides and then makes a decision. Whereas arbitration is binding, ACAS mediation makes formal but non-binding recommendations intended to provide a basis for settlement of the dispute (ACAS 1995).

Most ACAS conciliators come to ACAS from other government posts in the field of employment and industry and attend in-service training courses at appropriate intervals. They are usually full-time permanent employees.

From April 2000 the Employment Rights (Dispute Resolution) Act 1999 changed the way cases are processed by employment tribunals (formerly called industrial tribunals). It introduced a voluntary binding arbitration procedure, and powers for ACAS to develop a new national arbitration service. There are also new powers for the Chair of an Employment Tribunal to refer the case back to the employer, to be dealt with more informally.

Family mediation

The roots of family mediation go back to the 1970s. In 1973 the Finer Committee examined the situation of the growing number of one-parent families and proposed a Family Court with a Conciliation Service attached to it to tackle the issues arising from separation and divorce, which often led to poverty. The issues needing attention were children, finance and property. However, the government did not respond to these recommendations and professionals dealing with these problems became increasingly frustrated (Fisher 1993).

Two voluntary initiatives in the late 1970s attempted to address these problems. Senior court welfare officers in Surrey and south east London set up a system of volunteer conciliators as an alternative to the ordering of welfare reports by the courts. In 1978 the first independent Family Conciliation Service was set up as a pilot project in Bristol, to help separating or divorcing parents agree arrangements for their children.

More initiatives followed suit and in 1981 they came together to form the National Family Conciliation Council (NFCC), with about twenty local services, of which ten took referrals directly from the public. Although initially the word 'conciliation' was used (perhaps because of the ACAS usage), as time went on the word 'mediation' began to be used more often, and both words described the same process. In recognition of this, NFCC changed its name in 1992 to the National Association of Family Mediation and Conciliation Services. This was abbreviated to National Family Mediation (NFM), which is now its formal title.

The Solicitors Family Law Association (SFLA) was formed in 1982 to encourage a settlement-seeking approach in matrimonial proceedings, and many members of the SFLA were involved in their local family conciliation services (Parkinson 1997).

Within NFM, family mediators were initially qualified social workers or trained Relate (formerly Marriage Guidance) counsellors, although recently these criteria have become more flexible to include a wider range of people. Most mediators are paid sessionally and undertake their training partly with their local service and partly at the annual national training course.

Most local family mediation services only mediated in cases where a separating couple had children, and dealt with issues around children, but not property or finance. The Family Mediators Association was launched in 1988 by Lisa Parkinson (one of the original co-founders of the first Family Conciliation Service in Bristol) and a management board (Parkinson 1997). It aim was to provide mediation in respect of property and finance issues, which were often stumbling blocks preventing agreement concerning the children. The FMA offers the help of two mediators who work together as a team – one an experienced family solicitor, the other a qualified professional with experience in marital and family work, both with mediation training (FMA undated). It is a fee-paying service for any couple with or without children. However, the need to make this service pay for itself means that these fees are out of reach for many people.

The 1989 Report of the Conciliation Project Unit on the Costs and Effectiveness of Conciliation in England and Wales recommended that family mediation should not be restricted to issues directly connected with arrangements for children. In response, National Family Mediation developed pilot projects in five areas which already had family mediation services. These pilot projects were evaluated between 1990 and 1993. The report published in 1994 showed that users of 'all-issues mediation' gained greater benefit by sorting out all the issues, and saw mediation as a cost-effective alternative to the traditional legal process (Joseph Rowntree Foundation 1996).

There are now 70 family mediation services affiliated to NFM, of which 58 offer 'all-issues mediation'. They are grouped into seven regions, covering England, Wales and Northern Ireland. There is a separate organisation Family Mediation Scotland which covers Scotland. On 1 January 1996, the three main family mediation bodies (National Family Mediation, Family Mediators Association and Family Mediation Scotland) jointly founded the UK College of Family Mediators, to promote family mediation, establish recognised standards of training and make available details of registered mediators (UK College of Family Mediators 1996).

The Family Law Act 1996 introduced no-fault divorce proceedings and a staged process for divorcing couples to follow. Section 29 of the Act makes provision for legal aid for mediation in the same way as for legal representation (NFM 1996). To claim legal aid for divorce, couples must first attend a meeting with a mediation service, to see if mediation is suitable. In practice, if either party is unwilling to go to mediation, it is deemed unsuitable and the couple can then claim legal aid for the court case, using solicitors in the traditional way.

Mediation is now available from National Family Mediation, the Family Mediators Association, Family Mediation Scotland and an increasing number of solicitors who have trained in family mediation (encouraged by the formation of the British Association of Lawyer Mediators, BALM), provided that they are awarded franchises by the Legal Aid Board, for which they must meet quality standards. The SFLA offered its first training course for members in all-issues mediation in June 1996 (Parkinson 1997).

The Family Law Act also included, as a first step for all couples, an information meeting to ensure full understanding of what divorce involves; and to give infor-mation on the availability and advantages of mediation, so as to encourage the use of mediation rather than litigation, where possible. These meetings were piloted but stopped prematurely in June 1999 when their results were not deemed satisfactory, and this has delayed implementation of the Act. However, the claiming of legal aid via Section 29 has not been affected.

Another fairly recent development is screening for domestic violence, arising out of research on family mediation services and domestic violence (Hester, Pearson and Radford 1997). This means that family mediation services now offer separate interviews to each person to check for domestic violence, and determine whether this would make mediation useless or even dangerous (Allport and Bramwell 1999).

Mediation in the context of domestic violence is usually regarded as a taboo area, but Plymouth Mediation (a community and victim–offender mediation service) ran a successful scheme from 1995 to 1997, involving support for the victims, and work with the perpetrators by the local probation service, after which mediation was offered to those who wished. It ceased when its funding ended.

For the most part, family mediation services have concentrated on disputes arising from separation and divorce. For other family disputes, such as inter-generational disagreements, a variety of agencies may be called on. If family conflict is very entrenched and affecting the well-being of children, social or health services may become involved, using family counselling or therapy. Some family mediation services do provide a service for such disputes, and community mediation services in some areas also help. Additionally, there are some new specialist mediation services which mediate between homeless young people and their parents.

Schools conflict resolution and mediation

Conflict resolution work in schools started in the UK in 1981, with the Kingston Friends Workshop Group, which developed methods of teaching children how to resolve conflict peacefully. These workshops were taken up enthusiastically by teachers, social workers and managers in business and the community. A visit in 1982 from the Children's Creative Response to Conflict Programme in the USA gave the group many new training methods and materials, including mediation skills (Rawlings 1996). The materials developed by the group were compiled into the manual *Ways and Means* (1986), which sold out immediately, and several editions have since been produced.

Several other Quaker groups followed this example and two workers from Quaker Peace & Service, based at Friends House, London, gave support to such initiatives. One of the ways they did this was by hosting twice-yearly meetings for all those (not just Quakers) interested in conflict resolution in schools. They also helped to form the European Network for Conflict Resolution in Education (ENCORE) in 1990, when a group of interested practitioners met in Brussels, following the publication of a report on violence and conflict resolution in European schools (Walker 1989). ENCORE has held yearly conferences in different places in Europe since then (Belgium, Northern Ireland, Germany, Hungary, Romania). In 1991 the group formulated its aims (centred around supporting the development of conflict resolution and mediation skills in schools) and produced a leaflet in four languages – English, French, Russian, Spanish (Bentley 1997; ENCORE undated).

Schools work has grown gradually in the UK. Several independent projects have been set up to work in schools and quite a few schools have incorporated conflict resolution and mediation practices into their framework, either 'piecemeal' or, better, as a whole school policy. There are currently 45 school mediation projects (Mediation UK figures, August 1999), some working in several schools.

For the first few years most of the schools work concentrated on teaching children, usually in primary schools, about conflict resolution. More recently this work has developed to include school-based peer mediation training and schemes, in which children are trained to mediate in playground disputes. Most of the early schemes were in primary schools because of their more flexible timetables. Peer mediation has also now moved into secondary schools and a National Organisation of Peer Mediators for young people (13–25) had its launch meeting in February 1997. It ran six national conferences for young conflict resolvers and peer educators. These have led to a three-year Youth Network Project from 1999, designed and led by young people (Hazzard 1999).

As community mediation services became established, many felt that the logical extension of their work was to take it into schools and teach the next generation how to resolve conflict, as a preventative life skill. So there are now a considerable number of community mediation services which have a 'schools group' and, in fortunate cases, a funded schools worker to develop this work. Schools work may also be part of a 'crime prevention package' for intensive work on high-crime housing estates. Conversely, victim–offender mediation enthusiasts have started taking their restorative justice philosophy into schools. One county mediation service (Devon) has devised a way of spreading peer mediation to all schools in its area over five years, and has been asked to do the same for Cornwall.

A recent opening for mediation in schools has been created by the publication of the Crick Report (Citizenship Advisory Group 1998) recommending that all schools should study citizenship. The summary of the final report identifies three strands:

1.   Social and moral responsibility.

2.   Community involvement.

3.   Political literacy.

The revised statutory National Curriculum incorporates citizenship at Key Stages 3 and 4 (years 7–11 at secondary school) and suggests that schools should include practical opportunities to learn skills in these areas, including relationships in school (QCA and DfEE 1999). Clearly peer mediation is one excellent and practical way of meeting these curriculum requirements.

Several of the primary and middle school conflict resolution and peer mediation projects developed their own materials, so there is an abundance of good manuals and other resources to draw on. For secondary schools Mediation UK drew together a group of experienced people to produce a suitable manual, *Mediation Works!* (Mediation UK 1998a).

As peer mediation becomes more widespread, practitioners have started to think more about 'whole school approaches', in which peer mediation is just one part of a coherent philosophy based on conflict resolution principles and values.

Victim–offender mediation

The first interest in the UK occurred in 1972 when members of BACRO (Bristol Association for the Care and Resettlement of Offenders) considered victim–offender mediation as a means of helping offenders see the consequences of their actions. They realised they knew nothing about victims of crime and their perspective, so they started a pilot Victim Support group in Bristol. This raised awareness of victims' needs and led to many other similar schemes and the formation of the National Association of Victims Support Schemes (NAVSS, now called Victim Support) in 1979 (Victim Support 1982).

The first recorded victim–offender mediation and reparation service was started in 1974 by Mennonites in Kitchener, Ontario, when two young men apologised to their victims for 20 burglaries and paid compensation for all they had taken. Interest spread to the rest of North America and to the UK (Zehr 1990).

Victim Support took a lead in gathering the growing UK interest and helped to establish the Forum for Initiatives in Reparation and Mediation (FIRM, now Mediation UK) in 1984 (Reeves 1987). The increasing awareness of victims' needs also influenced the practice of victim–offender mediation and fostered interest in it.

A victim–offender mediation project was established in South Yorkshire in 1983 and four services were funded and researched by the Home Office between 1985 and 1987 (Marshall and Merry 1990). The Home Office took a great interest in the growing number of mediation schemes in the early 1980s, mainly with a view to diverting offenders from prison, which was beginning to be seen as an expensive and ineffective response to crime. As part of this interest, a senior Home Office researcher, Tony Marshall, undertook to update the NAVSS survey. This survey (Marshall 1984) showed the existence of five police-based reparation schemes, three court-based reparation schemes and two encounter groups (groups of victims and offenders meeting, not based on the same crime).

Things were changing so fast that the list of projects became out of date very quickly, and the Home Office published a new version only a year later (Marshall and Walpole 1985). The number of victim–offender mediation and reparation schemes operating or in the final planning stages had risen from 10 to 36.

Over the succeeding 12 years, an increasingly punitive criminal justice policy under a Conservative government had little interest in victim–offender mediation. Several services ceased due to financial cutbacks and a few new ones started, the total number of services remaining static. Despite this barren climate, three out of the four services originally funded by the Home Office between 1985 and 1987 went from strength to strength. Three large county areas have strongly supported victim–offender mediation, mostly funded by the probation service. The current number of services and projects is 46 (Mediation UK figures, August 1999).

Victim–offender services continued to develop their work. The Leeds service produced a training handbook (Quill and Wynne 1993) and Mediation UK issued guidelines on starting a service (Mediation UK 1993a). Research on the 1985–7 phase had shown a bias towards offenders, so services altered their practice to be more 'victim-friendly', so that victims, offenders and courts alike found the service very helpful. Several research studies were carried out, all of which showed positive experiences for victims, offenders and the courts, and a tendency towards reducing reoffending (Braithwaite and Liebmann 1997).

Victim–offender mediation has received a new direction with the election of the Labour government in 1997 and their decision to major on youth crime. The Crime and Disorder Act 1998 introduced Reparation Orders (and other orders in which reparation plays a part) in which young offenders (10–17) are required to make reparation to their victims or the community. Although victim–offender mediation is not specified in the legislation, the Youth Justice Board guidelines (1999) recommend it as the means to accomplish the reparation. The related practice of Family Group Conferencing, originating in New Zealand and Australia and involving the family and wider community in the process, is also spreading in the UK. The Youth Justice Board has granted funding to help start 47 new victim–offender mediation and conferencing projects during the year 1999–2000. This will radically change the face of victim–offender mediation in the UK.

With this expansion, many more organisations have become involved in victim–offender mediation, and the term 'restorative justice' has come into use to describe all the initiatives with mediation values. The recently founded (1997) Restorative Justice Consortium aims to bring together national organisations involved or interested in this field.

Community mediation

In the early 1980s, several well-known leaders in mediation and conflict resolution from the USA and Australia came to the UK and spoke to a variety of audiences. These meetings and contacts spread information about what was happening and at the same time brought together those in the UK who were interested in pursuing mediation, both in the community and neighbourhood context, and with victims and offenders in the criminal justice context.

In the 1984 survey (Marshall 1984) only two were community mediation schemes, Newham Conflict and Change Project and Edgware Mediation Service. At that time, mediation was virtually synonymous with victim–offender mediation.

By 1985 (Marshall and Walpole 1985), the balance had changed slightly and there were 7 community mediation services out of a total of 38. The earliest three services in this list were Newham Conflict and Change Project, London (1983); Southwark Mediation Centre, London (1984); and Sandwell Mediation and Reparation Scheme, West Midlands (1985) (undertaking both community and victim–offender mediation). These are all still in operation.

Mediation UK has taken a large role in helping to spread the practice of community and neighbour mediation, for instance, by publishing the *Guide to Starting a Community Mediation Service* (1993b), the *Training Manual in Community Mediation Skills* (1995) and the *Community Mediation Video* (1996a). There are currently 124 community mediation services (Mediation UK figures, August 1999) and the number of cases referred to these services rose from 7890 in 1997 to 11,504 in 1998 (Mediation UK figures, December 1999). The most common model is still the independent community mediation service, probably because this is how community mediation started and because it is seen as a good way of ensuring that mediation is seen as truly impartial. The situation differs in Scotland, where there are more in-house mediation services (Dignan and Sorsby 1999).

Much of this expansion has happened because local authorities have become convinced about the value of community mediation. The Department of the Environment booklet *Mediation: Benefits and Practice* (produced with help from Mediation UK, following a joint Noise Mediation Seminar), circulated in November 1994, was very influential in this respect. Although the Department of the Environment did not promise any funds for local mediation services, it gave the concept its blessing and encouraged local authorities to support or develop local initiatives. Local authorities pay keen attention to government circulars and this gave many of them the 'green light' to go ahead.

Whereas the first community mediation services were almost all to be found in inner city areas, some of the newer ones are based in small towns and rural areas. While some of the rise in neighbour disputes is due to the stress of urban living, there are also many neighbour disputes to be found in all sections of the community, e.g. boundary disputes, noise disputes and disputes between community groups.

From the early days, there were two strands of thinking that informed the community mediation movement, which are still present in current practice. The first is the 'grass-roots' aim of providing self-help schemes for people to sort out their own problems, rather than have them escalate into the hands of the law. This philosophy emphasises informality, volunteer help, benefits to the community as a whole and community-based independent management of mediation services.

The second strand is more 'agency led', a response by local authorities, and other statutory organisations to the ineffectiveness and expense of legal solutions to neighbour and community disputes. Moreover, if they provide the funding for the local mediation service, they want to see a degree of effectiveness, measured in their terms. This philosophy emphasises clear procedures, a degree of formality and measurable outcomes. Often such services are only provided for specific clients, such as local authority tenants.

As more local authorities decide that mediation is the way forward for them in handling neighbour disputes, many of them take the lead in starting them. Some of these services may be part of the line management structure of the funding agency (often a local housing department), but retain the independence of operation needed for impartiality and confidentiality in mediation. Independent services also receive the major part of funding from local authorities, often via a service level agreement, supplementing this with charitable funding (e.g. National Lotteries Charities Board). As community mediation becomes more of a mainstream option, quality assurance and accreditation will play a larger part and may become conditions of funding.

Research into community mediation in the UK has grown slowly. Early research on neighbour disputes pointed the way to mediation (Tebay, Cumberbatch and Graham 1986). Two early evaluative studies of mediation showed positive results (OPUS 1989; Quine, Hutton and Reed 1990), and an Australian study showed that community mediation resulted in a lower incidence of neighbour violence (Faulkes 1991). The Housing Association Tenants Ombudsman Service (HATOS), set up in 1993 to include mediation as part of their complaints procedure, used their research results (high satisfaction but low take-up) to improve their information system (Lickiss 1996). Research into the cost-effectiveness of neighbour mediation (Dignan, Sorsby and Hibbert 1996) demonstrated the scope for mediation to save costs, especially in some of the more intractable cases. This was followed up by a similar study covering Scotland with similar conclusions (Dignan and Sorsby 1999). The National Society for Clean Air (NSCA) National Noise Survey 1999 found that mediation was believed to be more effective than legislation in the long-term resolution of disputes, because it resolves underlying issues (NSCA 1999).

Commercial mediation

The initial idea for a commercial alternative dispute resolution (ADR) centre came to several prominent London lawyers in the late 1980s. They had heard of mediation being used in commercial disputes in the USA and wanted to bring these benefits to the UK. A chance meeting between Eileen Carroll, with ten years experience in international commercial disputes, and Karl Mackie, an ADR academic specialist and practitioner, at the American Bar Association conference in Hawaii, led to the idea of a centre in the UK. With the backing of the Confederation of British Industry (CBI) and several leading law firms in London, the Centre for Dispute Resolution (CEDR) was launched in November 1990 (CEDR 1996; O'Toole 1996).

CEDR handles cases where two (or more) firms are in dispute and would otherwise go to court. Mediation can save substantial costs and considerable time, especially if several parties are involved. The same principles apply as for other kinds of mediation. CEDR carries out its own training and accredits its own mediators.

There are several other organisations offering commercial mediation, such as the ADR Group, which started in 1991 as a network of 12 firms of solicitors (and now has many more) called ADR Net. The ADR Group headquarters staff provide training and act as a referral agency, either mediating commercial cases themselves or referring them to a member of their network who is geographically nearer the client.

The Academy of Experts, likewise, provides its own training and accreditation for neutrals from a wide variety of disciplines. It deals with personal, consumer and commercial disputes. There are also many firms of solicitors who have recently undertaken training in mediation, with a view to adding mediation to their repertoire of skills.

There have been several attempts to set up mediation attached to courts, such as the Bristol Law Society/ADR Group scheme, which took two years (1995–7) to obtain the Lord Chancellor's approval before it could start. The Central London County Court scheme was more fortunate. It began in May 1996 as a pilot scheme (made permanent in 1998) to allow mediation of civil disputes in the £3000 to £10,000 range, the next band above the informal small claims jurisdiction. Parties who opted for mediation did so without prejudice to their court-based rights and had a single three-hour session with a trained mediator from a recognised ADR provider, outside court hours 4.30 pm to 7.30 pm. Each side paid £25 towards the mediator's costs. The mediation was arranged within 28 days. The Patents County Court ran a similar scheme.

Professor Hazel Genn carried out detailed research to evaluate the scheme (Genn 1998). Although a disappointingly low number, 5 per cent, accepted the invitation to mediation (Genn 1998, p.40), the 160 cases going to mediation were successful: 80 per cent settled at the mediation session or soon after and 85 per cent said they would use the process again (Genn 1999, p.35).

The general success of mediation in the commercial sector (apart from the low take-up rate) has contributed to the recent reforms of civil justice (see pp.33–34), in which mediation will play a larger part.

Medical mediation

For some years many former Family Health Service Authorities (FHSAs, abolished in 1996) had been offering informal conciliation/mediation services to patients with complaints against their doctors. For example, the Leicester FHSA informal conciliation service was set up in 1991. Many complaints were resolved by conciliation, especially where they were based on misunderstandings, incomplete information or third party perceptions (Carmichael 1993).

In 1993 the Secretary of State set up a review of complaints procedures to ensure these were thorough, prompt and accessible – reducing waiting times and addressing the problems as close to the point of service delivery as possible. In 1996 the NHS issued a new complaints procedure for primary healthcare practitioners (covering GPs, dentists, pharmacists and ophthalmologists – but not hospitals or community services).

The aim of the new complaints procedure is to resolve most complaints at practice level, and the NHS Executive provided guidance packs for practices to develop their own procedures. However, if independent conciliation is thought to be helpful, this is available through the health authority. All health authorities have been asked to ensure that conciliation services are available to both parties to a complaint (NHS Executive 1996). Mediators are usually paid a small honorarium sessionally and are often experienced community mediators.

Complaints procedures for other parts of the NHS are under review, so there may be further moves towards mediation. There is also some use of mediation as an alternative to litigation, to resolve claims of clinical negligence against NHS trusts or health authorities (see case study in Chapter 12).

Environmental mediation

Environmental mediation has been used for many years in North America, to help resolve disputes concerning environmental and planning issues. Originally developed as a positive response from the corporate sector to high-profile campaigns by environmental organisations, it later blended in with developing ideas on consensus building and negotiation. These approaches are now used regularly in the USA in the planning of environmentally sensitive developments such as chemical works or logging projects.

Environmental mediation was pioneered in the UK in 1992, when several individual practitioners and the Environment Council (an independent charity which brings together groups concerned for the environment) came together (Baines and Ingram 1995). The emphasis in the UK has been on positive preventative consensus building, because this fits in better with UK public policymaking, which tends to develop generalised statutory procedures. However, this has meant that public sector agencies see this work as their business and are reluctant to involve independent neutrals (Sidaway 1998). The key features of environmental mediation are:

1. The large number of 'stakeholders': it is part of the process to decide who should be at the meetings, as all interests need to be represented. The mediator also has to ensure that these representatives communicate well between their group and the stakeholder group. Building consensus between all the stakeholders can take several months, so it can be a slow process – but the decisions made are usually better than those decided by just one party, possibly followed by massive protests and a public enquiry.

2. The complexity of the issues: these always include highly technical issues as well as those of personal values.

3. The uncertainty about the boundaries of the problem (and hence also its solution).

4. The fact that the environment itself is a form of 'stakeholder' (on whose behalf some, or none, may speak).

The two main organisations promoting this work are the Environment Council (through Environmental Resolve) and the Institute of Ecology and Resource Management, University of Edinburgh. Both undertake practical projects and provide training for practitioners (for instance, via the Environment Council's six-day course), and their work is helping to increase understanding of positive ways of managing environmental projects. There are the beginnings of a network to link practitioners, based on the wider concept of community participation.

There are overlaps between environmental and community mediation, which deals with many noise conflicts – part of the remit of the Department of Environment, Transport and the Regions. Community mediation services also carry out large multi-party mediations from time to time – whole streets, for example – which require similar techniques to environmental mediation (or vice versa).

Environmental mediation, from consensus building and prevention of conflict (often called 'stakeholder dialogue') to mediation of active conflict, has shown its value in saving time and money and in generating positive outcomes and trust for the future, in varied settings. These include:

- the de-commissioning of Shell's Brent Spar oil storage platform (Chapter 15), which led to a highly regarded set of guidelines (Acland, Hyam and Ingram 1999);

- influencing public sector statutory processes (DETR 1999);

- English Nature's development of planned programmes of mediation linked to a statutory land use plan (Keith 1999);

- the Planning Inspectorate's testing of mediation on some planning issues (Healey 1997);

- central government guidelines' recommendation of consensus building approaches in air quality management (Bishop 1999). This is the only example so far of a formal governmental recommendation.

Elsewhere in Europe, there is a strong tradition of collaborative working on environmental issues, especially in the Netherlands and Scandinavia, with recent growth in Italy, Slovenia and Latvia. Practice differs because of different cultural traditions, the structure and roles of voluntary and community groups and the relationship between central and local government. An influence towards consistency is the UN Local Agenda 21, which requires collaborative, consensus-based working towards sustainable development. This is likely to generate rapid advances in the amount, type and quality of mediation-linked work in the environmental field.

Elder mediation

The Elder Mediation Project (EMP) developed in 1991 from a Mediation UK executive committee meeting in which John Blinston, Yvonne Craig and other older members saw the need. This had become evident from the rising number of older people living longer, who were becoming involved in increasing conflicts in families, institutions and communities. A multicultural group of older volunteers was gathered to steer EMP and Yvonne Craig became its voluntary co-ordinator (EMP 1995).

The work is funded by small charitable grants. EMP has always had a commitment to empowerment and has run many workshops on 'Coping with later life conflicts', made presentations to multidisciplinary groups of professionals, contributed to publications and liaised with many other organisations. It has also undertaken over fifty mediation cases referred by these organisations and has successfully encouraged some of them to develop their own mediation services for older people.

EMP has many links with community mediation, having gathered its volunteers largely from these services. It therefore offers its workshops and training opportunities to those in community mediation, as well as to statutory and voluntary organisations concerned with older people.

Organisational and workplace mediation

Many organisational consultants have seen conflict resolution as part of their general remit in helping organisations move forward, especially as very often unresolved conflict plays a part in organisations becoming 'stuck'. More recently consultants have been undertaking mediation skills training to enhance their ability to resolve conflict, and mediators have been offering their services to organisations as well as to individuals. Many community mediation services also mediate between organisations or between groups within an organisation.

In 1995 the National Council of Voluntary Organisations (NCVO) launched a specialised Dispute Resolution Service for Charities and Voluntary Organisations, offering mediation for disputes involving staff, volunteers or committee members of these organisations (NCVO 1995). Another similar service started in 1996, promoted by the Association of Chief Executives of Voluntary Organisations (ACENVO) and CEDR (see above), concentrating on disputes between chief executives and their organisations (ACENVO/CEDR 1996). In 1998 these schemes amalgamated, re-starting in 1999, with NCVO providing information and passing on cases to CEDR to mediate (NCVO 1999). Mediation is particularly suitable for charities (rather than legal solutions) because the values of the organisation are at stake.

The first formal workplace mediation schemes started in 1996, in Lewisham Council's housing department and the Department of Health (Chapter 11). These were developed in response to the unconstructive grievance and disciplinary hearings of traditional workplace dispute resolution. The Local Government Management Board ran a conference in 1997 on the use of mediation in local government and since then several other local authorities and large employers (such as NHS trusts) have also developed workplace mediation schemes.

Mediation links – coming full circle

Early mediation practitioners linked with each other to explore mediation as a basic concept. Then the different sectors of mediation developed separately, as funding allowed. Now more and more links are being made across sectors. In the community-based sector, there have always been services providing more than one kind of mediation, often community and victim–offender mediation. An established community mediation service frequently becomes the base from which to develop other kinds of mediation, most commonly school mediation. Some have taken on schools work, victim–offender mediation, medical mediation and even family mediation. This has led to the emergence of 'multi-mediation centres', similar to many mediation centres in the USA. This could be particularly appropriate for rural centres, where there may not be enough referrals for one particular kind of mediation to make a single-type mediation service viable.

In addition, community mediation services have pioneered variations, extending mediation and its contexts in several ways. Examples include work with police, proactive work on high-crime housing estates to prevent arrests, multi-party mediations involving whole streets (overlapping with environmental mediation on occasions), mediation to prevent school exclusions, mediation between homeless young people and their families, mediation between parents and local education authorities for special needs students, to mention just a few. In several areas, community mediation services have become part of local authorities' antisocial behaviour policy, providing mediation before Antisocial Behaviour Orders are made under the Crime and Disorder Act 1998.

New developments in civil justice

The civil justice system in England and Wales has recently undergone its most radical rethink for more than a hundred years, and some elements of this will affect the development of mediation in several sectors. The Woolf reports on access to justice (Woolf 1995, 1996) endorsed the use of ADR wherever possible, and the Civil Procedure Rules (which came into force on 26 April 1999) established a unified procedural code for the High Court and county courts. Without making ADR compulsory, these rules lay an obligation on courts to encourage the use of ADR in appropriate cases. As a result, the number of mediations in civil cases (mostly commercial) has increased markedly during the second half of 1999.

In 1998, in a test case funded by the Law Society and the ADR Group, the Legal Aid Board decided that work done in mediating a dispute falls within the existing legal aid scheme. This removes an important barrier to mediation, as it means that disputing parties can claim legal aid for mediation in the same way as for solicitors' and court expenses. This had already been accomplished for divorce disputes by the Family Law Act 1996.

Following on from the Woolf Inquiry, a Green Paper on legal aid, *Legal Aid – Targeting Need* (Lord Chancellor's Department 1995), proposed block funding from legal aid for a variety of non-legal services. The government has set up the Community Legal Service, to co-ordinate legal services at three levels (information, advice and assistance) and rationalise methods of funding them (Lord Chancellor's Department 1999). The Legal Services Commission will succeed the Legal Aid Board and manage the Community Legal Service Fund which will replace civil legal aid; a draft Funding Code for ADR is under consultation. Funding for mediation could be made to any mediators or organisations who demonstrate competence, and this might include community mediation services as well as commercial mediators.

The Civil Justice Council was set up in 1998 as an advisory body to propose and monitor changes to the civil justice system (Civil Justice Council 1999). Among its five subcommittees to look at priority areas is the ADR Subcommittee chaired by Professor Martin Partington. In addition, the Lord Chancellor's Department issued a discussion paper on ADR (ADR Policy Branch, LCD 1999), asking for responses (by 25 February 2000) on key areas such as quality control, increasing take-up and whether an element of compulsion should be introduced.

Standards and accreditation

National mediation organisations have always tried to foster high standards in their members, and put considerable time and resources into developing practice standards. Many of these are only available within their own organisations, but some are available to others, such as the *Practice Standards* (Mediation UK 1998b) and the *Standards for Restorative Justice* (SINRJ 1998).

As mediation has moved from the margins to the mainstream and is paid for in some situations by public funds, the question of standards and accreditation has become crucially important. Most mediation organisations have accredited their own mediators from their own training courses, but from now on a National Vocational Qualification (NVQ) at Level 4 will be available for all mediators in England, Wales and Northern Ireland, with a Scottish equivalent SVQ. These *Mediation Standards* (CAMPAG 1998) have been developed by co-operation between the major national mediation organisations. The new Community Justice National Training Organisation is also developing national occupational standards, some of which will include community and victim–offender mediation (Community Justice News 1999; Schofield 1999); there will be links between these and N/SVQs.

There are also accreditation/affiliation schemes for services, for instance, family mediation services by National Family Mediation and by the Legal Aid Board for franchised services; and community mediation services (including some victim–offender and schools work) by Mediation UK. The proposed Quality Mark for the new Community Legal Service (Legal Aid Board 1999) could include community mediation services very quickly by linking in with Mediation UK accreditation; this is under discussion.

Some mediation courses have also achieved national accreditation, for instance, the Mediation UK *Training Programme in Community Mediation Skills* (1996b), accredited by the National Open College Network. There are likely to be further developments in this area in the near future, for instance, in the area of victim–offender mediation by the Community Justice National Training Organisation.

Conclusion

This exciting stage in mediation brings up many questions. One of these is how to dovetail a community-based system with a court-based system. Where is the boundary between services that are public (and free of charge) and services that are private (and paid for)? If services are paid for by the government, does this mean that some degree of compulsion to use the cheapest form (i.e. mediation) must be accepted? There are dangers that the values and benefits of mediation may be compromised.

So, while most of the recent developments are welcomed by the mediation world, there are some expressions of anxiety that mediation will be co-opted as 'cheap compulsory justice' or become 'routinised' and lose its potential for transforming relationships. There is some evidence that this has occurred in some areas in the USA, so lessons can be learned and preventive steps taken. There is a place for mediation at all levels from the court room to the grass-roots.

Acknowledgements

Some parts of this chapter have already appeared in *Community and Neighbour Mediation* (ed. M. Liebmann), 1998, London: Cavendish.

I would also like to acknowledge the help of the following in reading or updating this chapter: Marigold Bentley, Tony Billinghurst, Jeff Bishop, Mark Bitel, Sue Bowers, Mike Coldham, Yvonne Craig, Thelma Fisher, Meg Griffiths, Belinda Hopkins, Leap Confronting Conflict, Karl Mackie, Judith Moran, Damian Murphy, National Family Mediation, Carl Reynolds, Jill Roberts, Roger Sidaway and Marion Wells.

References

ACAS (Advisory Conciliation and Arbitration Service) (1995) 'Preventing and resolving disputes.' ACAS leaflet. London: ACAS.

ACAS (1996a) '20 years of improving industrial relations.' ACAS leaflet. London: ACAS.

ACAS (1996b) 'The role of ACAS.' ACAS leaflet. London: ACAS.

ACAS (undated) 'How ACAS started.' ACAS leaflet. London: ACAS.

ACENVO/CEDR (1996) Dispute resolution scheme information leaflet. London: ACENVO/CEDR.

Acland, A., Hyam, P. and Ingram, H. (1999) 'Guidelines for stakeholder dialogue.' Unpublished. Produced for Shell International Ltd.

ADR Policy Branch, Lord Chancellor's Department (1999) *Alternative Dispute Resolution: A Discussion Paper*. London: LCD.

Allport, L. and Bramwell, L. (1999) *Safe Solutions: A Resource Pack for Mediators and Others Working with People Affected by Abuse in the Home*. York: Pavilion Publishing for Joseph Rowntree Foundation.

Baines, J. and Ingram, H. (1995) *Beyond Compromise: Building Consensus in Environmental Planning and Decision Making*. London: The Environment Council.

Bentley, M. (1997) *ENCORE: The European Network for Conflict Resolution in Education*. London: Quaker Peace & Service.

Bishop, J. (1999) *Consultation: The How To Guide.* Brighton: National Association of Clean Air.

Braithwaite, S. and Liebmann, M. (1997) *Restorative Justice – Does It Work?: Digest of Current Research on Victim–Offender Mediation and Conferencing.* Bristol: Mediation UK.

CAMPAG (1998) *Mediation Standards.* Biggleswade: CAMPAG.

Carmichael, R. (1993) *First Report of Leicestershire FHSA on Informal Complaints: Helping Patients and Doctors to Listen to Each Other.* Leicester: Leicestershire FHSA.

CEDR (Centre for Dispute Resolution) (1996) 'Profile of Eileen Carroll.' *Resolutions* 15.

Citizenship Advisory Group (1998) *Education for Citizenship and the Teaching of Democracy in Schools.* Final report of the Advisory Group on Citizenship. London: Qualifications and Curriculum Authority (QCA).

Civil Justice Council (1999) *Annual Report 1999.* London: Lord Chancellor's Department.

Community Justice News (1999) 'National Occupational Standards.' *Community Justice News,* July, 3.

Department of the Environment (1994) *Mediation: Benefits and Practice.* London: DoE.

DETR (Department of Environment, Transport and the Regions) (1999) *In Touch with the People.* London: The Stationery Office.

Dignan, J. and Sorsby, A. (1999) *Resolving Neighbour Disputes through Mediation in Scotland.* Edinburgh: Scottish Office Central Research Unit.

Dignan, J., Sorsby, A. and Hibbert, J. (1996) *Neighbour Disputes: Comparing the Cost-effectiveness of Mediation and Alternative Approaches.* Sheffield: Centre for Criminological and Legal Research, University of Sheffield.

EMP (Elder Mediation Project) (1995) Information leaflet. London: EMP.

ENCORE (European Network for Conflict Resolution in Education) (undated) Information leaflet. London: Quaker Peace & Service.

Faulkes, W. (1991) 'Community mediation as a crime prevention strategy.' Plenary address, Forum for Initiatives in Reparation and Mediation Annual Conference, 2 July.

Fisher, T. (1993) *The History of Family Mediation Services.* London: National Family Mediation.

FMA (Family Mediators Association) (undated) Information leaflet. London: FMA.

Genn, H. (1998) *The Central London County Court Pilot Mediation Scheme: Evaluation Report.* London: Lord Chancellor's Department.

Genn, H. (1999) *Mediation in Action.* London: Calouste Gulbenkian Foundation.

Hazzard, S. (1999) 'What is this network all about?' November update. London: Leap Confronting Conflict.

Healey, P. (1997) *Collaborative Planning.* Basingstoke: Macmillan.

Hester, M., Pearson, C. and Radford, L. (1997) *Domestic Violence: A National Survey of Court Welfare and Voluntary Sector Mediation Practice.* York: Policy Press for Joseph Rowntree Foundation.

Joseph Rowntree Foundation (1996) 'The longer-term impact of family mediation.' *Findings Social Policy Research 103.* York: Joseph Rowntree Foundation.

Keith, B. (1999) 'Mediation – a new way forward.' *Site Lines,* autumn.

Legal Aid Board (1999) *The Community Legal Service Quality Mark.* Explanatory leaflet. London: Legal Aid Board.

Lickiss, R. (with Giddings, P., Gregory, R. and Karn, V.) (1996) *Setting up the Housing Association Tenants Ombudsman Service: The Debate and the Outcome.* Research Report 2. London: Housing Association Tenants Ombudsman Service.

Lord Chancellor's Department (1995) *Legal Aid – Targeting Need.* London: HMSO.

Lord Chancellor's Department (1999) *The Community Legal Service: A Consultation Paper.* London: LCD.

Marshall, T. (1984) *Reparation, Conciliation and Mediation.* Home Office Research and Planning Unit, Paper 27. London: HMSO.

Marshall, T. and Merry, S. (1990) *Crime and Accountability.* London: HMSO.

Marshall, T. and Walpole, M. (1985) *Bringing People Together: Mediation and Reparation Projects in Great Britain.* Home Office Research and Planning Unit, Paper 33. London: HMSO.

Mediation UK (1993a) *Victim Offender Mediation Guidelines for Starting a Service.* Bristol: Mediation UK.

Mediation UK (1993b) *Guide to Starting a Community Mediation Service.* Bristol: Mediation UK.

Mediation UK (1995) *Training Manual in Community Mediation Skills.* Bristol: Mediation UK.

Mediation UK (1996a) *Community Mediation Video.* Bristol: Mediation UK.

Mediation UK (1996b) *Handbook for the Mediation UK Training Programme in Mediation Skills.* Bristol: Mediation UK.

Mediation UK (1998a) *Mediation Works! Conflict Resolution and Peer Mediation Manual for Secondary Schools and Colleges.* Bristol: Mediation UK.

Mediation UK (1998b) *Practice Standards (for Mediators and Management of Mediation Services).* Bristol: Mediation UK.

NCVO (National Council of Voluntary Organisations) (1995) NCVO Dispute Resolution Service for Charities and Voluntary Organisations information leaflet. London: NCVO.

NCVO (1999) *Resolving Disputes by Mediation.* Service leaflet. London: NCVO/CEDR.

NFM (National Family Mediation) (1996) *The Family Law Bill: The Importance for Mediators.* London: National Family Mediation.

NHS Executive (1996) *Complaints Guidance Pack for General Medical/ Dental Practitioners.* London: NHS Executive.

NSCA (National Society for Clean Air) (1999) *NSCA National Noise Survey 1999.* Brighton: NSCA.

OPUS (Organisation for Promoting Understanding in Society) (1989) *Newham Conflict and Change Project, Evaluation Report.* London: OPUS.

O'Toole, K., CEDR (Centre for Dispute Resolution) (1996) Telephone conversation, October.

Parkinson, L. (1997) 'Some landmarks in the history of family mediation.' In L. Parkinson *Family Mediation.* London: Sweet and Maxwell, Appendix H.

QCA (Qualifications and Curriculum Authority) and DfEE (Department for Education and Employment) (1999) *National Curriculum for England: Citizenship Key Stages 3 and 4.* London: QCA and DfEE. (Also available on www.nc.uk.net)

Quill, D. and Wynne, J. (1993) *Victim and Offender Mediation Handbook.* London: Save the Children.

Quine, C., Hutton, J. and Reed, B. (1990) *Community Mediation of Disputes between Neighbours.* Report of an evaluation study on the work of Southwark Mediation Centre 1987–89. London: The Grubb Institute.

Rawlings, A. (1996) *Ways and Means Today.* Kingston: Kingston Friends Workshop Group.

Reeves, H. (1987) *Mediation from a Victim Support Perspective.* London: Victim Support.

Schofield, H. (1999) Telephone conversation, 3 December.

Sidaway, R. (1998) *Good Practice in Rural Development No 5: Consensus Building.* Edinburgh: Scottish Office Central Research Unit.

SINRJ (Standards in Restorative Justice) (1998) *Standards for Restorative Justice.* London: Restorative Justice Consortium.

Tebay, S., Cumberbatch, G. and Graham, N. (1986) *Disputes Between Neighbours.* Birmingham: University of Aston, Applied Psychology Department.

UK College of Family Mediators (1996) Information leaflet. London: UK College of Family Mediators.

Victim Support (1982) *Victim Support: The First Ten Years.* London: Victim Support.

Walker, J. (1989) *Violence and Conflict Resolution in Schools.* Strasbourg: Council for Cultural Co-operation, Council of Europe, ref. DECS/EGT (89) 24.

Lord Woolf (1995) *Access to Justice: Interim Report to the Lord Chancellor on the Civil Justice System in England and Wales.* London: HMSO.

Lord Woolf (1996) *Access to Justice: Final Report to the Lord Chancellor on the Civil Justice System in England and Wales.* London: HMSO.

Youth Justice Board (1999) *Guidance for the Development of Effective Restorative Practice with Young Offenders.* London: Home Office.

Zehr, H. (1990) *Changing Lenses.* Scottsdale PA and Waterloo, Ontario: Herald Press.

2

Family Mediation
Working to Support Separated Families
Marion Stevenson

Introduction

Family mediators assist in cases of family breakdown. They help separating or divorcing couples to discuss and, where possible, decide for themselves any issues that arise from the separation or divorce. This may relate to arrangements for children, finances or the legal process itself. Mediators can also assist where disputes arising from the breakdown occur between other members of the extended family.

Legislative background

In July 1974 the Finer Report (from the Committee on One Parent Families) identified the destructive nature of conflict in divorce matters, particularly from the point of view of children involved. It recognised that resolution of specific disputes through the legal process often exacerbated or failed to deal with underlying conflict. The report recommended 'conciliation' as a process that would assist parents to reach agreement about matters relating to the breakdown of the marriage and thus reduce the conflict between them, for the benefit of all the family members. Court orders at this time specified 'care and control' (where a child would live), 'custody' (who had responsibility for decisions concerning education, religion and health — joint custody orders were therefore common) and 'access' (how the child would keep in touch with the non-resident parent) in every case.

Two pieces of subsequent legislation have undoubtedly influenced the development of mediation in divorce matters, as well as being in themselves influenced by what was already taking place in terms of existing practice. The Children Act of 1989 enshrined the concept of equal parental responsibility for children on the part of both parents after separation. The family court now expects parents to agree arrangements for children, and only intervenes to make a specific order about where children should live (Residence Order) or how they should keep in touch with each parent (Contact Order) if it is convinced that this is necessary because the parents cannot reach agreement.

Thus the Children Act places emphasis on the requirement for parents to negotiate about arrangements for children and to make joint plans. Obviously this negotiation can be very difficult for parents around the time of their separation or divorce. Therefore many parents have been encouraged by solicitors and courts to make use of local mediation services, where they exist.

The Family Law Bill received the Royal Assent in 1996, and pilot projects are currently under way (May 1999) relating to Section 29 of the Act. This Section makes legal aid available for mediation for the first time. A consequence of this is that people are only eligible for legal aid for their divorce once they have met with a mediator, who assesses their suitability for mediation. These assessments are carried out by (Legal Aid Board) franchised mediators. Most mediation providers are very keen that involvement in the mediation process itself should remain voluntary. Therefore assessment for suitability includes discussing with the client whether – having had the process fully explained – they wish to opt for mediation. They are not denied legal aid for the divorce simply because they do not choose mediation.

At the time of writing (October 1999), the implementation of Part II of the Family Law Act has been delayed, due to disappointing results from pilot projects for the Information Meetings at the outset of the divorce process, where couples are given information on all the options, including marriage counselling and mediation. Part II includes the revision of the whole divorce process from a fault-based system to a system which simply acknowledges the fact of marital breakdown. Now that the future of the Act is unclear, many organisations in the field are lobbying the Lord Chancellor's Department to implement the new Act.

The development of mediation services

The first independent conciliation service was set up in Bristol in 1978 and other services soon followed. In 1981 the National Family Conciliation Council (NFCC) was set up to support services, to co-ordinate practice and training, and to provide national publicity and liaison for the movement. At this stage conciliators were solely assisting parents to reach agreements concerning arrangements for children after the separation. In 1990 a pilot project to include the settlement of financial arrangements was initiated, and after this many services undertook training to offer 'All Issues Mediation' (AIM) alongside the child-focused work. However, AIM still represents a very small proportion of most services' work and this chapter therefore deals mainly with mediation concerning children's issues. The process involved in AIM is explained briefly at the end of this chapter.

NFCC was renamed National Family Mediation in 1993, when most services also changed their names to include the word 'mediation' instead of 'conciliation'. There are currently 70 NFM-affiliated services in England and Wales (August 1999), all of which are either independent charitable organisations, or are sponsored by other independent charities. In Scotland similar developments took place and Family Mediation Scotland (FMS) was set up in 1992. There are 12 affiliated services.

A separate national body, the Family Mediators Association, was inaugurated in 1989. FMA uses a co-working model with a family mediator working alongside a lawyer mediator. It offers training to individuals who are suitably qualified and who then practise independently and privately in the field. Latterly FMA has trained some practitioners – both family and lawyer mediators – as 'solo' workers.

The UK College of Family Mediators came into being in 1996 as a result of the co-operative work of NFM, FMA and FMS. The College has developed national standards for training, selection and accreditation (Booth 1997).

Principles and assumptions in family mediation

Family mediation takes as its starting point the principles that underpin the mediation process in general: the confidentiality of the process, the impartiality of the mediators and voluntarism on the part of the parties. Family mediation is also underpinned by current beliefs about people's welfare and development in the circumstances of family breakdown.

Over one-third of marriages currently end in divorce. Figures five years ago showed that one-half of 'non-custodial' parents had lost touch with children after two years. Family mediation bases itself on the following premises:

- that children, where possible, need a continuing relationship with both parents;
- that co-operation between parents fosters healthy adjustment in children;
- that continuing conflict between parents is damaging to children;
- that parents can be enabled to make their own joint decisions.

Research has supported these premises. Many studies bear witness to the harmful effect of parental conflict, whether within or without a marriage. A study in Cambridge (Lund 1984) looked at 30 families with children aged 6 to 9, two years after their parents' separation. The families fell into three groups. Those children who had no contact with the absent parent (usually the father) appeared to have the highest level of emotional problems and the lowest self-esteem. Those children whose parents had achieved harmonious co-parenting arrangements had the lowest level of emotional problems and the highest self-esteem. Those children whose parents continued in a high level of conflict but who were in contact with both parents were in between. The conclusion was that frequent and conflict-free contact is profoundly helpful to children's adjustment.

The aim of family mediation is to help parents manage their negotiations with each other in order to foster continuing parental involvement with children and constructive co-operation between parents.

The expertise of the family mediator

Mediation is a process that is distinct from other activities such as counselling, arbitrating, judging, giving advice, investigating or making assessments. It may involve skills that are useful in some of these activities but in mediation they are brought together in a unique way.

To simplify a theme that is developed more fully elsewhere in the book, the mediator functions mainly by using the following strategies:

- organising diverse information and ideas into manageable themes;
- asking questions rather than making statements;
- eliciting further information in order to come up with ideas;
- summarising what a person is saying or where the discussion has reached;
- reframing – i.e. negative statements into positive requests;
- asking what people would like to happen now – i.e. future focus;
- helping build chosen options into a specific plan.

Possibly the most important of these skills is the ability to organise material into useful and manageable themes. This involves disentangling, separating out and defining different threads of the discussion, and being able to distinguish those that can be safely ignored, those that need acknowledgement but not discussion, and those that will be fruitful in terms of the negotiation. The mediator needs to be constantly alert – often in very highly charged situations – to the different possibilities for shaping the discussion so that effective problem solving can be facilitated.

Strategies in the mediation session are not brought into play in a haphazard way: timing is of the essence. It is this sense of timing, the ability to use the right strategy at the right time, that distinguishes the effective mediator. The skill of the mediator develops through practice. Mediation is not an easy thing to do. Even people who are skilled and experienced in other related fields are often surprised at how long it can take to feel competent and confident as a mediator.

Family mediators are selected for aptitude and often have at least five years' experience of working with families, in a social work or legal setting, or in relevant counselling work. They are usually educated to degree level. NFM mediators are recruited and selected by a local service before being formally selected and screened by NFM itself. After a period of supervised work (alongside an experienced mediator) they undertake the NFM core training programme in mediation. Family mediators have specialist knowledge of: the divorce process, both from an emotional and a practical point of view; child development and children's perspectives in family breakdown; current research in the field of divorce.

The mediation process

Mediation models vary slightly from one service to another. For example, one service arranges a two and a half hour session, during which each of the parents is seen separately for twenty minutes or so; they are then brought together to outline the agenda for the remainder of the meeting. Another service always sees parents individually for an appointment before setting up a joint meeting. Another service gives parents a choice as to whether they have individual appointments first or meet jointly from the outset.

At the time of writing, some standardisation of process is taking place in response to concern about mediation in situations where domestic violence or intimidation is an issue. The Legal Aid Board, for example, requires franchisees to see legally aided clients on their own (even if only for a short time at the beginning of a meeting) in order to assess the feasibility of mediation.

Despite these variations, the principles of practice behind the service delivered are constant. For the sake of clarity, I have described a typical model of practice in an NFM service and have followed a case example focusing on arrangements for children, to illustrate the stages of the mediation process. Mediation covering all issues (financial and children's issues) follows the same basic framework. The stages of the process are: intake; individual sessions; joint meeting.

Intake

Intake is the process by which referrals are taken by the service. Competent intake work is a vital part of the service. For many clients it will represent the first contact with mediation and the first experience of the principles of mediation in practice. If the worker does not observe these principles from the outset, the trust of the client in the integrity of the service can be adversely affected.

Parents either get in touch with the service themselves or are referred by a third party, usually their solicitor or the court. Where a parent contacts the service directly, by telephone in most cases, the intake worker explains the principles and process of mediation.

The intake worker explains the charging system (a sliding scale based on gross income) and establishes whether the person wishes to use the service. If another service seems more appropriate (e.g. counselling, legal advice, etc.), the worker gives information on these. It may be necessary for clients to explain a little about their circumstances in order to establish whether mediation is the right service at this point. However, they are discouraged from 'telling the whole story', since they will have to repeat themselves when they meet with a mediator.

If the parent wishes, a letter is sent to the other parent. This letter explains the principles of mediation and invites the person to telephone to discuss the possibility of using the service or to make an appointment. If the service does not receive a response within about three weeks, then the first parent is informed and offered an individual appointment to think through their options at this point. The option remains to use the service at a later stage if the other parent changes his or her mind. All appointments, whether for individual meetings or joint meetings, take place at the office.

Where a referral comes directly from a solicitor or the court, the intake worker writes to each of the parents in the same format as above, inviting them to get in touch. If they do not do so, the service will let the solicitor or court know.

Case example

Sarah and Jim's story (1)

Sarah contacted the service by telephone. She explained that her husband had just left her and had gone to live with a woman whom he had met through work. Their two daughters were 10 (Shirley) and 8 (Lorraine). The girls were extremely upset. Shirley was refusing to see her father at all after a row between the parents on the doorstep, when Sarah's husband had threatened her. Lorraine had been out with him on one further occasion but it had been a disaster and Sarah had had to cope with a terrible scene that night. She was at her wits' end.

The intake worker explained the mediation process and principles, stressing that the mediators would not give advice or take sides, but would help the parents to discuss the situation from all angles and look at possible ways forward. She also explained that the process was confidential and voluntary. She offered Sarah the opportunity to talk things through with a mediator in an individual appointment. She explained the charging system and fixed a time.

Individual sessions

Individual sessions with parents give the parent the chance to explain the problems as they see them, without the anxiety or distraction of the other parent being present. The mediator engages with the client by demonstrating understanding of the concerns and feelings in an impartial way, and the parent is helped to clarify the main issues that they may wish to discuss. The mediator has a chance to explain mediation fully. The mediator starts to encourage the 'future focus' that will ultimately be the key to a successful resolution, by asking the parent what they would like to achieve and different ways of getting there. The mediator can also raise other possibilities for the parent, such as counselling or divorce support groups, if appropriate.

The mediator checks the suitability of a joint meeting for the parent concerned, particularly where domestic violence has been (or still is) an issue. The main issue here is whether the parent feels able, with the support of the mediator, to express a view freely, without fear or pressure. It is also important to be clear about such practicalities as whether parents wish to arrive and leave separately.

Case example

Sarah and Jim's story (2)

Sarah came for her appointment with the mediator. She explained some of the background to the situation. The other woman (Linda) was someone whom she knew, had met at office parties and had even invited to her house. Her husband (Jim) had obviously been having an affair for quite a while but had denied it. He had left quite suddenly. She was shocked and angry. The girls had been devastated. They too had had no warning. To begin with they had agreed to see their father but they had become increasingly reluctant, particularly after meeting Linda on one occasion, which Sarah thought incredibly insensitive. They were now refusing outright to see him. Sarah knew that they needed to keep in touch with their father but felt very stuck about what to do.

The mediator helped her identify the main issues for discussion with Jim. These were: the ending of the relationship; how to help and support the children; the girls' contact with their father; the role of the new partner. Sarah's aim was to achieve a consensus over the plans for the children, so that they were not subjected to the kind of distressing scene that occurred on the previous occasion.

The mediator checked that Sarah would feel safe to voice her point of view in the mediation meeting. Sarah felt that the threat which Jim had made had been out of character and showed just how difficult the situation had become.

The mediator agreed to write to Jim, inviting him to contact the service, and to get back to Sarah to let her know whether a joint meeting could be arranged.

Jim responded to the letter from the service by telephoning and asking for an appointment. The intake worker explained the process in the same way as to Sarah and made a convenient date and time.

Jim came for the appointment with the mediator. He explained the background to the situation from his point of view. He had not planned to leave Sarah. In fact he felt terribly guilty. The trouble was that he had actually been unhappy in the marriage for some considerable time. The situation with Linda had developed over time and he had not felt able to talk about it with Sarah because he knew what her reaction would be. He had never explained to her about his unhappiness. Leaving had been the most difficult thing he had ever done and the pain went on and on. The children had sided with their mother. She did not encourage them to see him – in fact he felt she was really preventing them by making them feel guilty if they went with him. On the few occasions they had come out, they had all had a lovely time. The children had seemed to enjoy going to the fair with Linda and her children. Jim said he would eventually like to arrange overnight stays with him for both children.

Jim's issues were summarised as: the ending of the relationship; the position of the children and how to help them; the contact arrangements. His aim was to sort out the situation sufficiently to enable him to have a continuing relationship with his children.

Jim agreed to come to a joint meeting. Convenient times were identified and the mediator agreed to contact Sarah to make the arrangements to suit everyone. It was explained that there would be two mediators present at that meeting.

The joint meeting

In the model described, mediators generally co-work with another mediator. One mediator is the 'lead' mediator who chairs the meeting and is responsible for overseeing the process. The other mediator concentrates particularly on the individuals, coming in with any questions that might help clarify feelings, information or options. The second mediator also has a watching brief on the process and may make suggestions about direction, or suggest the mediators take a break. Because mediation is an extremely focused activity and meetings often proceed on several different levels at once, co-working can be considerably less stressful than solo working, as well as having a better chance of achieving all the aims of the session.

The joint meeting is scheduled to last an hour and a half. Further meetings can be arranged as necessary. Most parents have between one and three joint meetings. The joint meeting has a structure which is similar to the structure used in other fields of mediation. This is not always followed chronologically, but where there are diversions from it the mediators will normally know where they are in the process.

At some point during the meeting there is a five or ten minute break. This enables both parents and mediators to think quietly about what is being said. Parents are offered the choice of waiting separately (with one going to the waiting room) or remaining together. Mediators use the time to discuss how best to help parents in the second part of the meeting. Often the meeting changes in atmosphere after the break and sometimes unexpected progress can be made. The structure of the joint meeting is as follows:

1. Introduction to the process and setting of ground rules.

2. Invitation to parties to outline issues for discussion.

3. Clarifying the issues and making an agenda.

4. Exploring the issues and generating options.

5. Building the agreement.

6. Closure and follow-up.

INTRODUCTION TO THE PROCESS AND SETTING OF GROUND RULES

The mediator explains the principles (as above) and process. Ground rules are suggested. This usually involves saying something along the lines of: 'It will be important to each of you to be able to speak without being interrupted and to be talked to with respect. You need to give us the responsibility to manage the meeting in order to make sure you have an equal chance to put your point of view and to hear the point of view of the other parent. So we may ask you to stop, or wait for a minute, or try and put something in a different way. Is that all right with you?'

INVITATION TO PARTIES TO OUTLINE ISSUES FOR DISCUSSION

The mediator asks each parent to outline the issues that they would like to discuss, discouraging too much detail at this stage by explaining that they will have a chance to do this when they start discussing them one by one.

CLARIFYING THE ISSUES AND MAKING AN AGENDA

The mediator checks understanding of the issues raised. In making the list he or she will try to find mutual problem definitions, rather than just listing statements or complaints from each parent. The list might include some of the following, for example: explanations to the children; concern about a particular child; what is said in front of or to the children; schooling; handovers; communication/consultation between the parents; new partners; attendance at school functions; relationships with the extended family; contact schedule; activities during contact; safety issues; discipline; routines, etc.

EXPLORING THE ISSUES AND GENERATING OPTIONS

These two stages are usually listed separately. Exploration of an issue (what happens, who does what when, what is the concern actually about, etc.) normally precedes the mediator's shift to 'What would you like to happen differently?' or 'How could X help with that?' or 'What do you think would help to resolve that?' Unless people have a reasonably clear idea about what is difficult about something, they will not be able to think constructively about what would help make it easier. However, the two stages can overlap, because the exploration of the detail of the issues often throws up the options.

For example, a parent complains that the other parent often comes late for contact. When the mediators ask what happens, it may transpire that the children are always ready on time and quickly become anxious and disappointed. Mediators then ask both parents about what might help and are likely to receive such suggestions as: letting the children know that the other parent will be there between certain times (perhaps a half hour time band); the contact parent letting the home parent know if he or she will be late; changing the time to a more convenient one; the home parent not getting the children ready until the other parent arrives, etc.

Contact schedules themselves often emerge from a painstaking process of gathering information about everyone's commitments and detailing what they would really like to achieve for the children and for themselves.

BUILDING THE AGREEMENT

The agreement is built brick by brick from the options that parents choose on each of the issues. Every single plan made by parents is different from any other plan made by other parents. This is because the mediation process gives parents the chance to tailor their plans precisely to their own and their children's needs.

The mediators' contribution to this stage of the process is to help the parents weigh each of the options against their objectives and test for practicality. Mediators do not evaluate the options themselves, but may ask challenging questions about the consequences, to ensure that these are properly assessed by the parents. Once options are chosen on each issue, the mediators summarise and check understanding.

CLOSURE AND FOLLOW-UP

At the end of the meeting all the proposals are summarised again. Points of difference are also noted. A 'without prejudice' summary letter to both parents is offered. The mediators discuss with the parents whether to arrange a further meeting. It depends largely on the stage reached as to whether this is appropriate. Sometimes all issues are resolved satisfactorily in one meeting. Sometimes parents have made a start and would like to come back to continue the discussion. Sometimes parents have made a plan to try out and want to set a date to review the situation. Nowadays agreements are rarely ratified by court, because the court usually only makes orders where parents cannot agree the children's arrangements.

If parents cannot agree, the mediators discuss with them possible next steps, with the aim that each is clear about what will happen next. Sometimes parents decide to think over what has been said, stay with the current arrangement, or take legal advice. Often the mediators still offer them a summary letter, which details the common ground as well as the matters that are unresolved. This 'narrowing the area of difference' can in itself sometimes lead to resolution by the parents themselves, or their solicitors, after the meeting. This may be because having the difference narrowly defined makes it more amenable to resolution; or because the parents are able to accept 'less than best' once the difference has been properly registered.

If there is a clear decision to ask the court to decide the best course of action, the parents often take the summary letter from the mediators, in a form agreed by both, to their solicitors, or copies can be sent direct to the solicitors if the parents wish. The letter itself is never sent without the express permission of both parents. Since it is a 'without prejudice' letter, it cannot be used as evidence in court. However, it may help the solicitor to give informed advice concerning possible court orders. Parents are normally told that they are welcome to contact the service again at any time if they need further help.

Case example

Sarah and Jim's story (3)

> *Jim and Sarah came to the service for a joint meeting. The atmosphere was tense. The mediators explained the principles and process, and checked agreement on the ground rules* **(introduction to the process)**. *Both parents were then asked to outline the issues that they wanted to discuss* **(invitation to outline issues)**. *Sarah spoke again of the shock to the family caused by Jim's sudden departure, of the girls' distress and of the problem arising from the outing with Linda. She said she did not know how she was going to persuade the*

children to see their father. Jim spoke mainly of his contact with the children and how he felt this was being effectively blocked by Sarah. He recognised that he had done a terrible thing to Sarah in leaving so suddenly, but felt that the real problem was between the adults and that the children should be kept out of it.

The mediators summarised and outlined the following agenda for the meeting, checking each heading as they went along and writing the list on the flip chart: the ending of the relationship; the children and how they were at present; how to help them; contact – what, where, who? **(clarifying the issues and making an agenda)**.

The mediators chose to itemise the 'ending of the relationship' in this case because it was clear that this was currently casting a very long shadow over the situation. The aim was not to counsel the parents but to give them a chance to ask any questions and acknowledge the situation sufficiently to be able to separate out the children's needs from their own. Sarah asked Jim why he had not warned her. Jim said he realised that this had been the wrong way to go about things, and was sorry about all the hurt he had caused, but at the time it had seemed the only thing he could manage. The mediators asked each parent whether they thought the marriage was over. Sarah said that now she accepted it was; it was not her choice, and she would have liked the chance to work on the problems Jim mentioned. However, even if Jim wanted to come back now, she felt it was too late: too much had happened and it would be better for them all if they tried to build separate lives. Jim said he did feel the marriage was over. The mediators asked whether either was thinking of taking any formal steps. Sarah planned to consult a solicitor shortly for advice about the legalities. Jim was not in a hurry for a divorce but would accept what Sarah decided on this.

Jim and Sarah then spent some time talking about the children, describing their particular characteristics in a very similar vein: both bright girls with Lorraine being a bit more outgoing than Shirley, who tended to be quite sensitive. Sarah then talked about their reaction to the separation. She said Shirley was very angry with her father and said she hated Linda. Sarah knew Shirley loved her father but did not know how to help her with her anger. Lorraine was a bit more 'happy-go-lucky' but she had been upset by the angry scene at the end of the last visit and was now also saying she did not want to see Jim. Jim said that both children had seemed to enjoy their time with him and he was at a loss to understand the current refusal.

The mediators asked both parents what they thought might help the children at this point. Sarah said that the parents should avoid letting them see any arguments and Jim agreed with this. The mediators asked what would help them achieve this. Sarah asked that if Jim were coming to the house he should be on his own. Jim said that it would help if they avoided raising any issues other than those relating to the children, and thought they should both try and speak civilly to each other at the handovers.

The mediators then asked what the children had been told about the separation. Jim said that Sarah had obviously said it was all his fault. The mediators asked what he would really like Sarah to be saying. Jim thought a more general explanation might be helpful, such as: 'Mummy and Daddy can't live together any more, which is very sad for us all, but it is just one of those things that sometimes happen.' Both parents agreed that they should not say negative *things about each other to the children, and that the children needed to be reassured that, although their parents had stopped loving each other, they would never stop loving them.*

The parents then talked about the contact. Sarah said that she felt that, for the time being, it would be better if the children did not see Linda. She realised that in time they might need to, but it was too difficult for them all at present. Jim agreed to see the children on his own, or to take them to his parents' house. The mediators asked what suggestions each had for restarting the contact with the children and their father. Jim thought that if Sarah really encouraged them to come with him, there would be no problem. Sarah disagreed. She felt Jim had not taken on board the degree of feeling involved. The mediators asked how she felt Jim might help the situation now. Sarah suggested that Jim might offer to take them out for the day on a Saturday, perhaps planning a special trip. Jim was willing to try this, as a starter. The mediators asked Jim what he would like Sarah to say to the children about the outing. Jim said perhaps she could explain that it would be just the three of them, what time they would be back, and that this had been organised and agreed between the parents. Sarah agreed to say this to the children **(exploring the issues and generating options).**

The mediators asked when they would like to plan the outing. Sarah suggested that if Saturday suited Jim, they could try this Saturday. Jim asked to collect the children at 10.00 am, saying he could bring them back at 6.00 pm. Sarah suggested 5.00 pm, so that she could give them their tea and have a chance to chat to them before bedtime. Jim agreed. The mediators summarised the plans and offered to send a letter to both parents outlining the arrangements. Both parents thought this would be helpful **(building the agreement).**

The mediators offered a follow-up meeting to review the arrangements. Jim and Sarah thought they could try this arrangement for the next few weeks, and that then it would be helpful to come back to the mediation service to talk about the next steps. An appointment was therefore made for four weeks' time.

At the follow-up meeting the parents reported the successful operation of the plan. They brought up some minor problems and planned a few adjustments, adding in a midweek visit when Jim would take the girls out to tea. They agreed to review the question of overnight stays in three months' time **(closure and follow-up).**

This case demonstrates the usefulness of mediation in supporting co-operative parenting at a very critical time in the family's development. Because of the circumstances, and the understandably powerful feelings that were generated, the parents' ability to communicate effectively about parenting issues was impaired. As a result the children were in limbo: loving their father, angry with him, missing him, anxious for their mother, and frightened of the conflict between their parents. Yet both parents loved the children, both recognised the children's need to have two parents and – crucially – both had the courage to use the resource of an impartial third party who could guide their discussion and enable them to plan effectively.

Consultation with children

Some services consult directly with children during the mediation process, although it is still relatively rare. Meetings with children take place without parents present, after agreement from both parents. Children are not asked to take responsibility for decisions, but are asked for views on what feels comfortable or uncomfortable. Mediators agree with children on what they would like fed back to their parents, and whether they would like to be present at the meeting. Consultation sessions with children certainly seem to be helpful on occasion: children can express their thoughts to an independent outsider and receive reassurance about the normality of their feelings. They are often relieved that their parents are working to sort things out for them and pleased to be able to give their views directly to the mediator.

Mostly, however, parents tend to deal with any disagreements about what children say through the mediation process. This often involves trying to take into account what the child says to each parent, on the assumption that each version has a certain validity which needs to be taken seriously. Parents also discuss how they can support and help the children, for example, by letting them know that they are working together to decide the best plans for everyone.

All issues mediation

All Issues Mediation (AIM) assists parents to discuss and decide all relevant issues relating to the divorce, including the finances. Mediation of finances is a longer process, which involves the painstaking gathering of all the financial information (with supporting documentation), the display of that information and the consideration of the options for settlement. This normally takes between four and six meetings. The mediation model described above applies to AIM, but the stages of clarifying (information gathering) and exploring the issues and generating options (understanding the information and its implications in terms of possibilities) take several sessions.

Mediators recommend to all parents who opt for AIM that they retain their own solicitors, to consult during the process (and bring advice back to the mediation) and always at the end. Mediators prepare a financial statement and a 'Memorandum of Understanding', which is a legally privileged document outlining the parents' proposals for settling the finances. This is then taken to both solicitors for checking before being made the basis of any final settlement, either as part of the divorce process, or as a Separation Agreement.

Conclusion

Family mediation has significantly influenced the divorce process over the last twenty years. The culture in this country has changed over that time and has moved away from the establishing of fault and blame to an acknowledgement that divorce is a reality, and that fostering co-operation between parents is profoundly helpful to children. Mediation is a powerful process which has enabled many parents to continue as effective and supportive parents at a time when their relationship as partners has broken down.

What does the future hold? The current picture is complex and uncertain: the pace of change is rapid. It is currently not known, for example, whether the main body of the Family Law Act has been shelved temporarily or permanently. Consequently the nature and extent of the role of mediation in the divorce process is still unclear.

All this uncertainty and change of course creates a degree of anxiety. However, nobody can doubt that there has been a sea change concerning dispute resolution in divorce, and that mediation as an option is here to stay. The fact that mediation will be a permanent feature of the divorce process is a hugely significant and exciting development.

References

Booth, Dame Margaret (1997) 'A short history of family mediation.' In *UK College of Family Mediators Directory and Handbook* (1997–8). London: FT Law and Tax.

Lund, M. (1984) 'Research on divorce and children.' *Family Law 14*, 198–201.

3

Conflict Resolution and Peer Mediation in Primary Schools

Elizabeth Lawrence

Introduction

There is a dream that is shared by people everywhere – the dream of a peaceful, harmonious world. Keepers of this dream, including young people, are dreaming it into existence in schools, transforming them into communities of people based on equal rights, justice, caring and respect for each person as a unique and special member of the human race. Creating reality out of that dream requires many things, not least co-operation, effective communication, high self-esteem and an understanding of difference and conflict. These are the core elements of a training programme for developing conflict resolution skills and peer mediation in schools. Such a programme can be a major component in transforming schools to just and caring learning communities. Many schools in the UK, USA, South Africa, New Zealand, Norway and Northern Ireland now have peer mediation programmes, and new ones are starting as their effects become more widely known.

Conflict

Conflict is inevitable. It is neither good nor bad – it is part of living. How we handle it makes a difference to how we live our lives. There are costs if it is handled negatively, in terms of poor relationships, time, money, damage to people and property, self-esteem and feelings. All these costs are manifested in schools, as well as the costs of underachieving and alienated pupils and the subsequent waste of potential.

For most people conflict has negative connotations. The Chinese word for crisis or conflict is made up of two characters which mean 'danger' and 'opportunity'. This gives a refreshing perspective on conflict. If it is seen as an opportunity for learning and development, it takes on a positive view which opens up more positive approaches to handling conflict.

Conflict in schools

The context in which schools operate is, at times, daunting. We live in an unequal, aggressive, adversarial society which is highly competitive. Its aggression is revealed daily in behaviour which ranges from sarcasm, put-downs, offensive 'jokes' to threats, physical attacks and murder. Society is reflected to varying degrees in schools. The good news is that a change to a more equal, caring and co-operative society is beginning and mediation, including peer mediation, is spreading throughout the UK.

Managing difference

Difference often has negative connotations attached to it. The acceptance and understanding that difference is the norm, and is positive, is essential for children in helping them relate to each other on a basis of equality and deal with conflict constructively. We are all unique and the differences in our opinions, interests, values and needs often cause conflicts.

Understanding difference and the part it plays in conflicts is crucial to constructive conflict resolution. Ignorance and lack of understanding about differences are two of the factors leading to prejudice and discrimination. Understanding the roots of prejudice and discrimination and how they affect all of us reduces conflicts arising from them. Every person has the right to be safe, to be treated as an equal and with respect.

Name-calling

Name-calling in schools is deeply embedded in school culture and much of it involves using difference to hurt and establish power relationships. All children I have worked with dislike name-calling and express strong feelings about it, e.g. sad, lonely, afraid, unhappy, mad, miserable.

'I feel so hurt especially when they say things about my family.'

'I just pretend that I'm not bothered but I am. I am really hurt. I feel like punching them or I get very angry.'

'I feel disgusted and sad and I hate it.'

'When someone calls you a name you are hurt and the other person that called you a name knows so they keep on doing it so you call them a name and before you know it's a fight so I don't like name-calling.'

I have frequently been told by minority ethnic children that they do not report racist name-calling and other incidents, because most teachers do not understand racism and consequently often fail to handle such situations constructively.

In one school with a peer mediation programme, a racist song upset a white pupil, Jane, who said the song was insulting her cousins. The incident went to peer mediation (run by pupil mediators), but it had to be stopped because Jane was too upset and angry to co-operate. The mediators went to the head teacher, who explained the racist and offensive nature of the song to the pupils who had been singing it. She also discussed the song with the older pupils (who had done some work on racism the previous year) and this led to a general discussion of other incidents. The school felt this kind of incident would not have come to light prior to the mediation training programme.

Children need to know that racist or sexist name-calling (and other kinds of name-calling) and bullying are unacceptable and will be dealt with promptly and effectively. Both the offenders and the victims require support. The offenders need to understand the racist and sexist nature of such name-calling and the consequences for individuals and groups. The victims need support in handling incidents. Conflict resolution skills help to raise children's self-esteem and give them more confidence to handle such incidents, although some of the more serious ones will require the intervention of a teacher. Whole school policies which actively promote equal opportunities and understanding diversity are key elements in creating schools where prejudice and discrimination are at a minimum.

Responses to conflict

We all respond to and manage conflict in a number of ways. We can respond aggressively, passively or assertively/co-operatively. The first two are the basic 'fight and flight' reactions which cover a range of responses from murder to finger pointing, from withdrawal to avoidance. Aggressive and passive reactions are not very effective ways of responding to conflict, particularly in the long term. They usually result in a win–lose situation where one party is left feeling dissatisfied and aggrieved. Consequently the relationship between the two parties is unlikely to be very positive and the conflict may erupt again. Assertive/co-operative reactions are more constructive ways of responding and help to create or enhance good relationships.

Often the difficulties in resolving conflicts satisfactorily are due to poor listening and communication skills, and low self-esteem. These in themselves may also lead to conflict. In addition, disputes often have histories which affect the current disputes. In schools these can also affect the classroom environment adversely. It is important, therefore, to deal with long-term relationships as well as the specific conflict.

Pupils often lack the skills of co-operation, and the fact that most schools are hierarchical and competitive also increases the likelihood of disputes. Conflicts in schools may be both interpersonal and intergroup. Some of the most common causes are jealousy, name-calling, exclusion from friendship groups, threats, teasing, put-downs and bullying. Factors which escalate a conflict include jumping to conclusions, personal abuse, not listening, threatening and blaming.

Two important conflict resolution skills which help pupils handle their conflicts constructively are active listening skills and understanding that there is more than one perspective on any conflict. Listening to and discussing 'The Maligned Wolf Story', an alternative version of Little Red Riding Hood told from the wolf's point of view (Kingston Friends Workshop Group 1996, p.64) is an eye-opener for many children. They begin to learn to put themselves in other people's shoes and understand that there is more than one viewpoint in any situation.

Self-esteem

Adults and children will achieve up to a ceiling of their belief in their ability to achieve. If we can raise the ceiling of their belief in their own ability, we can raise their level of achievement. (Stacey and Robinson 1997, p.52)

Developing self-esteem and the ability to affirm self and others is a continuing part of a training programme in conflict resolution. High self-esteem is essential for children and adults alike. Part of high self-esteem is having an integrated, secure identity which is not threatened by behaviour such as name-calling. Increased confidence and self-esteem are evident at the end of such a programme, particularly with children who are regarded as less academically able.

Emotional intelligence

Schools are learning communities and should not be driven by market forces and a narrow definition of success in academic achievement, which condemns the majority of pupils to 'failure'. To be successful as adults, both in the world of work and the personal domain, requires high self-esteem and a range of social and emotional competencies. Daniel Goleman (1996), in *Emotional Intelligence: Why It Can Matter More Than IQ*, has drawn attention to the crucial importance of emotional intelligence and skills for dealing with life positively and effectively. Many of these skills are developed in conflict resolution.

Constructive conflict resolution

Question: 'What do peer mediators have to be good at?'

Answer: 'Ifryfing!' ('Everything') – Primary 6 (age 10) pupil at the end of a mediation training programme.

This is quite a challenge but one which children meet with relish. Although people have been practising mediation and conflict resolution skills for hundreds of years, their development in schools is relatively recent. Peer mediation programmes were set up in schools in the USA in the late 1970s, and the Kingston Friends Workshop Group introduced such programmes to the UK in 1981. Constructive conflict resolution is based on a number of beliefs:

- Pupils can take responsibility for their behaviour and have the ability to resolve conflicts constructively.
- Conflict is a shared problem.
- All parties to a conflict should participate in its resolution.

- Aggression and violence are not acceptable ways of handling conflict.
- Mediation skills empower pupils to handle their conflicts in constructive ways.

As conflict is a normal part of life, learning conflict resolution skills is as essential and as educational as learning the 3Rs.

Initially it is not essential for all these beliefs to be held by the whole school community for conflict resolution and peer mediation to be effective. If key figures are willing to take them on board and if the majority of the staff are open to new ideas, development will follow. However, a number of conditions are needed in a school for conflict resolution and peer mediation programmes to be effective and sustainable in the long term on a whole school basis:

- Conflict resolution and peer mediation should be integral to personal and social education programmes and a whole school policy on raising self-esteem, promoting positive behaviour and discipline.
- The majority of the school staff accept the beliefs underpinning mediation.
- The teaching and learning styles are open to the programmes.
- The ethos of the school is, or is beginning to be, congruent with constructive conflict resolution.
- There is co-operation and commitment of the head teacher and key staff.
- Raising self-esteem is recognised as a key element for the success of the programme.
- A named person has responsibility for the programme and subsequent training and support.
- Parents are aware of and accept the programme and take part in workshops for them.

There are many links with other areas of education, e.g. citizenship, personal and social education, anti-bias education, co-operative learning, creative thinking and problem solving, raising achievement and anti-bullying strategies.

Caution

A word of caution – introducing conflict management and peer mediation training programmes are not a quick fix, a bolt-on package or a magic wand. They will not transform a school overnight or solve the problem of bullying. Bullying is a complex matter which needs to be tackled on a broad front.

However, conflict resolution skills help young people to deal with bullying and the fear of bullying, by building up their self-esteem and giving them some coping strategies. The programmes also help to create a school climate where bullying is unacceptable, where both bully and victim know this and know they will receive the support they both need.

Dealing with concerns

A fairly substantial investment in time and commitment is necessary for change to take place, and for the benefits of conflict resolution and peer mediation to be realised. They are additional strategies which are part of a whole school policy on discipline and positive behaviour – they do not replace the school disciplinary procedures. Certain disputes are not handled by children, e.g. theft, drugs, abuse and serious bullying. Children, staff and mediators know which disputes are mediatable by them and which need to be referred to teachers. Teachers will also be using the conflict resolution skills, as well as the more traditional ways of handling disputes.

Training and research findings show that children are capable of and skilful at handling their own conflicts. They have a greater knowledge and understanding of the culture and relationships in schools than adults. In peer mediation programmes children are empowered and empower their peers, because they have to confront themselves, take responsibility for their feelings and behaviour and find mutually acceptable outcomes to their disputes. It becomes the norm and acceptable to talk through feelings and problems. Many children feel more confident in opening up to peers rather than teachers (Primary 6 – age 10 – evaluation answers):

- 'Teachers and children don't think the same.'
- 'Teachers sometimes take sides.'
- 'Teachers mostly blame.'
- 'Mediation is better because you don't get rows and don't feel frightened.'
- 'Some children talk more to children than adults.'
- 'Children sort it out in their own time.'

There may be a few occasions when mediation takes time out of a class but if conflicts are successfully mediated less time is lost overall in disputes and classrooms will be more peaceful and co-operative places.

The teacher's role

The teacher's role is of paramount importance to the success of conflict resolution programmes. Teachers model the behaviour so that children see the skills and qualities in action and receive positive feedback when they use them. Teachers too need high self-esteem and to be prepared to develop more equal relationships with children. Incidents in the classroom and elsewhere can be used by the teacher to demonstrate how to use the skills.

Peer mediation and conflict resolution training programmes

Aims

The aims of training programmes in conflict resolution and peer mediation are:

- to enable young people to take responsibility for conflicts and their resolution in constructive ways;
- to improve communication, co-operation, relationships and self-esteem;
- to encourage positive behaviour, self-discipline and the positive management of emotions;
- to reduce conflict;
- to reduce the amount of time teachers spend on minor conflicts and discipline;
- to enable teachers to have more time for teaching;
- to improve the classroom climate so it is more peaceful and co-operative and so enhances learning.

Training programmes

Training programmes are designed, in collaboration with the staff, to meet the needs of an individual school. Most programmes start with general conflict management training and then move on to peer mediation training if the school wishes to do so. Training programmes are age appropriate, so clearly the exercises in a programme for Primary 6 (age 10) or Primary 7 (age 11) will differ from one for infant or Primary 1 (age 5) (Table 3.1). They build on existing good primary school practice. The core elements of a training programme for any age are based on the iceberg principle. There are two icebergs, the conflict iceberg and the mediation/conflict resolution/problem-solving iceberg (based on a model taken from the Kingston Friends Workshop Group 1996, p.5).

Table 3.1 Numbering of primary classes in Scotland, England and Wales		
Age	Scotland	England and Wales
5 years old	P1	R – reception
6 years old	P2	Y1
7 years old	P3	Y2
8 years old	P4	Y3
9 years old	P5	Y4
10 years old	P6	Y5
11 years old	P7	Y6

The conflict iceberg

We only see the tip of the iceberg – the conflict (Figure 3.1). There are hidden elements underneath which can cause the conflict, keep it going or are contributing to it not having a satisfactory outcome. The hidden elements need to be exposed in order for conflicts to be resolved satisfactorily.

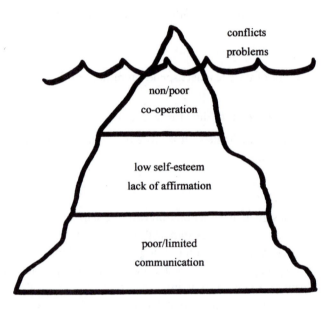

Figure 3.1 Conflict iceberg

The mediation iceberg

This iceberg is the opposite of the conflict iceberg. Positive outcomes rest on many skills and attributes (Figure 3.2). Training programmes based on the iceberg consist of developing communication, affirmation and co-operation skills, raising self-esteem, understanding conflict, feelings, difference and learning the mediation process. In each major element there is a range of skills and qualities for development. Communication skills would include active listening and responding, empathy, clarifying, summarising, open questions, evaluation and 'I' messages. 'I' messages are statements which begin with 'I' – 'I feel upset when I'm pushed around'. The person takes responsibility for their feelings, opinions and behaviour rather than blaming the other person – 'You made me feel upset.' Programmes are taught through a variety of methods such as circle time, drama and games as well as class, group and individual work.

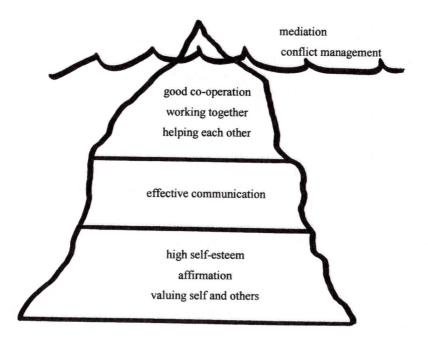

Figure 3.2 Mediation iceberg

Circle time

In circle time pupils and teachers sit in a circle which emphasises equality and co-operation. There are no barriers between pupil and pupil or between teacher and pupils. The major focus of work done in circle time is on raising self-esteem and developing communication and co-operation skills.

The basic ground rules for circle time are established by the children and teacher together. They will include: only one person speaks at a time, no interrupting, listen carefully, right to pass, no put-downs or name-calling. The teacher may well find her/himself mediating fairly punitive ideas about what should happen when people are finding it difficult to keep the rules. One suggestion from a class with a particularly high number of disaffected pupils was that two pupils should sit in the centre of the circle to keep watch and send out anyone who broke a rule.

A structure of rights, responsibilities, rules and respect (the four Rs) needs to be established in the classroom by the pupils and teacher working together. For example, one right could be: I have the right to be safe. This has the responsibility that I may not use aggression and violence, which results in the rule 'no aggression and violence'. If rules are broken, it is these rights and responsibilities that are referred to.

Children then decide how they like to be treated by other people and the class chooses the six ways they consider to be the most important ones to form 'Our Respect Charter'.

Once pupils have adapted to circle time (usually quite quickly), and have internalised the rules and trust the group, it becomes a powerful process for delivering conflict resolution and peer mediation programmes. Rounds are used where everyone takes it in turn to speak and be listened to. Pair and small group work, drama and discussion are also used within the circle.

Examples of exercises

At first pupils (like adults) find it difficult to say positive things about themselves (affirmation). The first time I used a round asking each pupil to say something they were pleased with about themselves, only half could find anything to say. After a few weeks everyone could find something to say without being embarrassed. There are numerous affirmation exercises. One which always delights children is for each child to draw their hand. This is passed round for others to write affirmations on the fingers, thumb and palm. Each child in turn stands at the front of the class and reads out the affirmations and receives a round of applause. This was the turning point for one child who had low self-esteem and rarely contributed to circle time. He came to me with a broad grin, his eyes shining, saying, 'Look they say I'm skilful!' From that moment his self-esteem and confidence grew. Another boy drew two thumbs on his hand so that he could get more affirmations!

An exercise which encourages listening, co-operation and imagination is the creation of a group story. One person in the circle starts with two words, e.g. 'Last night...' and each person in turn adds another two words to build up a story. Near the beginning of circle time, I always use a round to encourage pupils to express their feelings. They are asked to say how they are feeling on a scale of 0–10, with 10 representing feeling very happy and good about everything. If they wish, they can also explain why they are feeling that number. Most children find this a non-threatening way of expressing even very strong feelings, and they reveal situations which they might not otherwise do. The teacher can then follow up on these if necessary and the rest of the class can give support and understanding. A relaxing exercise to encourage the imagination is a round where each pupil finishes the sentence, 'If I had a magic carpet, I would...' One pupil said she would fly under all the waterfalls. Another said he would fly up high, then fall down and die so that he could join his grandfather who had recently died.

The mediation process

The mediation process for children is very similar to the adult process and usually consists of five broad stages:

- *Stage 1*: introductions, mediator's role, ground rules. The ground rules are no interrupting, no put-downs, no swearing or name-calling, try to be honest.
- *Stage 2*: each party tells their story uninterrupted and expresses their feelings.
- *Stage 3*: the parties question each other and discuss the issues.
- *Stage 4*: the parties put forward suggestions for workable solutions.
- *Stage 5*: the parties agree on one or more solutions. A written agreement is drawn up and signed by the parties and the mediators.

The mediators guide the parties through this process and support them in coming to an understanding of how each person feels and that they have a shared problem to which they can together find a workable solution.

In my experience, primary age children work through the process much more quickly than adults and are more open about their feelings and what they think about the situation. They usually find solutions quite easily and quickly, sometimes because they want to get back to the playground as quickly as possible!

Part of the training includes difficult situations and ways of handling them. For example:

Question: What does a mediator do if they are asked to mediate a dispute which involves their best friend?

Answer: They find another mediator.

Question: What does a mediator do if a disputant calls names?

Answer: They are reminded of the mediation rules and given a warning. If they persist, the mediators stop the mediation and try to find out why the pupil is behaving in this way. If necessary, they refer it to a teacher.

Delivery of programmes

Delivery of a training programme can be done in a number of ways and is always a collaboration between the school and the consultant/trainer, so that it meets the needs of a particular school. There are several general ways of delivering training programmes:

1.   The conflict resolution training programme is delivered by a consultant/trainer with the class teacher over a period of approximately eight weeks. If the school wants to set up a peer mediation service, a number of children who have completed this programme are selected to do further training to learn the mediation process and the role of mediators. Much of this is done through role play.

2.   At least two teachers attend a two-day course and then implement the first stage of the programme. Then they periodically attend workshops and return to their classes to implement the next stages.

3.   The staff of the school are trained in the use of circle time and conflict resolution skills and then implement a programme on a whole school basis, primarily through circle time.

In each case, if required, there is ongoing support from the consultant/trainer. The long-term aim is the embedding of the beliefs and skills in the curriculum, management and ethos of the school. It is essential to have a follow-up programme for the first year with additional training, a monitoring scheme and regular evaluation. A programme of workshops for parents runs parallel with the children's training, both to understand what the children are doing and so that they can be involved in conflict resolution programmes if they wish.

We all learn primarily by doing. The training programme is the first step towards handling conflicts constructively – the real work is the 'doing'. It is the real life practising of the skills which creates the change in attitudes and behaviour.

Case studies

School A in a rural area near a town and School B in an inner city area

In both schools a conflict resolution and peer mediation programme was run over a period of one term, half a day per week with Primary 6 (age 10) classes. A number of preliminary meetings were held with the head teachers and a day's workshop with the class teachers of Primary 6. There were meetings with all the staff and workshops were run for parents.

The delivery of the programme was a collaboration with the class teacher and consultant/trainer with the teacher being trained on the spot. The teacher also carried out follow-up work between the sessions. This often linked with curriculum work already timetabled.

Circle time was introduced to the children, who quickly adapted to it. At the time of Dunblane (when, in 1996, a number of primary school children and a teacher were killed in Dunblane by a gunman), School A abandoned the normal school day and every class used circle time to discuss and deal with what had happened. When I went there the next day to work with the Primary 6s, they decided they wanted to use part of circle time to continue discussing Dunblane. They were able to express their feelings and views openly and with maturity. They ended it by having a minute's silence. It was one of the most moving experiences I've had, and to this day I cry when I recall it.

Initially each programme session focused specifically on one element of the iceberg, e.g. self-esteem. After about three sessions, aspects of all three elements were included in each session. Work on difference, feelings, conflict and the causes of conflict was an essential component of the programme.

After the basic conflict resolution skills had been taught, the mediation process and role of mediators was introduced and practised, mainly through role play. The teacher, secretary and myself did a demonstration role play about a neighbour dispute. The pupils found this totally fascinating as the teacher and the secretary got right into role and gave very convincing performances, making my role as mediator somewhat tricky. The questions afterwards concentrated on such weighty issues as whether Miss really liked the pop singer 'Meat Loaf' or not!

At the end of the programme there was a special assembly where each child received a certificate to show they had been trained in conflict resolution skills. The children then decided who they thought would make the best mediators. Interestingly, their choices were virtually the same as those of the teachers. Several children said they did not want to be mediators – they knew they were not ready for the role. Those who were not school mediators were able to do other jobs such as helping with administration of the peer mediation service and asking children in dispute if they would like to try mediation.

Even before the mediation service was up and running, some of the younger children were asking the head teacher when they (the mediators) were going to help them. Peer mediation services were set up in both schools, with mediator support groups, monitoring and evaluation schemes, ongoing further training and plans for training the next year's Primary 6s. Mediators always work in pairs, usually girl/boy, on a rota basis. Mediation takes place in a designated room where confidentiality can be assured. To varying degrees, conflict resolution skills are now being taught to most of the classes through circle time.

All the children enjoyed the training, with the highest vote in School A going to the co-operative games.

'I enjoyed doing the frog game. I liked it because it was the first time I had ever been on a boy's back!' (Primary 6 girl) Most of them said they would use the skills outside the school, e.g. with family or when they see conflicts. Mediators from both schools have given demonstrations to teachers from other schools and they assist with the training of the Primary 6 classes.

An example of a school dispute – spreading lies

Disputes about spreading lies and rumours often occur in primary schools. In this particular dispute, four boys were spreading lies about five other boys, one of whom had his name, spelt incorrectly, written on a toilet door. A couple of other children suggested they should all go to mediation, which they agreed to do. Two mediators, a boy and a girl, listened to the stories from both groups and found it a difficult situation because the four boys were denying they had done anything. They were also disagreeing among themselves. The mediators asked each of them to write down the name of the boy whose name was written on the toilet door. One of them spelt it incorrectly! After that they all admitted they had been spreading lies. They acknowledged it was not a nice thing to do and agreed not to spread lies or write names in future. They also apologised. A few weeks later they were all asked to come to a mediation meeting to check if the agreement was holding. It was and they were all getting on well together.

Follow-up questionnaire

Approximately one year after the training, School B gave a questionnaire 'Has Mediation Made a Difference?' to the Primary 3–7 pupils and teachers. There was a very positive response with 68 pupils agreeing that it was helpful to have mediation to help them solve their problems; only four disagreed. One of the questions was: Question 7: Is there anything you would like to say about mediation? Examples of the answers were:

'I think mediation has helped the school a lot because there is hardly any fighting any more. I think we should keep mediation going.'

'I like mediation because I don't get battered any more out in the playground.'

'It helps people to be friends who have been in conflict for a while.'

'It is good because it stops the teachers wasting precious time sorting problems out.'

'I say it is brilliant because it helps me at home too, not just in school.'

'Mediation has made the whole school a much calmer and more secure place for all children' (teacher's comment).

Comments from the head teachers and class teachers

School A – Head teacher

It's incalculable the pride I felt as a head teacher in the success of the pupils in this pilot project as they moved towards becoming articulate, mature and supportive in handling conflict situations. The whole school benefited from the training of a class of pupils because everyone reaped the reward of their ability to support their peers in handling conflict situations successfully. Surprisingly, among the most accomplished mediators were pupils who had once found pleasure in bullying.

School A – Class teacher

The children support each other more and are more considerate. They have developed empathy and think more as a group. They also co-operate with each other in their work. I have a more equitable relationship with them. I'm relaxed and I just happen to be the person who co-ordinates the group. Some children have changed their behaviour outside school. Some parents have said their children are more reasonable at home and aggression is reduced.

School B – Head teacher

The training has cut down on the amount of conflict in the playground and at break times. The mediators deal with the disputes and the pupils themselves are beginning to talk through their disputes. They are able to stop minor disputes escalating. Their self-esteem is much higher and they have increased self-confidence. They also have higher expectations of themselves and I have as well. They still get involved in disputes at times. All classes are developing conflict management skills especially communication skills and raising self-esteem through circle time. It has also improved my communication with parents.

School B – Class teacher

The staff are spending less time dealing with conflicts. It has helped children to be more tolerant of others and more able to listen and hear other viewpoints. Circle time is very valuable. The children say things of a personal nature which they would not say outside the circle so I have become more aware of the personal lives of the children.

Research

Research on peer mediation in Northern Ireland at the Centre for the Study of Conflict at the University of Ulster has found pupil relationships have improved, as have communication skills, and co-operation and conflict has declined. Less able pupils in particular, have shown increased academic progress as a result of improved self-esteem (Hartop 1996).

There has been extensive research in the USA. Teachers and student mediators on a mediation programme in five schools in New York were evaluated and it was found that:

99 per cent of the teachers agreed that the mediation component had given children an important tool for dealing with everyday conflict, 85 per cent agreed that mediators' participation in the mediation component had contributed to increasing the mediators' self-esteem, 88 per cent said that mediation helped students take more responsibility for solving their problems, 84 per cent of the mediators agreed that being a mediator had given them skills they can use for their whole life. (Metis Associates Inc 1996)

Conclusion

We are all children of the planet Earth and we are entitled to live in a peaceful and harmonious world. Conflict resolution and peer mediation training programmes are strategies which will help equip children to live their lives constructively and harmoniously. There will always be some conflict. What is needed are schools (and adult institutions) where this is at a minimum and the norm is for conflict to be talked through and handled constructively by everyone in the school community. The research and evidence from head teachers and class teachers shows that this is being achieved in some schools, and there is no reason why it should not be achieved in many more, given the necessary conditions. An effective and sustainable conflict resolution programme will enable the principles of constructive conflict resolution to be reflected in the policies and practices of the school. Such programmes, as part of whole school policies on raising self-esteem and promoting positive behaviour, can make a significant contribution to enhancing the learning of children and the development of positive relationships and life skills.

References

Goleman, D. (1996) *Emotional Intelligence: Why It Can Matter More Than IQ.* London: Bloomsbury.

Hartop, B. (1996) *Peer Mediation as an Expression of Education for Mutual Understanding – Facilitating Change, Annual Report 1995–1996.* Londonderry: The EMU Promoting School Project.

Kingston Friends Workshop Group (1996) *Ways and Means Today.* Kingston-upon-Thames: Kingston Friends Workshop Group.

Metis Associates Inc (1996) 'The resolving conflict creatively program, 1988–1989: summary of significant findings.' In L. Lantieri and J. Patti (eds) *Waging Peace in our Schools.* Boston: Beacon Press.

Stacey, H. and Robinson, P. (1997) *Let's Mediate.* Bristol: Lucky Duck Publishing.

4

Mediation in a South London Secondary School

Mark Bitel and Delia Rolls

Introduction

This chapter describes the development and progress of mediation in Sacred Heart School in Camberwell, London. A 1997 Office for Standards in Education (OFSTED) inspection of the school praised the school's approach to conflict resolution as 'innovative and exceptional'.

With five years' experience, Sacred Heart is probably one of the longest running school-based mediation programmes in Britain. Mediation at Sacred Heart is integrated into a package of conflict resolution approaches that are now embedded in the school culture, and the role of the peer mediators has progressed beyond purely conducting mediations. This is an account of the successes and lessons learned since the spring of 1993.

Background to the school

Sacred Heart School is a Roman Catholic mixed-gender secondary school located in the London Borough of Southwark, one of the most deprived inner city boroughs. Sacred Heart shares many of the benefits and challenges of an inner city school and with its caring ethos is a positive beacon in the community.

There are 580 students at the school in Years 7 to 11. The students come from a wide range of ethnic, cultural and national backgrounds with 27 language groups.

The school has a well-developed 'special needs' department, which includes a full-time school counsellor on the staff. It is within this department that the conflict resolution programme is based, with the school counsellor taking the lead responsibility for its development and operation.

Setting up the mediation scheme

Mediation was introduced to Sacred Heart by Southwark Mediation Centre, the local mediation service, which employed a part-time schools project worker. Sacred Heart was picked as one of the two schools for the pilot programme and the schools project worker liaised closely with the school counsellor to initiate the project.

The project began in the 1992 autumn term, with lessons for Year 9 students (aged 13 to 14) examining the meaning of conflict and alternative ways of dealing with disputes. At the end of this term an election was held to choose ten students to be trained as mediators.

The training took place over a period of three months. A two-day introductory workshop was held at Southwark Mediation Centre for both pilot schools and subsequent weekly training sessions took place in the individual schools. The school counsellor was jointly responsible for the training because of her special interest in this area. The school management supported the school counsellor through additional training in other conflict resolution programmes, including 'Playing with Fire' and 'Training for Trainers' (youth and conflict courses offered by the Leap Confronting Conflict). The school counsellor's voluntary work with the 'Alternatives to Violence Project' also provided a useful foundation in developing conflict resolution programmes at Sacred Heart.

In the first year, the training was conducted during school time and the trainee mediators were released from their classes to attend. The training encompassed listening and other communication skills, what it meant to be a mediator, working with a co-mediator and the form and structure of mediation sessions. Learning how to use the structure and the ground rules (see Box 4.1) was a key element, as this supported the mediators and enabled them to keep their mediations on track, preventing conflicts between the disputants from getting out of hand during the session. During the training, the student mediators reached 'an impressively high standard in their mediation skills' (Southwark Mediation Centre 1994).

By the end of the summer term, the first student mediators were ready to mediate and received their certificates for their National Record of Achievement (NRA) portfolios. They were issued with their triangular mediator badges (Figure 4.3) so that they could be identified as mediators in the school. A special summer celebration workshop was held for the mediators by the school counsellor and an outside trainer, to consolidate their achievements and further develop the group's confidence.

The mediation scheme was launched that summer with presentations in school assemblies and a poster competition. The launch of the mediation scheme resulted in a trickle of cases that enabled the mediators to build their confidence gradually, as each case was successfully mediated.

After the long summer break, another workshop was held by the school counsellor and the outside trainer to refresh the mediators and rekindle their enthusiasm. Cases continued to trickle in and requests for mediation peaked immediately after each of the anti-bullying sessions (see 'Other conflict resolution programmes in the school', p.78).

Mediations were generally conducted during lunch breaks and all mediators were required to attend weekly after-school support sessions with the school counsellor. This weekly commitment proved to be too demanding for some of the mediators and

Box 4.1 Structure and ground rules for a mediation session

STEP 1: How to introduce the mediation session

Welcome to Sacred Heart School's Mediation programme. My name is...
and my co-mediator's name is...

Thank you both for attending. Am I right in saying that both (all) of you are here because you wish to resolve a problem? Look for agreement before moving on.

Anything you say will be treated in the strictest confidence.

Now we will tell you how the mediation session will run:

1. *In a moment we will outline the ground rules.*

2. *Then each of you can give your account of what has happened with no interruptions.*

3. *We will then summarise what you have said.*

4. *Then we will discuss all the points, one by one, and the feelings you may have about them.*

5. *Towards the end, we may find areas of agreement and write them down.*

6. *The ground rules are as follows:*

    we ask you to treat each other with respect
    we ask you not to interrupt
    we ask that you give us permission to bring the mediation to a halt if needed.
    we would like to remind you that all the facts discussed during the mediation will be confidential, unless you tell us about any abuse, which we will need to bring to the attention of the school counsellor*.

7. *Do you understand these ground rules? Do you agree to be guided by them? You must seek agreement before you move on.*

STEP 2: Listening to the stories – finding out the facts and feelings

Which of you would like to give your account first? Thank you... (A)

After (A) gives his/her account, summarise (A)'s account. Look directly at A. Then swap round and ask (B) to give his/her account. After (B)'s account, summarise what (B) has said. Look directly at (B).

Remember at this stage to summarise: the facts; the feelings; and the points for discussion.

STEP 3: Working towards agreement

Start with the point that is *not* the most important point but one on which you will get agreement. Then work through the points, one by one, focusing discussion on that one point and the feelings that each party have about that point.

* This is a statutory requirement under the Children Act 1989.

Figure 4.1 Start of mediation session: disputants face away from each other

Figure 4.2 End of mediation session: disputants face towards each other

Figure 4.3 Mediator badge: The border, outlines and word 'Mediator' are in gold letters and the circles are coloured in two different shades of red

four of the ten trained mediators dropped out of the project, leaving a core of six mediators: five girls and one boy.

As with all successful development projects, Southwark Mediation Centre was gradually able to withdraw as the pilot project became established within the school. During the transitional period, Southwark Mediation Centre was able to pay the school to cover two hours of the counsellor's time each week to co-ordinate the project at Sacred Heart, until the mediation scheme became integrated into the school's own budget.

The first group of mediators enjoyed the profile and status of being among the first student mediators in Britain. They spoke at local and national conferences and were delegates at the 1994 Mediation UK conference.

Getting the boys involved

The first group of mediators were predominantly girls and it was seen as vital for the success of the mediation scheme to get more boys involved, to have a more balanced gender mix among the mediators.

The mediation co-ordinator decided to change the method of recruiting the mediators. Instead of an election, students in Year 9 were encouraged to put themselves forward to be trained as mediators. The school counsellor/mediation co-ordinator positively encouraged some of the more popular boys who were good

Figure 4.4 Mediators in Year 10 (1997–8)

at sports in Year 9 to become mediators. In order that the mediators would have credibility throughout the school, it was also seen as essential that they were representative of the different abilities in the school, rather than relying on the students with the best educational or behavioural attainments. The mediation scheme was seen as a way of increasing student responsibility.

This approach was successful and many boys came forward to be trained as mediators, including some of the 'coolest' boys in the school. This was a major breakthrough, as it increased the credibility of mediation throughout the school (Figure 4.4).

By the end of this process, 25 pupils had been recruited into the second group to be trained. Due to the large number being trained, the establishment of mediation as part of the school's normal activities (rather than a high-profile pilot project) and the pressures of the National Curriculum, the mediation training was moved to an after-school activity.

Training peer mediators

Every week for ten weeks, the trainee mediators attended a one-hour training session. Box 4.2 shows the outline topics of the training course. The training is experiential, fast-moving and fun. Each session builds on learning from previous sessions and there are frequent opportunities to practise the skills in order to reinforce the learning.

Box 4.2 Outline topics of the peer mediators' training

Session 1 Introduction and community building

Session 2 Listening skills

Session 3 What is conflict? What is mediation? Being a mediator

Session 4 Introducing the three steps to mediation. How to introduce a mediation session and the ground rules (Step 1)

Session 5 Active listening

Session 6 Listening to disputants and working towards agreement (Steps 2 and 3)

Session 7 Role play: mediation practice

Session 8 Demonstration of mediation skills

Session 9 Celebrating difference

Session 10 Mediation practice

The ten sessions are followed by proficiency tests and weekly meetings for further learning and supervision.

A written test is given in Session 9. After the formal training ends, trainee mediators are required to pass a practical demonstration (in a role play) of their ability to mediate. Occasionally, a trainee will have to undertake more than one practical demonstration of their mediation skills, until the trainer is satisfied that they have the confidence and ability to mediate in the school.

The fact that the sessions took part after school meant that trainee mediators had to give a real commitment. About ten dropped out during the training, leaving a core group of 15 newly trained mediators. After the initial training, they continued to attend weekly practice sessions until they had passed a proficiency test and received their mediators' badges.

Keeping the momentum going

Mediation cases began to come in thick and fast. Sometimes the mediators would witness conflicts in the school and invite the disputants to attend mediation; at other times one student in dispute with another would come to a mediator and ask for mediation. Written agreements were rare, with most agreements being verbal. The mediators followed up successfully mediated cases several days after the agreement, to ensure that the agreements were being kept to.

Weekly lunchtime and after-school support sessions were provided for mediators to share their experiences and receive support and advice from their peers and the mediation co-ordinator.

The most common cases tend to involve name-calling or 'cussing'. Other common types of case involve disputes between friends, which without mediation would develop into long-term conflicts. Some typical cases are described below. (Names have been changed to protect the identities of the students involved.)

Two typical mediator-initiated cases

CUSSING AND GOSSIP

A pupil in Year 7 was getting bullied about her name by a boy in her form. The mediators invited them to mediation and they both agreed.

After listening to their stories it emerged that the boy, Nathan, had asked Agnes out and she had refused. Agnes then told Nathan's girlfriend about this and he was therefore really angry. He expressed his anger by cussing Agnes. The mediators used their skills to get the disputants to listen to each other. Agnes then acknowledged that she shouldn't have spread gossip by telling Nathan's girlfriend, and she apologised. Nathan then said sorry for cussing her and the matter was resolved.

FRIENDSHIP IN PERIL

Two girls, Norma and Vera, were arguing about an incident that happened at the weekend.

The exchange was becoming very heated and one of the mediators who was on duty became involved. She asked the girls if they wanted to go to mediation and they agreed. Another mediator was found and the session began.

Having listened to the stories, it emerged that Norma had been caught smoking while staying the weekend at Vera's caravan. Vera's mother was annoyed and the girls had started arguing, and were continuing that argument in school on Monday.

At first Norma could not see what all the fuss was about and was not taking any responsibility for smoking. Vera then explained about the strict no-smoking rule on the camp site and that her mother was angry because not only was Norma under age, but had also broken the rule.

Vera said her mother was afraid that they might be asked to remove their caravan if the site manager found out. Upon hearing this, Norma said she didn't realise and was sorry she had upset Vera's mother. The girls felt that for the time being they didn't want to be friends, but agreed to a follow-up meeting in a week's time. The meeting was held and in fact the girls were friends once more and planning the next weekend!

It has been the experience at Sacred Heart that young people respond well to peer mediation. If conflicts can be mediated at an early stage, when the underlying causes of conflict are relatively fresh, young people can use mediation as a way of listening to and hearing what is really going on in their relationships with others. When they can hear what is really going on, they can use the structure of mediation to find acceptable ways forward to reduce the conflict.

Mediation does not seek to turn all student disputants into 'best friends', but it offers them opportunities to take responsibility for sorting out their own conflicts and learning from them. However, with some frequency, surprising things can happen in mediation and unexpected outcomes occur that go beyond 'face saving' or simple 'win–win' solutions (Box 4.4).

An example of a mediation with an unexpectedly good outcome
YER MUM!

> *Two boys, Adrian and Toby, had a fight in an art lesson. The boys had been cussing one another and generally winding one another up. It was at the point when they both cussed each other's mothers that the fight broke out.*
>
> *The art teacher stopped the fight and suggested that they go to mediation. At first both boys were somewhat reluctant to attend, but eventually they agreed.*
>
> *The two mediators went through the process and listened to both boys' stories. What materialised was that both of their mothers were ill: one was disabled and the other abused drugs. The mediators skilfully helped the boys to realise the commonality between them, and how not knowing about the other person's circumstances led them to the cuss, provoking the fight, as both boys were extremely protective of their mothers.*
>
> *The situation was positively resolved and the boys became a great support to each other.*

Responsibility for the scheme falls totally on the mediation co-ordinator and the mediators, so keeping the momentum going requires considerable commitment. Regular lunch time and after-school training and support sessions are vital to keep the scheme in operation.

Each year slight modifications and improvements are made to recruitment and training. There is now such strong demand to be trained as a mediator among Year 9 students that prospective mediators are asked to complete an application form and attend an interview. Applicants are asked why they want to be a mediator, about their commitment and why they should be chosen. It can be a very difficult task indeed choosing a maximum of 20 trainees per year, but this is the largest group the co-ordinator can manage during training.

Other developments are added each year in order to keep an element of newness and excitement in the scheme. These activities have included composing a peer mediation rap song (1994), writing a training manual (Rolls 1996), regular overseas visitors to see the scheme in action (ongoing), an exchange programme with student mediators in Norway (1997) and a reading support scheme (1998). The latter two developments will be described in more detail in later sections.

Current developments include participation in a three-country European Union school mediation project. From this three-year programme which commenced in

1997, Sacred Heart hopes to establish regular dialogue with mediators in Norway and Denmark via the internet, develop a vocational qualification (such as NVQ – National Vocational Qualifications) for school-based peer mediators and improve the training manual.

Other conflict resolution programmes in the school

The mediation scheme at Sacred Heart sits within an overall framework of conflict resolution approaches, as shown in Box 4.3. These conflict resolution approaches support and dovetail into each other, offering students a wide choice of ways to address their problems with other students. Giving students a choice also requires them to take responsibility for deciding how they wish to address any such problems.

Box 4.3 Conflict resolution at Sacred Heart

Anti-bullying workshops

All Year 7 students attend six sessions to reduce peer approval for bullying; introduction of concept of a *telling school, No Blame Approach* and *peer mediation*.

No Blame Approach

Offered by school counsellor to all students as a constructive way to resolve problems between students, with no sanctions if instigator takes responsibility to sort things out, makes things right and ceases to cause the problem.

Peer mediation

Mediation is an option for all students to resolve student–student conflict. Mediators selected and trained in Year 9. Mediators become active in Year 10 and reduce involvement as they approach their GCSE examinations in Year 11.

More punitive sanctions against anti-social student behaviour are also available, if students experiencing problems with other students wish to report incidents to teachers and heads of year (which may result in letters home to parents of the perpetrator and eventual exclusion).

School policy ensures that students have a choice in deciding how to deal with conflicts with other students.

The anti-bullying workshops began in the autumn of 1993. Although bullying was not a particularly apparent problem at Sacred Heart, a student survey conducted in 1993 demonstrated that a great majority of pupils were concerned or worried by the issue of bullying. The independent trainer who had earlier been involved in the special beginning and end of term workshops for the initial group of mediators was paid to work with the school counsellor to develop anti-bullying workshops. A programme of six workshops was developed (Bitel and Rolls 1995). Each workshop lasts for one hour and takes place every half term. It is delivered by the trainer and the school counsellor several times on the same day, so that each class in Year 7 can attend.

The participatory workshops take the form of circle time and small group work on the issues of reducing peer approval for bullying. They do this by looking at the roots of bullying, helping each student to have a voice and know that it is safe to tell if they are experiencing problems, encouraging responsibility and celebrating diversity. Peer mediation and the 'No Blame Approach' (Robinson and Maines 1997) are introduced and role plays used to show how they work.

The school counsellor offers students the opportunity to work confidentially through their conflicts using the 'No Blame Approach'. A student who is experiencing problems with other students can describe this to the counsellor. With the student's permission, the school counsellor then contacts the other student(s) involved. In a process parallel to mediation, the disputants get to hear each other's stories and the feelings associated with the dispute. Those causing the problem are then told that if they can take responsibility to sort out the problem and cease causing it, then the matter will go no further. They are asked for suggestions and an agreement is made. The school counsellor then checks back with both parties to see if the agreement is working out, and if it is the matter ends there.

Virtually all disputes taken through the 'No Blame Approach' are satisfactorily resolved. However, in the rare cases when the disputes have not been resolved, the matters are referred to the school's senior managers to deal with, following traditional behavioural sanctions such as detention, letters home to parents or exclusion. However, the 'No Blame Approach' offers the opportunity to get the dispute resolved at the source and decreases any vicious cycles of punishment, anger and revenge.

However, if the school counsellor were to try to deal with all the conflicts in the school, her role would be completely unmanageable. This is where the mediators play an invaluable part. Students experiencing conflicts with other students at Sacred Heart have a choice of to whom to go to talk about their problems. This choice usually depends on the nature of the conflict and whom they most trust to help them resolve it. Sometimes they choose to go to the school counsellor; some students choose to speak to their form tutors and some go to the mediators.

Importance of the whole school approach

If there is a weak link in the conflict resolution framework at Sacred Heart, it is the fact that there is no consistent whole school approach to conflict. Different members of staff deal with student–student conflict in different ways.

The roots of this date back to the introduction of the peer mediation programme. Although the conflict resolution framework has always had the broad support and backing from the head teacher and deputy head teacher, the peer mediation scheme and other approaches can sometimes be marginalised as they are based within the

Learning Support Team. Because of this, these approaches are somehow never quite seen as 'mainstream'.

The school counsellor/mediation co-ordinator has repeatedly requested In-service Education and Training (INSET) time to present the conflict resolution framework to the full staff, but this has been difficult, due to all the other important pressing needs for staff information and training during INSET.

One of the greatest lessons learned from the Sacred Heart peer mediation scheme is the importance of a whole school approach. If this were achieved, it would make it more likely that the mediation programme would be supported and valued by all staff and lead to greater consistency across the school. Nevertheless, many staff at Sacred Heart are aware of the range of conflict resolution approaches and demonstrate their positive view by referring students to the mediators or the school counsellor.

Through the anti-bullying programme, all students know about the alternative approaches to resolving their conflicts with other students and the choice rests with them.

A whole class mediation

Mediation at Sacred Heart is routinely used for student–student conflicts. There are no formal structures to address student–teacher conflicts through mediation. Due to the asymmetries of power between students and teachers, mediation is very often not appropriate. But one day in 1997, a situation arose between a teacher and a whole class of Year 7 students (aged 11 to 12) that needed resolving. By complete coincidence and serendipity, this situation occurred immediately before the beginning of an anti-bullying workshop, so there were two adult mediators on hand to deal with this most unusual occasion.

This case, described below in detail, demonstrates a very powerful point that mediation can sometimes be used to solve student–teacher conflicts, though skilful adult mediators are likely to be necessary. It would be quite inappropriate for students on their own to mediate a student–teacher conflict (these effects could be mitigated by using a team of student and staff mediators – but this is not the practice at Sacred Heart). This case also points to the power of mediation to get to the bottom of things and heal broken relationships. All involved in this mediation came out of it feeling better about themselves than before the mediation.

Case example

A teacher had been accidentally knocked unconscious by a ball being thrown in her classroom. As a result of her losing consciousness, she was taken by ambulance to hospital.

Several days later the teacher returned to school, where she was due to take the same class during the first lesson of the day. Although the school management did not require her to return to work as she was leaving to return to her home overseas at the end of the week, this was a brave but necessary thing for her to do, in order not to lose her confidence in teaching.

However, once she was in the classroom, the students acted very stupidly and cruelly, asking her if she had lost her memory and if she could remember their names. Although there was some element of them trying to make sense and understand what it means for a person to lose consciousness, the effect was that the teacher felt bullied by the whole class and had to leave the room.

The same class were due for their anti-bullying workshop in the second lesson. The incident was reported to the school counsellor and trainer who were next due to take the offending class. A decision had to be made to run the workshop programme or to deal with the conflict that was present.

The team made a decision to deal with the class conflict. The class sat in a circle and were told that the teacher would be joining the group and links were made between the previous workshop topic, responsibility, and the incident that had just occurred. At that point, a senior member of staff entered the room and singled out one student with a history of problems as the culprit and removed him from the class. Exclusion was highly probable.

Then the teacher was asked to come and join the circle. First, the teacher explained what had happened. Then the facilitators suggested that it was unlikely that only one student had been involved in the incident, and quite likely that all students had contributed in some way to causing the teacher distress. As it went round the circle, each student owned up to his or her own degree of responsibility in what had happened. Most of the students owned up to having played a part in the conflict and spontaneously apologised to the teacher.

After each student had spoken, the teacher was encouraged enough to tell the class that the only reason she had returned to school before she went back to her country was that she had really enjoyed teaching that class for the year and she did not want to leave without saying goodbye. She was able to tell the class how much she had valued them. Had it not been for this process, the class might never have known this.

After the teacher had left the room, the facilitators went round the circle asking each student what could be done to make amends. Suggestions were offered, and although the class wanted to buy her something, they felt that making her something would be more valuable as it would be more personal and long-lasting than chocolate! Each student agreed to make her a card or write a letter to thank her for all she had taught them during the year.

At this point the bell sounded and it was time for the next class. But this extraordinary matter did not end there. During the lunch break, a small but significant number of students from the class voluntarily and spontaneously went to the head teacher and confessed their actions in the incident, saying that it was not fair that only one boy should take all the blame and be excluded.

The head was so surprised at this sudden burst of honesty that he referred all the students (including the troublesome boy, who was facing a final exclusion) back to their form tutor to deal with the matter in a way that did not result in any exclusions.

An exchange programme with student mediators in Norway

During an overseas conference where the school counsellor was giving a presentation on peer mediation in secondary schools, an invitation came to develop a student exchange programme with Norwegian school mediators.

Orders for copies of the training manual (Rolls 1996) were taken at the conference to raise funds to cover air fares. Additional money was raised through numerous other fundraising events including cake stalls, a Valentine's Day disco (organised by a parent) and a small grant from a local grantmaking trust.

The Sacred Heart and Norwegian pupils began exchanging letters almost as soon as the schools were linked up. Four months later, ten Year 11 Sacred Heart mediators flew off to visit Sandbeken Skole, Lillestrom, just north of Oslo.

The Norwegian host families showered hospitality on the visiting mediators, who were made to feel like celebrities (including an appearance on television and a civic reception lunch with the mayor). After much socialising, the Sacred Heart mediators ran their own workshops for the trainee Norwegian mediators and all of them answered each other's questions.

After three days in Lillestrom, the Sacred Heart mediators went to Oslo to run a workshop for the Oslo Mediation Board. After a serious grilling about mediation by the participants, the mediators themselves were surprised by how much they knew about mediation and in such depth.

Throughout the trip their confidence shone through and it was an amazing 'trip of a lifetime' for all concerned. Since leaving the school, two of the students involved in the exchange have been involved in initiating and setting up a peer mediation project in their sixth form college.

Other exchange visits have since happened or are currently in the pipeline. In January 1998 a group of trainee student mediators visited from a vocational school in Oslo. Further student exchanges are currently being planned to the European Union project partners.

Getting the mediators involved in reading schemes

A current development at Sacred Heart is to get student mediators involved in reading schemes. A high percentage of Year 7 students at Sacred Heart come to the school with a reading age three or four years below their age level. The mediators spend some of their lunch hours listening to these children read, in order to get their reading level up.

Their mediation training is helpful for this activity as they have learned to be patient listeners and are positively motivated to help others in the school to solve their problems – whether conflicts or low reading ability.

So with all the sacrificed lunch hours and staying late after school, what do the mediators get out of all these activities?

Benefits for the mediators

The benefits for the peer mediators are substantial:

- *Confidence*: mediation training helps young people to be more confident.
- *Self-esteem*: the training helps them to build greater self-esteem, which is sustained by successful mediations, knowing they perform a useful role and visits to and from other groups.
- *Responsibility*: being a mediator is a very responsible role and can help students who in the past have behaved less responsibly. Many young people have been 'turned around' by this.
- *Skills*: the training in communication skills is increasingly more useful as we move into a post-industrial economy where information is of primary importance.
- *Being part of a constructive group*: being a mediator offers young people an opportunity to be in a tightly bonded group with a constructive purpose and peer pressure to stay out of trouble.
- *Enhanced job applications and CVs*: mediation is still quite an unusual skill that makes the mediators' job applications and CVs stand out.

Peer mediators who leave Sacred Heart often return to tell the scheme co-ordinator how having been a mediator has helped them get into college or get a job. Some have also returned to help train other young people as mediators. In March 1999, the student mediators won a community award from the Metropolitan Police in recognition of their work.

Reflections and conclusions

The learning from five years' experience of implementing peer mediation and other conflict resolution approaches at Sacred Heart School can be summarised by the following five points:

1. *Whole school approach*: getting the whole school to understand right from the beginning how mediation works and its potential value is vital, and can make the difference between running a very successful scheme and struggling to keep it going.

2. *Selection of students*: getting the mediators to reflect the school's student population is also vital. This includes gender, race, culture and the full range of academic abilities.

3. *Commitment*: sustaining a successful mediation scheme requires enormous commitment on behalf of the staff involved and the students selected and trained. This commitment must include regular support and supervision.

4. *Constant innovation:* the scheme must be seen to be constantly improving, evolving and developing new ideas, to keep the energy to sustain a successful scheme.

5. *Training:* training must be sufficient, fun and of high quality in order to enable the mediators to mediate successfully.

Mediation offers schools a constructive way to involve young people in taking greater responsibility for their lives. The school gains an additional approach for reducing student conflicts and addressing conflicts early before they get out of hand. The mediators gain confidence and skills that will help them throughout their lives, as well as offering them a constructive role to play at school and in their communities. The community as a whole benefits from responsible young people who serve as role models for others, and a valuable route to training the potential leaders of tomorrow.

References

Bitel, M. and Rolls, D. (1995) 'Responding to bullying: a report on the first year of the anti-bullying workshops at Sacred Heart School, London SE3, September 1993 to June 1994.' Unpublished report.

Robinson, G. and Maines, B. (1997) *Crying for Help: The No Blame Approach to Bullying.* Bristol: Lucky Duck Publishing.

Rolls, D. (1996) 'Mediation training: a 10-step approach to training young people to become mediators.' Unpublished training manual.

Southwark Mediation Centre (1994) *Annual Report 1993/94.* London: Southwark Mediation Centre.

5

Community Mediation in an Urban Setting

Graham Waddington

Introduction

This chapter describes in general terms what community mediation services do and some of the cases that have come to one urban service, Cardiff Mediation. While many cases have ended in a positive outcome, I have also described some of the difficulties that services can experience while becoming established, often by taking on disputes which could be viewed as less suitable for mediation.

In the last five years community mediation has become one of the largest growth areas within the field of mediation in the UK. Figures from Mediation UK (the national umbrella organisation for most community mediation services) show that there were 11 community mediation services in 1991, whereas in 1997 a total of 85 operational services was recorded (Mediation UK 1997).

Community mediation services deal with community and neighbourhood disputes. The latter have recently received much media coverage and the term 'neighbours from hell' has become a growing social construct often sensationalised by press and television journalists. Terms such as 'neighbour nuisance' and 'anti-social behaviour' are now everyday terms used by welfare professionals and statutory agents such as the police and housing staff, who often bear the brunt of community conflicts.

Community mediation services generally have three broad principles of operation: they are independent, confidential and non-legal (Acland 1995). They can be organised in a number of ways. There are independent services which use trained volunteer mediators, employ one or two paid staff and are run by voluntary management committees. A few services have paid staff who also carry out mediation work.

Many services are constituted as charities and often limited companies as well. In other places local authorities have adopted in-house mediation as part of an overall strategy for neighbour nuisance. Sometimes housing sector staff are trained to carry out mediation work as part of a social housing service for tenants. Finally, there are a few independent self-employed mediators who carry out community mediation for agencies and local authorities, where services are needed on a smaller scale.

Common to all these types of delivery is the principle that community mediation should be free of charge at the point of delivery; and that mediation should be widely available and accessible to the public across a wide range of community groups. This is particularly significant in urban settings where the population make-up is often disparate, transient and diverse.

Mediation is one of many options of dispute resolution open to neighbours experiencing difficulties with each other, and has several advantages. It is non-legal, so that people have the opportunity to settle their disputes out of court and, more importantly, out of the public eye. Mediators act impartially, not taking sides and with no vested interest in the outcome of the dispute. They are only there to help facilitate an agreement which is mutually beneficial to all parties concerned. The parties involved agree to mediate and are invited to represent their own interests. It is estimated that around 80 to 90 per cent of neighbours who participate in a mediation meeting come to an agreement.

Most community mediation services are fairly new. Cardiff Mediation is a city-wide community mediation service which has been fully operational since April 1996. The service primarily takes referrals from housing, statutory and voluntary agencies on behalf of neighbours in dispute. There are also a large number of self-referrals from disputants. The service is independently constituted as a charity, has two full-time members of staff (a co-ordinator and a case manager) and operates with approximately 30 to 40 volunteer mediators (Cardiff Mediation 1997).

Many community mediation services start with just one paid member of staff (the co-ordinator) and a few services start with two. When Cardiff Mediation was initially set up, there was great optimism but little understanding about what mediation could do. Other new city-based services will know that it is difficult to provide a confident and coherent service initially, due to lack of experience and a proven track record in the field. This difficulty is part of the wider issue that mediation is still at a comparatively early stage of development in the UK.

This chapter also looks at mediation as a community strategy, working in conjunction with other agencies. Mediation services can provide so many benefits to other agencies. Mediation is a relatively private service for individuals and therefore provides a different approach from other more public methods of dispute resolution. Confidentiality and privacy are key motivating factors for people coming to mediation. Providing there are no issues which need to be disclosed to authorities, many disputes involving lifestyle clashes and behavioural difficulties can be resolved without the problems being taken further afield. The agencies that have contracts with Cardiff Mediation have found it enormously beneficial to involve an independent service which specialises in settling disputing behaviour.

The neighbourhood dispute

So what can happen in neighbourhood disputes? Unfortunately constructive and proactive conflict management is seldom sought at an early stage. Often the individuals involved or the agency staff dealing with the dispute will exhaust other formal or legal procedures before thinking about mediation as an option. As a result, some individuals referred to mediation services are a year or two into the life of an ongoing dispute. They experience a devastating degree of emotional pain, have a general mistrust of the world, exert extreme psychological defences against any sort of positive conciliation and, in some cases, have become completely isolated from the communities in which they live (Cardiff Mediation 1998).

Case example

In October 1996 two neighbouring families telephoned Cardiff Mediation and reported allegations and counter-allegations of violence, vandalism and theft. Their two stories almost mirrored each other exactly. Both families wanted help in their situation and had already involved the police, the housing agency, the environmental health department and their respective solicitors. Although they were interested in mediation, they had doubts about its effectiveness and were sceptical about reaching an agreement. Both families agreed to a joint meeting with me and a colleague as mediators. One party declined the meeting on the preceding day. Another meeting was arranged and the same situation occurred. We offered to act as 'go-betweens' (providing a 'shuttle diplomacy' process), allowing the parties to build an agreement without having to face each other in the same room. This process took a number of visits until a final agreement was constructed and written up.

The kind of statements made in the agreement were largely about future actions. They were simple, achievable and well within both parties' capabilities of carrying them out: actions like taking children's footballs back if they came over a fence, or talking in a non-abusive manner when informing their neighbours about noise levels. These sound like easy goals to achieve, but when situations are fraught with bad feeling, simple actions are almost impossible. The agreement was monitored by the mediation service for about six months, and during that time the families managed to sort out the tangible problems which had made them so untrusting towards each other and had caused so much conflict between their children, in-laws, other neighbours and friends. In retrospect we offered them two very simple things — trust and flexibility. It was surprising to see the level of commitment to creating a win—win situation, once both parties could move on from past events and look to the future.

The volunteer community mediator

The role of the mediator is an unusual one. The mediator is flexible, pragmatic and without a vested interest (but not uncaring) in the moral dilemmas and personal injustices that arise in disputes. Volunteer community mediators need to be highly trained. They are communicators between disputing parties and also managers of anger. They are information providers and the medium for all parties to work through.

Community mediators generally work in pairs. This is partly for health and safety reasons and partly because of the nature of disputes. Most neighbourhood disputes involve a multitude of issues, sometimes endless and difficult to categorise. When issues, subissues, subsidiary disputes and external previous conflicts pile up into one case, the mediator's role becomes daunting in deciphering and breaking down the component parts. John Crawley's feasibility study in the Hackney area of London discovered that: 'Over 100 different activities were described as causing neighbour nuisance. They covered almost the entire scale of human behaviour from "staring" to "assaulting with weapons"' (Crawley 1997a).

Volunteer community mediators play a valuable role for the places in which they work. Being impartial is not a particularly natural role to take on, in an existing environment of advocacy, representation and adversarial attitudes. The work of the mediator can remain a mystery to those enquiring and curious about mediation. In this climate, community mediators undertake an endless learning journey, with constant self-evaluation every time they intervene (and every second they interact) in a dispute as an impartial third person.

A landscape for mediation

In urban settings communities are often fragmented and constantly changing, and disputants (in many cases) will not know their neighbourhood well enough to have built up close relationships with the people next door.

Urban disputes can be very public, as there is often nowhere for individuals to hide in a compact terrace, small cul-de-sac or block of flats. For a number of disputants who come to mediation, there can be many eyes looking in on their dispute – their neighbours, the housing association, the police, family members, other local residents and the mediators. For many people living in densely populated areas, it is difficult to make conflict invisible.

Cardiff is a city with a diverse population. From the centre, to the north and east, there are long-established residential areas. Surrounding the city on all sides are local authority housing estates, and to the south there is the docks area – a relatively small region historically marked by trade, shipping, migrant cultures and the demise of coal and other pre-war export industries. Currently this region of Cardiff is a landmark of new economic growth heralded by the site of the Cardiff Bay Development.

Like most British cities, Cardiff is made up of 'communities'. Older areas such as Grangetown and Butetown consist of a range of well-established black cultures. Certain parts of Ely and Caerau to the west are sites of some of the older local authority housing estates. Some areas of Cardiff in recent years have been under the media microscope as communities plagued by riots, drugs, high youth crime, murder and many other social problems.

Because mediators are trained to be flexible in their approach and work in a diverse landscape of disputes, mediation becomes a way for people to keep their perceptual, social and cultural beliefs, while broadening their options to reconcile the differences prevalent in urban settings. This premise leads on to the unique relationship between disputant and community mediator.

The disputants

How individuals view themselves and how they think they are viewed, in relation to where they live, becomes a familiar dynamic in disputes and a priority focus for the mediator, who needs to uncover what people want to achieve and gain from the immediate community in which they live. Individuals are often dissatisfied with the community in which they wish to participate.

Case example

In January 1998 a referral came to Cardiff Mediation involving two sheltered housing tenants. The main issues in the dispute were about the shared communal living space and the shared facilities such as the washroom and garden. There had been a high degree of involvement from the housing agency and both parties' solicitors. This was an ideal case for mediation because the underlying issues and feelings were about social needs. Questions that were discussed in this case were: Whose friends should come to the house and use the garden? At what times should this happen? What were the codes of conduct about having friends around in a property which was shared?

The only modes of communication between the parties were their arguments, threats and cutting comments. Coupled with this style of communication were their expressions of fondness for their houses, their loved surroundings and their desire for things to be better (from their own perceptions, of course, and not from the other person's). Both had vivid visions of their ideal living situation and the kind of atmosphere in which they would like to live. For both of them, this was linked to the past, to a life based on a shared sense of community. At a joint meeting, the two parties expressed their wishes to be neighbourly and defined some common ground about what that meant for them. However, the agreement eventually broke down, due to continued bad feelings and external parties who declined the offer of joining the mediation.

Richard Hoggart wrote about northern, urban, working-class life and the idea of 'the neighbourhood'. In one account of a small town on the edge of Leeds, he described how the home was a deeply private space, 'but when the front door opens out of the living room on to the street, and when you go down the one step or use it as a seat on a warm evening you become part of the life of the neighbourhood' (Hoggart 1957).

Hoggart wrote in great detail about how northern urban neighbourhoods of pre-war Britain responded and adjusted to the structural changes of industry by living out a rich cultural existence. This view of community life in northern England is revisited throughout the book. From one town to another, a similar blueprint of community life is fermented by solidarity, and encoded social rituals are underpinned by a richly textured rapport and dialogue which moulds collective identity.

In the context of this example, community mediators provide a very important process for individuals who find themselves undergoing a process of societal change. Nearly every disputant who has contacted Cardiff Mediation in the last two years has described a concept of a neighbourhood or community in which they would like to live. This concept has either been visionary or part of the past.

Mediators work directly with the disputant to look at the future and focus on personal needs. The outcomes of settlement or resolution often mean some kind of personal change for disputants. In urban settings, the effects of housing policy and political changes are often more quickly experienced by tenants and residents than in rural situations. Some of the outcomes from the Housing Act 1996 (in some regions) has resulted in probationary tenancies and specific tenancy clauses about behaviour and harassment. These legislative measures are designed to modify and control behaviour, but can also breed a culture for complaints (HMSO 1996). The urban community mediator is someone who can work with individual values while helping neighbours process societal change collaboratively.

The next part of the chapter looks at how a community service like Cardiff Mediation attempts to make itself known to different and sometimes fragmented communities; what the limits of mediation are; how a mediation service can shape itself as a service; and offering dispute management in a diverse city.

Putting it back in the community

Starting out in mediation, I became aware of the view that mediation services could act as a catalyst to put back into communities the presence of an impartial third party. Many people perceive mediation skills as part of their working and personal lives, so finding skilled mediators should not be difficult. Surely services only need to advertise for people who are good listeners, have the ability to be fair, impartial, non-judgemental, with good communication skills and can work as part of a team?

However, finding individuals who can apply the mediation process in different community settings is difficult. Mediators are not counsellors or advocates, although some of the communication and interpersonal training on mediation courses are also used in those professions.

Actively being impartial is not a natural working role and is difficult to demonstrate in training and practice. It is my belief that community mediators should not mediate close to where they live because of the implications for impartiality. So, in that sense, community mediation services are not putting back permanent figures who can mediate in their own neighbourhoods, but training people who can replenish and respond to the need for non-legal, informal dispute resolution.

Recruitment, training and practice

Mediators work in difficult and complex situations, so the basic training in mediation needs to be challenging. Some services have difficulties in recruiting mediators to represent different communities. Mediation often attracts educated professionals working in related fields, which can lead to mediation acquiring a white middle-class image at the outset. In addition, some social groups prefer to retain anonymity and autonomy from outside intervention or involvement.

Mediation services are sometimes in competition with legal processes and other formal modes of conflict resolution. Mediation is new, relatively unknown and will take time to filter into public consciousness. While addressing this with help from groups such as residents' associations and the Race Equality Council, Cardiff Mediation is also working towards recruiting a body of individuals from the different social and minority groups around Cardiff. Even where services have achieved broad representation from the community, all mediators need to be comfortable and competently trained to work in different environments and be culturally sensitive.

Mediation may be voluntary but it is by no means amateur. The mediation service needs to know at the recruitment stage that individuals can maintain a commitment to the work. The emotional upheaval of the personal learning in carrying out the final role play, after an intense and tiring five days' training, nearly always promotes elements of personal self-doubt, humility and anticipation about taking on a first case. This is coupled with excitement and joy that the course is finally over. The self-reflection and revelation on mediation courses is immense. This personal reflection on skills and abilities is intensified on the first case visit to party A, as they may be met with seemingly impossible impasses from an unwilling, non-negotiating, distressed and angry disputant.

When we train and work as mediators, we learn that a visit to a party in a dispute will involve listening carefully to 'their story' and this is precisely what we hear – a narrative, told to us live by the author. It contains a whole spectrum of human morality, social happenings leading to a central plot, indented by subplots, twists of fate and numerous characters.

Mediators are faced with the challenge of trying to uncover the key interests and needs of the storyteller. They also use skills to dialogue with the disputants and develop an awareness of the disputant's sense of community. One of the ultimate tests for mediators is to communicate coherently what mediation can do and how it can benefit their situation.

Facilitating personal change is central to the role of the mediator. Perhaps it will become less likely that mediators will match up to or represent a community, but be more adept at working with the complex picture of urban living, by being adaptable and flexible third parties, modelling lateral thinking towards dispute resolution and personal or social intransigence.

With housing development and urban regeneration, there is a high degree of mobility and transience within urban landscapes, challenging any notion of community in a more traditional sense. This makes it difficult for users and providers of services to equate their older perception of 'community' with current reality. In this way, community mediation provides a service which can help individuals cope constructively with social conflicts and look towards personal change.

A question of responsibility

Mediation has been cited as a way of increasing community interaction and building better relationships between people. Many of the written agreements drawn up by neighbours coming to mediation have largely been about accepting and living with each other's differences or defining space and territory. Disputants request space, peace and quiet; they sometimes say they cannot (or do not want to) reciprocate the level of sociability offered by their neighbour. A large number of disputes that have come to Cardiff Mediation service have been settled not by co-operative action, but by negotiating personal boundaries so that there is little further contact between neighbours.

Dispute referrals come from registered social landlords, the local authority housing department and the police (at Cardiff these sources of referrals constitute about 50 per cent of the total). The self-referrals also frequently have a history of statutory agency involvement throughout the course of the disputes. Although most neighbourhood conflict nationwide seemingly goes unreported (Dignan, Sorsby and Hibbert 1996), action taken by the disputants that do complain is often accompanied by the use or threat of authority. The intention is often to establish a resounding victory, inflict damage or create fear. Disputants also use authority for protection, safety and to gain a sense of control and personal identity.

Here are some typical responses given to mediators by disputants, with reference to their understanding of authority or coercive action. These statements have been gathered during initial telephone contact, office visits or individual party visits in disputants' homes:

> If she carries on it, won't be mediation – I'll have the police, the housing association and environmental health round there.

> I've spoken to my solicitor and I agreed that mediation was a very good cause, so I'm going to pop a little something in the post to you for your kindness. It won't happen again, my solicitor said he'll have the housing association up in court.

> I don't want to waste your time, you must have other things to do. This is down to the housing. I appreciate your time but I've tried mediating with these people and they aren't able to respond to reason. They're animals!

It seems that a social coding is set in urban cities. If people have a dispute with their neighbour, they go to an authority as the first step. People's adherence to and wish for authoritarian measures is sometimes unstoppable. The statements above have come from cases which have (to varying degrees) gone through mediation. Many of these types of statements tie into huge impasses which disputants bring up because mediation services are not seen as an authority – more as a charity or voluntary service, with 'nice people' who are trying to do their very best. This perception causes difficulties for the neighbourhood mediator. Many issues may be mediatable, but the neighbour refuses to consider this, because their pattern of resolving disputes has been to pass on the responsibility to authority.

So how can disputants be encouraged away from adversarial action? Once people arrive at mediation, it is essential that mediators do not impose any authority, other than the authority needed to manage the stages of the process. However, because authorities are often disputants' first port of call, those agencies can provide the boundaries for mediation to work within. Mediation becomes one option within a range of processes for handling complaints.

Referral with the help of authority

It has been possible to develop ways of working very efficiently with authorities. Existing authorities can endorse the local mediation service. Mediators are taught to pitch to the tone and velocity of anger, handle situations involving aggressive outbursts and cope with the emotionally charged atmospheres created by energy and anxiety.

Disputants want action when they call in the police, the local authority or housing association. It is at this point that officials make critical decisions over what action to take. It is also the defining moment when mediation can either be put high on the agenda of a disputant's options, or become a solemn leaflet next to a take-away menu in someone's hall. The difficulty that agencies have with neighbour disputes is defining who will take action:

> Depending on the seriousness and nature of the complaint(s), the personal circumstances of the parties involved and the tenure of the property they live in, a neighbour dispute might involve one or more of the following agencies: the police, local authority housing, environmental health. (Dignan *et al.* 1996, p.6)

Finding a place for the mediation service within other agencies' complaints and policy procedures means that tenants and residents become aware of the mediation service, because it is being offered by a familiar body through which they do most of their complaining.

One housing association in Cardiff made a clear policy statement about mediation and this helped the mediation service, the tenants and the housing association. The statement articulated that they (the housing association) would contract in the local mediation service to deal with disputes that were based on lifestyle differences and conflicts which the harassment clause in their tenancy agreement did not (by definition) cover. This strategy was supported by providing the association with workshops in mediation and clear referral guidelines. Consequently, the number of complaints which were taken at the office decreased overall. The tenants had clear information about mediation, officers had information about referring and the mediation service gained good publicity.

In these circumstances independence is always in question. Agencies do need to be aware that when they employ or contract mediation services they are paying for independence (Crawley 1997b). This means that they are investing financially in something which demands consent and ownership from the disputants involved. For statutory agencies this is a risk, but that risk is weighed against going ahead with harassment or eviction procedures, which can be costly, time consuming and ultimately produce a punitive outcome.

Agency staff are human and genuinely want to help. Juggling with their many tasks, they frequently express frustration and anguish when faced with polarised positions. They often feel stuck in the middle, being called on as the voice of authority to make a decision and come down on one side.

This is a good point of connection between the mediation service provider and the contracting agency. Working with an authority does not mean compromising principles or independence. It involves careful contracting about where to intervene in a dispute and creating a clear consistent message to the user.

The authority of the mediator

Not many newly trained mediators go out on their first case feeling confident about what they are meant to do, as they have no experience yet of seeing the process working. They see the principles, envisage the rationale and know that mediation is, fundamentally, common sense. Going out there and doing it well is a different reality. This is where linking with other agencies through a referral process is essential. Mediators need thorough training in how to apply mediation processes in different settings. They need to be competent not only at face-to-face meetings, but also in shuttle diplomacy, working with individual parties, monitoring disputes and carrying out follow-up visits to disputants after cases have been closed. These are all-powerful and valid ways of managing conflict and defusing disputes.

Part of working in an urban landscape of conflict is being aware of and seeing mediation services as part of a chain of ways to deal with conflict. Once mediation is adopted at a policy level by referring agents, it provides a strong mechanism to help those seeking assistance in resolving disputes. Neighbours who come to mediation often find a point at which they decide whether or not they can live with difference. Mediation provides them with the opportunity to know more about their neighbour, even if they do not reach agreement. Through being encouraged to have greater awareness of their own values, disputants become more able to take individual responsibility for how they react when they are in conflict.

Conclusion

A language for urban mediation

There is a link between the older sense of community described earlier and terms such as 'conflict resolution', 'collaborative problem solving' and 'win–win' (mutually agreed) solutions. Although these are valuable aims for any mediation service, they may also give rise to disbelief or unrealistic expectations about what mediation can do. The application of these principles (in an ideal sense) relies on stable structures, such as a sense of community and collective identity, cohesive cultural codes and communities with a solid economic base. In urban settings these principles are difficult to practise and can be seen as an unachievable panacea, because of the fluid nature of modern urban living. Many referrals involve people who have never politically, socially or culturally lived out 'a sense of community'. I feel that as mediation providers our task is to develop a language which reflects more closely the nature of urban conflict as it exists now. In Cardiff and other urban centres the need for mediation is great. The ease of mediation's transition 'from fringe to mainstream' will depend as much on how mediation is communicated and validated as how it is practised.

References

Acland, A.F. (1995) *Resolving Disputes Without Going to Court.* London: Century.

Cardiff Mediation (1997) *Annual Report 1997.* Cardiff: Cardiff Mediation.

Cardiff Mediation (1998) *End of Year Case Report 1998.* Cardiff: Cardiff Mediation.

Crawley, J. (1997a) *Neighbours, Nuisance and Mediation.* Heydon: Conflict Management Plus.

Crawley, J. (1997b) *Making the Most of Mediation.* Heydon: Conflict Management Plus.

Dignan, J., Sorsby, A. and Hibbert, J. (1996) *Neighbour Disputes.* Sheffield: Centre for Criminological and Legal Research, University of Sheffield.

Hoggart, R. (1957) *The Uses of Literacy.* Harmondsworth: Pelican.

HMSO (1996) *The Housing Act 1996.* London: HMSO.

Mediation UK (1997) *Annual Report 1997.* Bristol: Mediation UK.

Further reading

Acland, A.F. (1990) *A Sudden Outbreak of Common Sense.* London: Hutchinson.

Liebmann, M. (ed.) (1998) *Community and Neighbour Mediation.* London: Cavendish.

6

The Rural Mediation Service

Sue Bowers

Introduction

Whereas the early community mediation services in the UK appeared in the towns and cities, the 1990s saw a movement into rural areas. Twenty-three new projects opened across the country in 1997, with a similar expectation for 1998; by July 1999 the total was 150.

Mediation UK does not identify the nature of its member services, but of the 97 listed at the end of 1997, 35 had addresses in rural areas, or in small towns with a rural hinterland. This chapter will offer a brief profile of one rural mediation service and then consider the characteristics of others with similar constituencies.

Profile of Mediation Dorset

The area

The county of Dorset stretches from Lyme Regis in the west to Christchurch in the east – a distance of about 56 miles; and from the south coast to Shaftesbury in the north; an area of approximately 1038 square miles. Predominantly rural, it includes the conurbations of Poole and Bournemouth and the country towns of Dorchester, Bridport, Gillingham and Wimborne. In April 1997 local government reorganisation divided the old Dorset County Council into two urban unitary authorities (Poole and Bournemouth) and a new Dorset County Council covering the rural area, which retained the district and parish councils.

Dorset Community Action carried out a Poverty Mapping exercise in 1997. Although usually seen as an affluent county, Dorset has a significant proportion of poorer people, scattered throughout the area, with small pockets of quite severe deprivation in both urban and rural areas. Tourism is an important source of employment, particularly near the coast, but is largely seasonal, a factor which affects housing as well as jobs; cross-channel ferries operate from the port of Poole. There are army camps at Bovington, Lulworth and Blandford; the closure of the naval helicopter base at Portland severely affected employment in the area. The Atomic Energy Establishment at Winfrith Newburgh has decommissioned most of its reactors and a new company is attracting fresh uses for the site.

The 1980s saw an influx of financial and commercial organisations into the urban areas, particularly in Poole, where they are the basis for continuing growth and prosperity. BP has been involved in extensive oil exploration and drilling, but advances in technology now enable oil to be extracted through pumping units, leading to a much smaller operation. BP made significant contributions to community activities, but employment is diminishing. The result of exploration by other oil companies elsewhere in the county is still uncertain.

In Dorset there are 2900 farms, but under 2 per cent of the total population is now directly involved with agriculture. There are several large privately owned estates, but these are no longer labour intensive. At the end of 1997 weekly earnings were significantly below the national average and 44 per cent of wage earners in the rural area were taking home less than £250 per week (Office for National Statistics 1997).

The population includes many retired people. There are few visible members of minority ethnic groups in the rural areas, so those who live there often feel isolated and unsupported. Dorset Racial Equality Network offers support and tries to raise awareness of racial issues. Dorset Development Education maintains a community presence, raising awareness of the growing diversity of the county's population. Poole and Bournemouth are venues for school holiday trips by foreign students who are sometimes the victims of aggression from local young people.

While many Dorset residents have elected to live in this beautiful county, others are trapped there by a lack of opportunity and choice, particularly young people in areas where transport makes it difficult to widen outlooks and increase social skills. Recent food safety crises, European Union agricultural pricing policy and the strong pound have very seriously affected the incomes of small farmers. The emergence of the Countryside Alliance, though representing very diverse views, has given a voice to their worries, and European funding has recently provided an improvement in local transport and support for activities for disaffected young people. Bournemouth was a recipient of Safer Cities funding until the end of 1998.

An increase in homelessness over the last seven to ten years is most visible in the larger towns. This can be attributed to a number of factors, including the downturn in the economy, legislation limiting housing benefit payable to people under 25 and changes in community care, particularly among people with a history of mental health or drug dependency problems.

Setting up the mediation service

The service was launched in September 1993, following a training course in mediation skills initiated by local Quakers. Twelve people completed the course and agreed to form a steering committee to set up a small-scale, independent mediation service. About half of them were in full-time employment, the others either retired, in part-time or casual employment, or caring for families.

There was no knowledge of other rural services to use as models, but Mediation UK's *Guide to Starting a Community Mediation Service* (1993) was helpful. No formal survey of need was undertaken at that time; each committee member was aware of potential demand within his or her field of activity and the decision was made to work from existing knowledge.

A start-up grant of £200 from Dorset Social Services, grants from two small charitable trusts and donations from interested individuals allowed the service to begin. A telephone answering machine was installed in the home of one of the committee members who offered to receive enquiries. Information leaflets were designed, printed and circulated to libraries, health centres, Citizens Advice Bureaux (CABs) and local churches. The aims of the service were defined as:

- to provide a conflict resolution service to individuals and organisations;
- to promote the understanding and growth of conflict resolution in the community;
- to develop and improve the skills of those interested in the mediation process;
- to promote the understanding and development of conflict resolution in schools.

Administration

Early administration was minimal. The original trainer became the co-ordinator and the treasurer's role was performed by the person receiving and processing enquiries. Someone undertook to seek funding. In the first year this team handled 128 enquiries, of which 53 were disputes. A second training course in Poole in January 1994 attracted ten participants, of whom six remained as volunteer mediators.

The need for charitable status was recognised early; an inaugural general meeting was held in November 1994, a more formalised committee structure was set up and a small office found in the Community Advice Centre in Poole. Charity registration followed in June 1995.

Over the next two years growth in mediation activity was slow, although training and work in schools continued. Ill health depleted both lead mediators and the administrative team. Balancing the mediators' workloads proved extremely difficult, particularly those without private transport living in out-of-the-way places. Experienced mediators were overworked while new ones waited so long for experience that their interest waned. By the end of 1995 the need for a salaried co-ordinator and a larger office had become overwhelming and a funding proposal was circulated to 20 statutory, commercial and charitable bodies. With the exception of a restricted grant for equipment and generous support from Quaker Meetings throughout the area, there was little response.

In October 1996 we surveyed 69 local organisations to identify levels of need and potential support. Forty-three respondents all declared a need; support was largely in terms of help with promotion. Several offered to stand for the management committee, mostly from housing associations. A number of statutory and community organisations became recognised referring agencies. The absence of offers of new financial support was striking.

A significant income boost came through a consultancy undertaken for a consortium setting up a nearby mediation service. The search for affordable accommodation ended when the local brewery offered rent-free rooms, surplus to their requirements, in a Victorian house in Dorchester. Well situated opposite the weekly market and handy for public transport, it is ideal accommodation, even more so as it is shared with the local volunteer bureau, a community resource. Lack of security of tenure is the only drawback.

In January 1997 an administrator on a three-month service agreement organised our move into the new office; a permanent co-ordinator was appointed on 1 April. We recognised that the 16 hours laid down in the contract were inadequate and the co-ordinator has consistently worked way beyond them. Funding to increase hours and rates of pay to a realistic level was a priority.

The office move and the co-ordinator's appointment transformed the service. Monitoring procedures were tightened and support for the mediators strengthened. The larger office enabled volunteers to work alongside the co-ordinator, although it has proved difficult to find enough administrative helpers. Publicity was restarted and referrals increased; an open day created and strengthened community links. One year later, the organisation was enthusiastic and purposeful.

The award of National Lottery Charities Board funding in April 1998 has been a further boost to morale. It has allowed the creation of 32 additional hours of salaried help to raise community liaison, quality assurance and work with young people to a standard which would not have been possible without it. National accreditation (with Mediation UK) of the service and preparations for an optional national qualification for mediators are under way. Additional trainers for the Young Mediators Project have been recruited and trained and an in-house accreditation procedure established for them. However, because NLCB funding must be used for new work, there is still a great need for stable core funding.

Management committee

The first committee consisted entirely of mediators. Additional members have been recruited but growth has been slow. Statutory authorities have been reluctant to nominate representatives. Member representation includes mediators, housing associations, CAB, further education and Equal Opportunities officers. One was the Diocesan Social Responsibility Officer and the secretary of the committee has a legal background.

Types of mediation undertaken

Most cases are housing or neighbour disputes, or family and partnership problems. Marital breakdown or separation cases are accepted only after checking that the client is aware of Relate (formerly known as Marriage Guidance) and has a reason for coming to us. Extremely co-operative relations were established with Dorset Family Mediators, who used to refer to us any case which lay outside their remit until their closure in 1998. (Since then Mediation Dorset has taken family cases where facilitated dialogue can help, but not cases concerning court or legal agreements.) Workplace disputes usually come through the CABs; group mediations have been undertaken for housing associations and voluntary organisations. Mediators have received additional training for the setting up of victim–offender mediation, in co-operation with Victim Support, funding for which has come from Dorset Probation Service.

Many clients refer themselves as a result of leaflets in public places or through one of the recognised referral agencies, that is, health centres, CAB, police, housing associations and departments, and some social services departments. Some examples, with details altered to prevent identification, follow.

Case examples

Cars and hedges

Mr and Mrs A lived in a large house on the outskirts of a village and had, some twenty years before, sold off a portion of their land to a developer. Mr B, who bought the resulting bungalow, repaired cars in his garden. The As allowed their hedge to grow much higher in order to screen off the 'junk yard', as they called it. Mr B complained that this was depriving him of light and view and demanded that the level be lowered. Mrs A went to talk to him one day while he was outside gardening and he hit her arm with his garden tools, causing her to go to hospital for treatment. Several solicitors' letters later, they were still extremely antagonistic. After initial separate visits, they met for mediation, and talked through the many petty annoyances that each had experienced over the years. As the atmosphere became less confrontational, each party agreed that they had been guilty of provocation, and apologised. Gradually they agreed that if Mr B moved the cars to a different part of his garden they would not be so visible to the As, who would then trim their hedge to its original height. Mr A wrote to the mediation service expressing the wish that he had come to us years earlier.

Loneliness

An elderly widow, living on the edge of an isolated village, was referred by the CAB, complaining that her neighbours' extension had blocked the stream flowing at the bottom of the garden and she was afraid of flooding. The neighbours declined to meet us or her, saying she was a troublemaker and they were doing nothing wrong. She was helped to contact the then National Rivers Authority, who confirmed that no regulations or good practice guidelines were being breached, but she still kept telephoning saying she did not know what to do.

During one of these long conversations, sensing that the caller was very lonely, we suggested a call to Age Concern. The idea was welcomed; at follow-up she was enjoying regular visits and had stopped worrying that the garden would flood.

Teenager–parent conflict

An 18-year-old girl contacted the office, saying she had left home after a quarrel with her parents. They lived in an isolated village with few occupations for young people. She was temporarily sleeping at her boyfriend's home. She was unrepentant but agreed to a meeting in the presence of mediators. One parent was keen for her to return home, but the other felt things had gone too far. The mediation shifted to the parents, who in the end decided that the time had come when their daughter was capable of living away from home, and that it would be best for all. She was referred to a housing association dealing specially with young people and, once the break had been made, they were able to rebuild, cautiously, a new relationship, based on recognition of their independence.

Two residents' associations

We were asked to help with a larger scale situation where two groups of tenants were in dispute with each other and the housing association itself. The residents' associations of two estates accused each other of improper action on the joint committee and the housing association of unfair handling of the situation. A day of separate talks with each party was followed by a joint meeting with a carefully agreed agenda and ground rules, chaired by the three mediators. Shortly before the scheduled end of the meeting, no movement had taken place and they were asked if, as they had been unable to reach agreement, they would each outline what their course of action might now be. Within minutes, a plan had been agreed to meet together with one of the housing association managers who had not so far been concerned in the problems. A few weeks later, a number of resignations had voluntarily taken place, procedures had been amended and a new committee was working well.

Cases where mediation could not help

Not all cases have happy endings. A violent disagreement over a presumed right of way, referred by a statutory authority appalled at the possible legal costs, could not be settled by mediation. As the two parties will, presumably, still be neighbours after the court battle, they have been assured that we would still be willing to help them to work out a way of living in proximity when the legal position is clear.

In another heavy neighbour dispute, a man had weedkiller poured on his garden and found his car alight in his drive one day. He sought our help when told that the police could do nothing without proof. Within an hour he phoned back to say his wife could not bear to spend another night in the house and they were putting it on the market.

A significant number of cases involve people who have mental health problems or have suffered abuse. They may be receiving psychiatric or social support but living on an open housing estate. Not formally ill, they are nevertheless very sensitive to noise and nuisance and vulnerable to low-level teasing or abuse. They often lack the confidence to deal with the rough and tumble of estate life in a confident way. Where parties are able to take part in the process meaningfully, mediation can foster greater understanding between all involved.

The most frequent cause of failure is that the second party is unwilling to become involved. Sometimes there is good reason, but we are continually considering how our approach can be made more encouraging without raising unrealistic expectations.

Training

In line with our aim to promote the understanding of conflict resolution in the community, introductory training is open to anyone. Fees are charged to cover costs, but kept as low as possible to encourage access, and bursaries are offered. The first two courses had fifteen sessions, but travel, particularly in winter over unlit country roads, was taxing and a new format was agreed. Two weekends, plus some guided reflection at home in between proved intensive but popular and such courses now take place twice a year, at alternate ends of the county. Additional evening courses have now been added to cater for differing wishes and availability. Places are limited to 16 and on average around 5 people per course apply to be volunteer mediators.

Ongoing training is continued through a programme of evening events plus occasional Saturdays. Content varies: sometimes there is a formal training input by the training co-ordinator or experienced mediators; at other times a sharing of experience, mutual support and guidance. Occasionally an outside trainer is engaged. Mediators are expected to attend an agreed number of training sessions per year to maintain their in-house accreditation (see below). Attendance at training events is problematical – the ever-present travel problems exert an influence.

Experienced mediators are encouraged to become involved in training others; a 'training for trainers' course covers basic training skills for trainers both in the community mediation service and in the Young Mediators Project.

Support and supervision

All mediators are encouraged to contact someone for advice, guidance or reassurance if and when they need to talk over some aspect of a case. This may be the co-ordinator or their supervisor. Supervisors are drawn from the more experienced lead mediators; Mediators meet quarterly in supervision/support groups, and approximately annually for review with the training co-ordinator.

In-house accreditation of mediators

Mediators are accredited at three levels: visitor, support mediator and lead mediator. All must have completed the training course and application procedure. Visitors are authorised to undertake initial visits with a lead or experienced support mediator. As they gain experience, their accreditation and training needs are reviewed in a meeting with the service and training co-ordinators. Occasionally, progress is slowed or halted when someone has lost touch through missing too many training events.

Two mediators are always assigned to a case. Originally, the same two would follow it through from initial visit to conclusion. As our caseload increased, a shortage of lead mediators developed and as many cases either failed to come to face-to-face mediation or were settled without the need for joint meetings, accredited visitors are now paired with experienced support mediators to make the initial visits, and a supervisor is appointed to the case. If these develop into face-to-face mediations, the supervising mediator is involved, either in place of one of the original mediators or, if appropriate, in addition. This has worked well both for the newly qualified visitors who are keen to gain experience and for clients, whose waiting time has been significantly shortened. It has also reduced travelling.

Schools work

Early in 1994, to mark the Year of the Family, the service received £670 from a local radio community trust towards a Young Mediators Project. The first course started with Year 4 (8–10 year olds) in a local primary school. Before the end of the course the children were mediating their own problems; at the school's request a further class was trained the following year. Thereafter, the school took on supervision and support of the mediators and the mediation service maintained a supporting role. In December 1995 the project received the South West Area award in the Home Office's 'Make A Difference' scheme and was presented with a plaque and a cheque for £1000 by the Home Secretary.

A Quaker local peace work grant funded a secondary school pilot scheme. Training at age 15 has to be fitted into a more demanding curriculum, but after trial and error a format was found and a peer mediation programme established. Another problem in a rural area is the difficulty in arranging after-school activities. If students from outlying districts miss the school bus they have no other means of transport home. However, the third generation of mediators has now been trained. Staff are seeking ways of extending the programme more widely throughout the school and support and supervision of the mediators has been strengthened.

Work is to begin in autumn 2000 at the tertiary college to which the secondary students transfer. A new course will develop the skills of the school-trained mediators and set up a mediation programme appropriate for a community college.

Work in schools makes a considerable drain on the energies of a small mediation service, particularly while the courses are running, and needs to be balanced against work in the wider community. Nevertheless, its importance is widely recognised and Mediation Dorset has been greatly encouraged by the response, believing that the foundation has been laid for continuing work among young people. The primary training models are now used elsewhere in the county and we hope that new legislation and the formation of Youth Offending Teams will offer new opportunities and resources for action.

European funding for a project with disaffected young people started at the end of 1999 extends the work beyond schools into the wider community.

Funding

The community mediation service, like most others, is free of charge to clients, although they are invited to make a donation and often do. Initial grants and small donations were sufficient for the first year of operation, but the move to an office increased the administrative outlay and the high travel expenses means that the average cost of a mediation remains high. Employing a co-ordinator continued the escalation.

Finding someone able to take specific responsibility for fund raising has been difficult and this vital job has been squeezed in between other functions by those with time and experience. Together with the delays involved in local government reorganisation, this has adversely affected income and underfunding continues to threaten the existence of the service.

Mediation Dorset's level of statutory support falls well below that of the majority of services. Despite the circulation in 1994 by the Department of the Environment of its booklet *Mediation: Benefits and Practice* (DoE 1994) to all local authorities, few of them are aware of its presence. However, the growing use of the service by statutory organisations will enable us to approach both staff and politicians with greater assurance and we believe it is only a matter of time before their support improves. The Rural Development Commission has not, so far, felt able to help as much of our work takes place in the urban areas, but significant help has come from Safer Cities for work in the Bournemouth area.

Fees for external training, consultancy and mediation for organisations have therefore played a significant part in our growth and survival. Three bands allowing for varying levels of resources make for a very flexible system. Mutual needs are discussed with clients, who respond positively, occasionally paying more than asked. Some fees are agreed on a 'one-off' basis, but service level agreements are being arranged and more are expected. At present, any organisation can refer clients indirectly by suggesting that they contact the service personally, with no consequent obligation to pay us a fee. Some have done that, but others recognise that under-resourcing makes it impossible to deliver a high quality service and that a measure of security and stability is in everyone's interest.

The decision to seek Lottery funding caused heart-searching to those of our members and funders who were opposed in principle to the National Lottery, some of whom were our most loyal supporters. Some expressed disappointment but none withdrew support, for which we have been grateful.

Future development

Longer term administrative structure

As a result of twice-yearly training courses and wider public understanding of mediation, the number of mediators has grown steadily. We expect that this will allow the formation of semi-autonomous local groups who meet in their own area for training and support, with a local link person who looks to the central office for administrative back-up. There would still be a need for joint and centrally organised events, but overall Mediation Dorset would become more of a resource base, with the work of the co-ordinating staff and volunteers adapting to meet the changing demands.

The viability of the service will require a measure of salaried staffing. In line with community mediation practice nationally, the service will continue to depend heavily on volunteer effort. However, the creation of paid jobs is seen as a beneficial objective, wholly compatible with the value placed on the work done by volunteers. Over-dependence on voluntary effort, even if it can be sustained, has implications for Equal Opportunities policy. A flexible staffing structure, offering a number of part-time jobs, creates possibilities for people with caring or other community responsibilities, and for those with a disability or some other reason which makes finding full-time employment difficult.

National accreditation

Mediation UK accreditation was gained in 1999. Although our in-house accreditation is designed to ensure high mediator standards, we would like to offer a national qualification to those who wish to work for one. This involves taking part in one of the schemes being developed for a National Vocational Qualification (NVQ) or National Open College Network certificate for individual mediators, and plans for this are under way.

Challenges and opportunities

The Young Mediators Project is based on the model pioneered in the 1980s by Kingston Friends Workshop Group (Surrey), which underpinned its schools work with parenting courses in the surrounding communities. Resources have not yet been available to extend the YMP work in that direction, but interest has been expressed by schools, individual staff, parents and youth clubs. Housing associations report that many of their problems stem from children who are out of parental control and they would welcome an initiative to work on individual housing estates.

Homelessness creates a recognised need among young people who have had difficulty in co-existing with parents, especially during parental separation or family restructuring. Mediation has been helpful and we would like to be more proactive in this area when resources permit.

In 1996 we were invited by Dorset Health Commission to submit proposals for addressing the high suicide rates among young males in the county, and trainers from the YMP were invited to attend a multi-agency conference. This work could not be taken forward without the recruitment of additional trainers and our priority has been the established schools work. Suicide among farmers and agricultural workers is also high; the service has been included among the helping agencies listed on a farmers' helpline card.

Working links have been established with Dorset Probation Service, which funded additional training to allow us to take on victim–offender mediation. This is done in co-operation with Dorset Victim Support. Early liaison with the county crime prevention officer ceased when the post disappeared after local government reorganisation, but contact has been made with the new Youth Offending Team. Co-operation with Dorset Police has resulted in the making of a promotional videotape; we receive regular referrals from local officers.

Comparison with other rural mediation services: A survey

The 35 services with rural or small town addresses were each contacted in January 1998 and asked if they would complete a questionnaire (see Appendix 1 at chapter end). Over half sent responses. They showed that there is no such thing as a typical rural mediation service, but there are strong trends and common features.

Only two of the twenty-two respondents saw themselves as wholly rural; two others dealt only with an urban constituency, so were not included. The rest covered either a rural area containing a sizeable centre of population, or an urban centre with surrounding countryside, and dealt with referrals from both areas. The size of the area varied considerably; the largest covered 2000 sq miles. Two were over 1000 sq miles, the majority were between 100 and 200 sq miles and the two smallest covered 50 and 70 sq miles respectively.

The earliest had started operating in 1990; there were two each starting in 1993, 1994 and 1995. Five had been launched in 1996 and eight in 1997. Several said they were set up in response to the circulation of advice by the Department of the Environment. Many are multi-agency initiatives, with local authorities playing a dominant part alongside housing associations and committees. Police, Victim Support, district and parish councils, tenants' associations, local churches and the 'voluntary sector movement' are also involved. Occasionally services were the initiative of one or two individuals, particularly those launched prior to 1997.

Population

An almost universal feature of the predominantly rural services was the small number of people from minority ethnic groups; isolated black, Asian or gypsy residents may have no communities to support them. However, services which combine rural and urban areas report a huge diversity of outlook and need; there are sometimes distinct local identities within a larger area. One service included a mix of rural communities and an urban overspill town. Villages may be tightly knit communities with large, extended families living in close proximity. Rural poverty was noted by a few, with families trapped in a cycle of deprivation, boredom and alienation.

Types of mediation undertaken

Neighbour disputes formed the most common, sometimes the only type of mediation. Other services reported a wide variety of presenting problems because of the relative scarcity of specialist agencies. All had a proportion, sometimes high, of self-referrals, together with cases referred by their funding bodies. Boundaries, noise, children and anti-social behaviour were the most commonplace problems. Other conflicts arose from confrontations between urban 'incomers' with sometimes unrealistic expectations of rural life and the local population in old often substandard housing areas with long-standing, entrenched problems, where people had lived in close proximity for many years. Case loads varied widely: apart from two services which handled an average of twenty cases a month, the majority dealt with between five and nine of which, overall, about 20 per cent came to face-to-face mediation.

Communication

The wide dispersal of both volunteers and clients has time and cost implications for all forms of communication. Travel restricts commitment and influences attendance for committee members and volunteers alike, and also affects recruitment of staff. Patchy public transport forces mediators into cars and excludes those without them. Summer traffic in tourist areas is heavy; an hour's mediation can call for up to three hours' driving. Telephone costs are high when many colleagues are beyond the local call rate. Isolation is also a problem for volunteers and clients alike.

Finance and funding

Post-1997, local authorities were frequently the largest contributors, either through grants, service level agreements or both. Housing associations were prominent among funders, as were the police. Urban Aid, Safer Cities, district and parish councils, probation services and churches, charitable trusts, fees, donations, fund raising and the National Lottery all figure among sources of grants. Funding levels varied widely. One service reported an expenditure below £5000. Most had needed between £10,000 and £15,000; two annual turnovers of £50,000 and £130,000 were unusual among respondents.

Promotion

The widespread nature of the rural constituency and the more conservative outlook of many of its residents call for greater effort in promotion and result in slower acceptance by the community. Talks need to be repeated in district after district and the rate of growth is slow.

Other common problems

Like Mediation Dorset, those serving wide areas could foresee the need to establish 'satellite centres' to aid communication. Experience of recruiting volunteers varied. Sometimes this was difficult because of time demands and a lack of public transport and, in one case, lack of a 'volunteering culture', but often a ready willingness was found. Despite attempts to encourage a wide cross-section, most services felt their volunteers were not representative of the community; many were older people or 'incomers', often with valued skills and experience. The service whose mediators came from the farming and local community was in the minority. Personal safety was a concern in one of the wholly rural services where volunteers visit isolated farms to see people who are stressed and have easy access to firearms.

An outside view, from the co-ordinator of one of the urban services, confirmed much that has been said. He offered reflections on work they had done in providing training for three rural services and a short excursion made into offering a service for a neighbouring rural housing department:

Undoubtedly the biggest difference was travelling times; for an urban service almost an afterthought, but for work in rural areas the prospect of spending up to an hour travelling each way, plus the cost, is daunting. Far fewer cases can be managed.

A second difference we noted was a problem with that aspect of village life where everyone knows everyone and everything, and has an opinion to match. There also seem to be fewer choices – to move house; avoid each other; change schools; alter other neighbours' viewpoints. There are more feelings of isolation and powerlessness; and more dependence on other agencies. The profile of volunteers is also different – more middle-aged/retired, and of a less diverse background than in an urban setting.

Also, and importantly, there are far fewer sources of funding!

Conclusion

Mediation Dorset has been described in some detail. Questionnaire responses have shown that there is no standard pattern for rural services; much of the work is indistinguishable from that done in city centres. However, many of the challenges and opportunities which we have experienced are also apparent in other schemes that serve rural communities.

The movement is in its early stages and growing steadily. Although problems of communication, isolation and funding figured largely in the responses and in our own experience, increased opportunities for networking will undoubtedly ease the task of those who are initiating and running services. There is a marked sense of energy, enthusiasm and pioneering spirit evident in the air. Mediation is here to stay, in the country as it is in the towns.

Acknowledgements

I would like to thank those who responded to the questionnaire for their generous help. Also Dorset Community Action and Bournemouth Churches Housing Association for their help with the brief sketch of the area. The services which responded to the questionnaire include:

Breckland Neighbour Mediation Service, Cambridge and District Community Mediation Service, Castle Morpeth Mediation, Fife Community Mediation, Guildford Community Mediation Service, Mediation Dorset, Mediation Norwich, Mediation Mid Wales, Mediation Somerset, Mediation West Cornwall, Mid-Devon Mediation Service, Mid-Surrey Mediation Service, Monmouthshire Mediation Service, New Forest Mediation, Oxford Community Mediation, Plymouth Mediation, Resolve Mediation Service (Workington), Resolve (West Berkshire Mediation Service Ltd), South Hams Mediation Scheme, Waverley Community Mediation Service, West Kent Independent Mediation Service, Whitstable Mediation.

References

Department of the Environment (1994) *Mediation: Benefits and Practice.* London: DoE.
Office for National Statistics (1997) *New Earnings Survey.* London: HMSO.
Mediation UK (1993, updated 1996) *Guide to Starting a Community Mediation Service.* Bristol: Mediation UK.

Appendix 1
THE RURAL MEDIATION SERVICE Questionnaire

1.   Do you consider your service to be

   - a wholly rural mediation service

   - covering part rural, part urban constituency

   - not rural at all?

   (If the latter is the case, there is no need to go further, as your information will not be relevant. Thank you for getting this far!)

2.   What is the approximate size of the area you cover? (however is easiest for you to describe – sq miles, km, or miles across, etc.)

3.   How long have you been in operation?

4.   By whom/what initiative(s) were you set up?

5.   Are you still managed by the same body(ies)?

6.   How are you funded?

7.   What is your annual financial turnover?

8.   What types of mediation do you offer?

9.   What is/are the commonest problem/s with which you deal?

10. How are they referred to you?

11. Approximately how many dispute enquiries do you deal with in a month?

12. About how many of these come to face-to-face mediation?

13. How many mediators

   - other volunteers

   - paid staff

   do you have?

14. In what way(s) would you consider that you are different from urban services with regard to:

   - the type of conflicts which come to you

   - your management and administrative structure

   - ease or difficulty in recruiting volunteers

   - age, ethnicity or other factors relating to your particular community

   - running costs

   - support from the community

   - other factors?

15. Any other comment you would like to make?

Completed by _____

For _____ Mediation Service

Thank you very much

7

Community Mediation in the USA

Current Developments

Deborah Boersma Zondervan

Introduction

Mediation can be defined as the process of using a neutral third party to facilitate constructive communication, de-escalate volatile emotions and focus disputants on productive problem solving. Mediation at the community or local level (as opposed to labour mediation) first appeared in the USA in the early 1970s. Since then, the community mediation process has grown to include programmes in nearly every state, and cover a wide range of conflict situations. This chapter will provide an overview of community mediation in the USA, the mediators who provide the mediation services, when and how mediation is used, and future trends for community mediation. The chapter will also present and discuss some of the current tensions in community mediation, as the community mediation process interacts with and is positioned against mediation in other arenas, such as courts, government agencies and private alternative dispute resolution systems.

History of community mediation

Among the first community mediation programmes in the early 1970s were the Columbus (Ohio) Night Prosecutor's Mediation Programme, the San Francisco (California) Community Board Programme and similar programmes in Rochester (New York) and Boston (Massachusetts). The Department of Justice used the Columbus programme as a model to replicate in various places across the USA, leading Attorney General Griffin Bell to establish neighbourhood justice centres in Atlanta (Georgia); Kansas City (Missouri); and Los Angeles (California). Common themes for all of these programmes were:

- to look for alternatives to court for the burgeoning number of court cases filed;
- to empower citizens to learn and use conflict resolution and problem-solving skills, rather than relying on third parties, such as courts, police officers or other community resources.

US Supreme Court Justice Sandra Day O'Connor is frequently noted for observing that: 'Courts should be the place of last resort, rather than the place of first resort.' Community mediation programmes are a crucial piece of the 'first resort' options.

Community mediation programmes often offer a variety of dispute resolution mechanisms, including the following (National Institute of Justice 1997):

- *Arbitration*: a dispute resolution process that empowers a neutral third party to impose a settlement upon disputing parties, following a hearing between the parties.

- *Conciliation*: any effort by a neutral third party to assist in the resolution of a dispute, short of bringing the parties together face to face for a discussion of the conflict.

- *Facilitation*: similar to mediation in the use of third party neutrals and face-to-face communication, but with the goal of designing dispute resolution processes, meeting agendas and/or meeting management for large, diverse groups.

- *Mediation*: an effort by a neutral third party to assist disputing parties to resolve the conflict through the conduct of a face-to-face meeting. In such meetings, the third party is not authorised to impose a settlement on the parties, but rather seeks to assist them in fashioning a mutually satisfactory resolution to the conflict.

Nonetheless, mediation is the cornerstone of most programmes. Hallmarks of community mediation are that it is characterised by:

1. Use of trained community volunteers.

2. Sponsorship by a private non-profit or public agency with a governing or advisory board.

3. Diversity of mediators and others involved to reflect the community served.

4. Direct access to the public.

5. Provision of services to the public regardless of ability to pay.

6. Promotion of collaborative community relationships.

7. Encouragement of public awareness.

8. Intervention during the early stages of the conflict.

9. Provision of an alternative to the judicial system at any stage of a conflict (Ray 1997, p.72).

As of 1996, there were more than 550 community mediation programmes in the USA, with over 19,500 active volunteers. These programmes handle over 97,500 cases referred each year, with the volunteers actually mediating over 45,500 cases (Ray 1997, p.73). States with the largest number of community mediation programmes are New York, Michigan, North Carolina, Massachusetts, California, Florida, Ohio, Texas and New Jersey (National Institute of Justice 1997, p.4).

Training and monitoring volunteer mediators

Goals of mediation/roles of the mediator

In most community mediation programmes, the mediator is conceived to be 'a neutral intervenor [who] helps people involved in a dispute develop solutions that are acceptable to them. Unlike a judge or an arbitrator, the mediator has no authority to impose a binding decision on the disputants. He can only persuade them' (Stulberg 1987). While the theoretical definition of mediation is generally shared by community mediation programmes and other types of mediation programmes, there is less consensus on the goal(s) of a mediation session. Goals of, or anticipated outcomes from, community mediation programmes range from clearing crowded court dockets, to increasing the parties' ability to communicate with each other, to saving parties' time and/or money.

This lack of agreement gives rise to one of the first tensions in the mediation field. Most community mediation programmes concur that a crucial goal of a mediation session is to provide a forum for participants to reach their own, mutually agreeable resolution to the issues(s) that brought them to mediation. However, many community mediation programmes are in situations where, due to funding or referral sources, there are other pressures on the mediation process. One of the biggest of these pressures is the use of mediation as a court docket-clearing tool, rather than a process to empower the participants. In some jurisdictions, community mediators are faced with mediations that are limited to 60 minutes because of court schedules. In other instances, there is pressure to use mediation as a fact-finding tool, rather than a dispute resolution process in its own right. In some court jurisdictions, a process called mediation is used as part of the court process, but what happens during the process is more akin to arbitration or early neutral evaluation (a process, usually court-annexed, where a lawyer or lawyers sets a monetary value or value range for a specific case).

The tension between these various approaches to mediation can be viewed as a continuum of 'evaluative' versus 'facilitative' mediation, depending on the extent to which the mediator helps fashion the outcome (Riskin 1996). Also, in either evaluative or facilitative mediation, mediators can define the problems or issues narrowly, or broadly. A narrow problem definition leads to a focus on position-based settlement, with a primary emphasis on legal claims and court outcomes. A broad problem definition leads to a focus on interest-based settlement, with much more discussion of underlying interests, such as how the parties wish to communicate, or future relationships between them.

Facilitative mediation promotes communication between parties, allows (or encourages) the venting of emotions, clarifies the interests of the parties and encourages them to invent creative options acceptable to both parties. In evaluative mediation, issues are clarified, information is traded and facts and data exchanged, arguments are streamlined (as compared to the full trial process) and possible legal outcomes are evaluated. Rather than being separate entities, pure facilitative and pure evaluative mediations could be viewed as opposite ends of a continuum, with most mediations falling somewhere between them. Community mediation tends to fall toward the facilitative end of the continuum, while mediation as part of a court settlement process tends to fall toward the evaluative end.

More recently, Folger and Bush introduced another conceptualisation of mediation in *The Promise of Mediation* (1994), where a mediation approach is 'centered on mediation's transformative dimensions: *empowerment* and *recognition*' (Folger and Bush 1994, p.263, author emphasis).

All these issues impact on how community mediators are recruited and trained, how they view their role and how they are evaluated. Because community mediation programmes have leaned more toward facilitative mediation, this leads to a training emphasis on communication and interpersonal skills, rapport building, empathy, reframing (structuring the mediation as something other than a win–lose proposition) and interest-based negotiation, in addition to learning the basic mediation process. Court-mandated mediation programmes are more evaluative, especially since their mediators are nearly always lawyers. In this setting, training emphasises more caucusing (private meetings with just the mediator and one party), trade-offs ('I'll give you X, if you give me Y.') and other mediation techniques that closely parallel labour mediation.

Clearly, there is room for all these approaches to mediation. The critical issue is for each programme or centre to define its goals, then to use those goals to define the appropriate mediation approaches.

Mediator qualifications

The topic of defining necessary mediator skills and background, and then evaluating specific mediators relative to these requirements, is hotly discussed, both in community mediation programmes and other mediation arenas. Approaches to this issue range from requiring an advanced degree in law or social work (Florida), to emphasising past experience or training regardless of education, to some combination leading to certification or credentialling by an individual state. In a recent survey of community mediation programmes, over half of the programmes (56.2 per cent) ranked *training* in basic mediation process and interpersonal communication skills as their most important qualification, followed by *other* (13.7 per cent and undefined), *certification* (7.5 per cent), *college degree* (4.1 per cent), *experience* (2.7 per cent), *background check* (2.1 per cent), and *mentor/apprentice* (0 per cent) (McKinney, Kimsey and Fuller 1996, p.155).

There is general agreement on the qualities and skills of good mediators: ideal mediators are perceived as impartial, trustworthy, good listeners, flexible, creative, patient, able to understand divergent points of view and able to analyse problems and identify key issues. What is far less easy to determine is the balance between training, knowledge, judgement and intuition that produces the ideal mediator.

Complicating the mediator qualification issue is the reality that various mediation programmes may have goals which differ, or goals which are actually in competition with each other. The Society of Professionals in Dispute Resolution (SPIDR) Commission on Qualifications (SPIDR 1996) lists eight potential goals of mediation:

- increased disputant participation and control of the process and outcome;
- restoration of relationships;
- increased efficiency of the judicial system and lower costs;
- preservation of social order or stability;
- maximisation of joint gains;
- fair process;
- fair and stable outcomes;
- social justice.

Obviously, while all these goals are appropriate at specific times and for specific situations, no one mediation programme can provide all of these all of the time.

So, for adequate, effective delineation of the necessary qualifications for mediators, from which training and evaluation are derived, a programme must first clearly identify the goals for that particular mediation programme, then work back from that to articulate what specific qualifications their mediators must possess. SPIDR provides a framework for assessing mediators based on three recommendations adopted in 1989:

- that no single entity (rather, a variety of organisations) should establish qualifications for neutrals;
- that the greater the degree of choice the parties have over the dispute resolution process, programme or neutral, the less mandatory the qualification requirements should be;
- that qualifications criteria should be based on performance, rather than paper credentials.

In 1996, SPIDR expanded on these points with five additional guidelines:

1.   Strengthening the availability of a variety of dispute resolution processes, practices and practitioners is important to best serve a diverse public and meet their special needs.

2.   If no single entity should certify general dispute resolution competence, then it is critical for those interested in qualifications to work collaboratively with [one another] to develop standards and models of best practice.

3. It is important to actively solicit the input of consumers, practitioners, programme administrators, educators, researchers and others to identify needs and develop standards of competence and excellence in practice.

4. Consumers need broad access to quality dispute resolution services.

5. Wherever possible, the Commission will seek to develop recommendations and approaches that are practical to implement and that define, enhance and inspire excellence in practice.

Building on these concepts, the state of California has proposed legislation that sets standards for certifying mediators. The legislation identifies training, experience and performance as three critical parts of competent mediation performance. Based on this, the San Diego Mediation Center (California) developed a credentialling programme for its mediators. The performance of a mediator is measured by evaluating specific behaviours used by a mediator in a simulated mediation session.

The Oregon Mediation Association is also developing options for ensuring competency of mediation services. The options range from certification, of either the mediator or the training, to a comprehensive public education campaign to educate the public on what to look for when choosing a mediator.

As with the issues of mediation styles and goals, the issues of what makes a good mediator, how we identify those traits in a particular mediator, and how community mediation programmes articulate these conclusions to consumers, are matters of ongoing discussion in the mediation community.

Getting referrals for a community-based programme

One of the challenges of any community mediation programme is the fact that volunteers tend to be much easier to find than disputants. Whether it is lack of familiarity with the mediation process, a preference for third party decision-making, a reluctance to let outsiders into a conflict situation, or other reasons, getting parties to the table can be a difficult process. Ideally, community mediation programmes would receive most of their calls directly from citizens who know of the centre and opt for mediation as their dispute resolution method of choice. In truth, though, mediation programmes need to cultivate a wide variety of referral sources. Most tend to be the front-line agencies that citizens contact – courts, police departments, city inspection departments, prosecutors' offices, consumer protection agencies and human service agencies. In some mediation programmes, reliance on court referrals, especially small claims cases, has led to intense discussions over whether mediation programmes should, formally or informally, align themselves with courts, on the theory that that is where the cases are, or whether too much reliance on court referrals will encourage courts simply to incorporate the mediation programme as another arm of the court.

Community mediation programmes are addressing these issues on two levels. First, work continues to retain current referral sources and to expand to non-traditional referral sources. 'Making effective use of mediation center capacity is still not what most elected or appointed officials think about' (Amsler 1997). Second, some community mediation programmes are working to educate the public about mediation in general, with the goal of raising the awareness level of mediation. Media campaigns, public access television programmes and public service announcements are used by community mediation programmes in many states; leading the way in this are campaigns in Hawaii and Oregon.

'Expanding the pie' for community mediation

Of the many recent trends in community mediation, one of the most critical to programme growth is the increasingly broad spectrum of cases brought for community mediation. Originally, community mediation programmes were designed to handle minor criminal neighbourhood complaints, as courts were not an effective forum in which to handle these disputes (National Institute of Justice 1997, p.2). Reflecting this orientation, some of the original programmes were called 'neighbourhood justice centres'. In the 20 years since these programmes began, however, the types of cases handled have grown to include both major and minor criminal and civil disputes. For most community mediation programmes, developing expertise in different types of mediations has been a reflection of the needs and interests of their local community.

The National Institute of Justice (1997, p.4) lists as typical types of community mediation cases: 'minor criminal, minor civil, school based dispute resolution, divorce/custody, inter-group, public policy, resolution mechanisms, victim–offender mediation efforts, and other specialized services'. Several types of non-traditional community mediation cases are profiled next.

Agriculture-related mediation

The US Department of Agriculture (USDA) has relied on mediation since 1988 to resolve some categories of producer–lender disputes. In the past, USDA has relied on individual mediators, often based in a state's capital city, to provide services needed statewide. More recently, USDA has contracted with the state of Michigan to provide agriculture-related mediation through the network of 28 community mediation programmes in that state. Types of cases mediated range from denied bank loans, in which the method of calculating assets or depreciation is in dispute, to inter-generational disputes over the sale or dissolution of a family farm.

Case example

A couple who had farmed for many years sold their farm to a daughter and son-in-law, trading houses with the younger couple in the process. After several years of farming, the daughter and son-in-law decided they did not wish to continue farming. There were many points of discussion over who was responsible for which loans, how the assets would be divided and how the housing situation would be resolved when the younger couple sold the farm and wanted their house back. Mediators met with the family over three sessions. Some issues were resolved; some were not. After the mediation process, though, the issues yet to be dealt with were clear and the two families were working together to solve them, rather than blaming each other for the pitfalls of the situation.

Victim–offender mediation

The use of mediation as a form of restorative justice, rather than punitive justice, is growing in the USA. Restorative justice focuses on addressing the needs of crime victims and the restoration of the offender to the community (primarily through restitution), rather than focusing on prosecuting the offender with a crime against the state, as is typical in traditional retributive justice. While originally used for first-time property offences, victim–offender mediations have been performed between offenders and families of drunk-driving victims and murder victims. Victim–offender mediation also now often includes post-adjudication mediation, which uses the mediation process to provide a final sense of closure to the court process, rather than as an alternative to the court process.

Case example

A father became very angry with his teenage daughter's boyfriend when he found out that the 16 year old was pregnant. During an argument with the boyfriend, the father, who used a walking stick because of a disability, hit the boyfriend with the stick. The boyfriend's glasses were broken and he required stitches to his face. Assault charges were filed. The judge, realising that the daughter planned to keep the child and that the boyfriend would continue to interact with the family as the father of their grandchild, recommended victim–offender mediation to set damages and restitution for the assault. The resulting plan for handling damages became part of the court file. The two men also talked about how and when they would interact, although that part of the mediation was not committed to writing.

School-based peer mediation

Many community mediation programmes are partnering with local schools to teach mediation and conflict resolution to students and staff. In the early 1980s, programmes often focused on setting up peer mediation, in which students were trained to mediate disputes involving other students. It became clear, though, that training a small group of students did not always have the desired impact on the school at large. Many programmes now emphasise a two-pronged effort to teach interpersonal communication and conflict resolution skills to all students and staff, then train selected students as mediators when the need arises. Leaders in this area are the San Francisco Community Boards Programme (San Francisco, California) and the New Mexico Center for Conflict Resolution (Albuquerque, New Mexico).

Case example

The assistant principal of a middle school had been working on conflict and rumour issues with a group of several 12 and 13 year olds since the beginning of the school year. In November, the assistant principal had the girls in her office yet again, for an incident which occurred that morning. As the girls talked, it became clear that two of the girls had broken, for the second time, a previously mediated agreement. The assistant principal became very frustrated with the girls as they had discussed this behaviour twice before, and stated that she didn't think she [the assistant principal] was neutral enough to finish the mediation. At this, a girl in the group who was new to the school that autumn said she had been trained as a peer mediator in her previous school. She offered to take over as mediator to facilitate the discussion between the two girls and the assistant principal. The mediation was completed, with the girls renewing their agreement. The assistant principal noticed over the coming weeks that the girls did keep their agreement this time.

Using the community mediation process in other state or federal systems

The Alternative Dispute Resolution Act (ADRA) of 1996 mandates a system of alternative dispute resolution for all federal agencies. While many agencies are creating these internally, often using some form of mediation as part of the process, other agencies are turning to local community mediation programmes to provide mediation services. Examples of this include:

- special education mediation;
- community mental health disputes;
- Equal Employment Opportunity Commission (EEOC) disputes.

SPECIAL EDUCATION MEDIATION

The Atlanta Justice Centre, one of the first community mediation programmes in the USA in the 1970s, began working with the Georgia Department of Education's Division of Exceptional Students in 1979, to mediate disputes over education issues under the federal Education for All Handicapped Children's Act (1975). In 1995, that legislation was rewritten as the federal Individuals with Disabilities Education Act (IDEA). In 1997, the Act was amended to require each state to develop and implement a statewide system of mediation when a request is filed for a due process hearing (National Association for Community Mediation 1997). In New York State, the special education mediation programme is offered through the statewide association of community mediation programmes.

Case example

A child had a one-hour commute each way to receive special education services in a programme located outside her town. The services she needed were not offered in her local school district. The parents filed a complaint, asking for the district to offer the programme in her local school district. In mediation, the parents and district reached an agreement to change the transport arrangements, so that the child's daily commute was reduced to 25 minutes each way, and made a plan to work towards having the child returned, with assistance, to her local school district.

COMMUNITY MENTAL HEALTH DISPUTES

As with many other federal and state departments, community mental health departments are formally including mediation as part of their dispute resolution process. In Michigan, the Community Mental Health Code, as amended in 1995, provides for mediation both in the recipient rights complaint process and in the formal appeals process (Michigan Public Act 290 of 1995). While mediation services may be provided by any mediator, several counties use their local community mediation programme to provide mediation.

Case example

A middle-aged man, a client of a community mental health programme, was told he was no longer eligible to receive services. The client's family filed an appeal. The client, his brother/legal guardian and a programme representative met in the presence of neutral mediators. During the meeting, the programme representative explained that the psychologist had determined that the medication the client had been receiving was no longer needed, so he was discharging the client from that particular programme, but not from the agency. The programme representative, guardian and client were able to set up a different treatment plan for the client.

EQUAL EMPLOYMENT OPPORTUNITY COMMISSION (EEOC) DISPUTES

The Civil Rights Act of 1991, Sec. 118, Alternatives Means of Dispute Resolution, states that: 'Where appropriate, and to the extent authorized by the law, the use of alternative means of dispute resolution, including…mediation…is encouraged to resolve disputes arising under the Acts or provisions or Federal law amended by this title.' Since 1996, EEOC offices in some states have been using community mediation programmes to settle some types of complaints. Cases filed are screened by EEOC staff and those deemed appropriate for mediation are referred out to community mediation programmes.

Case example

A person with a severe speech impediment applied for a position as a postal route carrier, and after both a written test and an interview was not hired for the job. He felt that it was because of the speech impediment, so he filed an EEO claim. The mediation was attended by the prospective employee, an advocate from the local disability rights commission and a Post Office supervisor, who was not the person who initially interviewed the applicant. In the interview, the supervisor explained all the criteria he used in making hiring decisions, including criteria of which the applicant was not aware, and the applicant was also able to explain his perspective. The Post Office supervisor then offered to hire the applicant as a temporary employee for six months. The disability rights advocate explained what resources the applicant could get, at no cost to the Post Office, to enable him to perform the job. Both parties were satisfied with the outcome and left with an agreement.

Beyond mediation: Getting conflict resolution into our communities

The diversifying nature of the work listed above indicates that training programmes in mediation, conflict resolution skills and violence prevention issues are also a growing part of community mediation programmes. Increasingly, community mediation programmes are viewed as resources for developing the interpersonal problem-solving capacity of communities, as well as a place to go when one-to-one problem solving fails.

Centres also look to training to provide income to support mediation programmes. While local funding and grants often provide basic programme support, mediation programmes are not seen as recipients of charitable contributions in the same way as services to children, homeless families, etc. So training provides a forum for community mediation programmes both to increase their own resources and to strengthen their communities.

Community mediation programmes are also working with innovative community collaborations to get conflict resolution skills into various institutional and organisational settings. On a national level, both the Girl Scouts of the USA and the federal Head Start programme for disadvantaged preschool children and their families are incorporating mediation and conflict resolution internally, with the assistance of community mediation programmes in several states.

The future of community mediation

Funding

One of the most critical issues facing community mediation is continued funding for mediation programmes. Despite the solid track record of conflict interventions by community mediation programmes, 72.6 per cent of the centres polled in a recent survey had between one and four full-time employees, while another 15.1 per cent had no full-time staff. Of these programmes, 56.7 per cent received primary funding through taxes or court filing fees, with another 16 per cent reporting receiving grant funding (McKinney *et al.* 1996). Also, 96.7 per cent of the centres responding to the survey listed themselves as non-profit agencies, which by mandate usually offer mediation either at no cost or very minimal cost. Thus, to continue to provide community mediation means continued commitment on the part of courts, governments and other funders.

Diversification / specialisation

The increasingly complex and specialised types of mediation listed above require mediation training beyond the initial basic training to qualify mediators to mediate in these specialised forums. While many community mediation programmes have developed these types of training, this also raises questions of certification, qualification, fees charged and whether or how programmes that rely on volunteers should charge for and pay mediators for cases that are not traditional community mediation cases.

Integration of mediation into systems or processes

A related issue is the increased use of mediation in formal agency or organisational procedures. Community mediation programmes play a part in some of these arenas. In some areas of the country, community mediation programmes are working with the US Postal Service to mediate internal post office disputes. Other community mediation programmes have worked with local courts to infuse juvenile detention centres or residential programmes with conflict resolution and problem-solving skills. Again, as community mediation programmes enter these arenas, additional training will be needed.

The Dispute Resolution Center (DRC) of West Michigan

The history and evolution of the Dispute Resolution Center of West Michigan, where the author works, exemplifies a typical community mediation programme. Opened in 1986 as the first community mediation programme in Michigan, the DRC was modelled on the Neighborhood Justice Center of Atlanta (Georgia).

In the early days of community mediation, there were various models, each of which was quite firm about their version of the vision of community mediation. In the neighbourhood justice centre model, one mediator per case was used and, nearly always, a caucus (separate meetings between the mediators and the parties individually). The rationale for a caucus was that a mediator never knew if there were any underlying issues unless they had caucused. Another well-known model, from the Community Boards Program, relied on panels of three to five community representatives as mediators and caucuses were hardly ever used. The rationale for this is that a main purpose of mediation is to teach parties more effective communication skills, which cannot be done if they are kept separate from each other.

Over the years, the DRC, like many other community mediation programmes, has melded these two philosophies. We now often use co-mediators, for two reasons. One is to train and coach new mediators. The other is that working with peers is one of the best ways for mediators to learn new techniques, receive feedback from other mediators, and as a quality control mechanism. Mediators sometime caucus, but often do not. Like other mediation centres around the country, we have tried to keep up with new research and skill sets and incorporate them into ongoing training and professional development for our mediators.

In many respects, the DRC is similar to the profile of a community mediation programme outlined in McKinney *et al.* (1996). While no specific professional background is required for mediators, potential mediators fill out a questionnaire and are interviewed (usually by a centre staff member and another mediator) prior to the training. Following the training process, an internship consisting of observation, co-mediation and mediating under the supervision of an experienced mediator is required.

A minimum of six mediations is required to complete the internship process. Sometimes, staff or supervising mediators recommend additional co-mediation time. Other times, the mediator prefers to continue as a co-mediator rather than a solo mediator. On occasion, a volunteer mediator's service has had to be terminated for a variety of reasons, which is always a painful process for all involved. Once mediators have completed their internships, they are asked each year whether they wish to re-commit for another year. Re-committing requires attendance at two of three in-service training sessions and mediation of at least four cases during the year.

Case referrals often come from the court system. There are many levels of courts: small claims, general civil, family, landlord/tenant and circuit (superior). The centre, like many other centres, makes many attempts to secure case referrals from other sources, with moderate success. The reality, though, is that many people turn first to court for assistance with disputes, so courts are often the first point of referral to mediation.

Geographically, the centre began in 1986 to serve one county, Kent, which contained the major city (200,000 inhabitants) and the majority of residents (600,000) of a metropolitan area. In 1990, the Michigan Legislature created a statewide Community Dispute Resolution Program, funded by a $2.00 increase in court filing fee per civil case filed in each county. Three years after that, the centre was asked to provide mediation services to five neighbouring counties, whose court filing fees ranged from $500 to $8000 per county per year, compared to the $60,000 per year generated by court filing fees in the original, urban county. Providing outreach and services to six counties, somewhat proportionate to their filing fee revenues, has been and continues to be a challenge. Residents and agencies in the original county have much more ownership of the mediation programme than do the other counties.

The centre is a non-profit organisation, administered by a 21-member board of directors. For several years it had a staff of three full-time employees; recently, a fourth was added to focus on new programme areas. There are about forty-five active volunteers at any given time, although maintaining a mediator base that is truly reflective of the communities found across six counties is a formidable challenge. The centre also relies heavily on college and university interns to assist the intake staff. In 1997, the hours logged by non-mediator volunteers amounted to the equivalent of a 0.75 FTE (full-time employee) staff person.

Like other non-profit agencies and other non-profit community mediation programmes in particular, the centre's future efforts will be directed to diversifying our funding sources (and thus our programme areas) and to continuing the work of mentoring, monitoring and supporting the mediators who are the backbone of any community mediation programme.

Conclusion

In the past 20 years, community mediation programmes have moved from what some critics perceived as a 'fad' to an integral part of many communities in the USA. In addition, the entire field of mediation and alternative dispute resolution has gained a much higher profile in the past two decades. This will provide increased opportunities for community mediation programmes to expand their services in their communities. It will also challenge community mediation in two key areas. First, as the non-profit, for-profit, government-based and private practice sectors of the mediation community continue to grapple with their respective roles in a rapidly changing culture, will mediation become a mainstream profession and reduce or eliminate the role of volunteers? Will states continue to support community-based programmes, or will the focus change to for-profit mediation providers?

A second and related issue is how community mediation programmes present themselves to their communities. Community mediation programmes are rich resources for communities – for conflict resolution services, training, resources and education. In some cases, though, programmes can frame their strengths (including volunteer mediators and their ability, as members of non-profit programmes, to handle cases at little or no cost) as limitations. This mindset limits the capacity of some programmes. It will remain a challenge for community mediation programmes to be able to define themselves, their services and the good they do to the public at large in their communities.

References

Amsler, T. (1997) 'Trends in community mediation.' *National Association for Community Mediation* autumn, 8.

Bush, R.A.B. and Folger, J. (1996) 'Transformative mediation and third party intervention: ten hallmarks of a transformative mediation practice.' *Mediation Quarterly 13*, 4, 263–278.

Civil Rights Act of 1991, Sec. 118, *Alternatives Means of Dispute Resolution.*

Folger, J. and Bush, R.A.B. (1994) *The Promise of Mediation.* New York: Jossey-Bass.

McKinney, B.C., Kimsey, W.D. and Fuller, R.M. (1996) 'A nationwide survey of mediation centers.' *Mediation Quarterly 14*, 2, 155–166.

National Association for Community Mediation (1997) 'Interview with Edie Primm.' *National Association for Community Mediation* autumn, 5.

National Institute of Justice (1997) *Community Mediation Programs: Developments and Challenges.* Washington DC: US Department of Justice.

Ray, L. (1997) 'Community mediation centers: delivering first-class services to low-income people for the past twenty years.' *Mediation Quarterly 15*, 1, 71–77.

Riskin, L. (1996) 'Understanding mediator orientations, strategies and techniques: A grid for the perplexed.' *Harvard Law Review 7*, 1, 57–58.

Society of Professionals In Dispute Resolution (SPIDR) (1989) *Qualifying Neutrals: The Basic Principles*. Washington DC: SPIDR.

Society of Professionals in Dispute Resolution (SPIDR) (1996) *Ensuring Competence and Quality in Dispute Resolution Practice*. Washington DC: SPIDR.

Stulberg, J. (1987) *Taking Charge: Managing Conflict*. Lexington MA: Lexington Books.

8

Victim–Offender Mediation in Practice

Jean Wynne

Introduction

Victim–offender mediation is a voluntary process of communication, conducted by a neutral mediator, which allows victims to express their needs and feelings, and offenders to accept and act on their responsibilities. This mediation process has benefits for victims and offenders at all stages of the criminal justice process because it deals with the personal effects of crime not usually addressed by the formal justice system. Hurt, pain and loss suffered by victims are acknowledged by offenders, and this acknowledgement is often the most healing part of the process. When victims know their pain has been heard, they stop reliving the event and begin to put the offence behind them.

Community mediation usually takes place between parties who blame each other, so mediators are neutral on who is to blame. Victim–offender mediation differs in the clear acknowledgement of responsibility, as the guilty party is known. Mediators can demonstrate their neutrality by giving equal respect to both parties.

The mediation process can be thought of as a continuum ranging from exchanges of information and feelings via the mediator, exchanges of letters, audio or video tapes or direct face-to-face meetings, with reparation by the offender as a possibility at any point. Victims are offered a series of choices and can stop the process at any stage.

Victims may also sometimes choose when the mediation takes place. For some it is important that mediation takes place before sentence so they can have a voice at court. Other victims feel strongly that they want to test out their offenders' sincerity and request that mediation takes place after sentence.

Mediation helps offenders to accept full responsibility for their behaviour, however painful it may be to face up to reality. Having heard their victims' feelings, offenders can no longer pretend that the offence was 'just a job'. This awareness is difficult for offenders at the time but helps them in the long term because it can act as a catalyst for change.

Mediation UK guidelines in training and setting up a service

Mediation UK, the national umbrella organisation for mediation services, has produced guidelines for the training of mediators and setting up new mediation services (Mediation UK 1993). The basic principles for these guidelines are that mediation must be voluntary and in the best interests of both victims and offenders. Offenders must accept full responsibility for the offence and mediation must be physically, psychologically and emotionally safe for all parties.

Mediation should be a neutral service carried out by trained mediators who have no other stake in the criminal justice process. It is not considered appropriate for social workers, probation officers or victim support workers to mediate with their own clients because they have a different relationship with their clients from the other parties and could not be genuinely neutral.

Mediation services should, if possible, have premises in a neutral location, not sited in probation, social services, police or victim support premises. It is considered essential that the service has an advisory or management group which includes representatives from police, courts, victim support, probation and social services. Monitoring and evaluation are crucial and services are expected to undertake them. There is now an accreditation scheme available for services through Mediation UK.

Training

There is no nationally organised training course for mediators at present. Some universities include a mediation option, but these courses usually cover the more theoretical aspects of restorative justice and mediation, rather than a practice teaching element. A mediation National Vocational Qualification (NVQ) based at level 4 has been developed and is now available through local NVQ centres. An NVQ in community justice will be available from autumn 2000 and will include three mediation units from the Mediation NVQ. Anyone wishing to undertake the victim–offender route of the mediation NVQ would need to train with one of the existing services in order to provide the necessary evidence of experience.

The Mediation UK guidelines recommend that mediators' training should include knowledge of the courts, sentencing, supervision of offenders, the criminal justice process, negotiation skills, report writing, mediation skills, listening skills, working with juveniles, handling violence and aggression, non-discriminatory practice and mediating specific offences such as deception, domestic violence and sexual assaults. This training usually takes place over a period of time.

Because mediation is such a new area of practice, much of the knowledge is held by experienced mediators, so 'on-the-job' training and case discussions are essential elements of mediation training.

Introductory training courses provided by existing services involve prospective mediators in role plays of assessment procedures, indirect mediation interviews and face-to-face meetings between victims and offenders. The role plays are based on actual cases and the trainees role play them from the three different perspectives of mediator, victim and offender. An essential part of the training course is self-reflection on attitudes and values. This helps mediators to become aware of their own values and how these fit in with the values of mediation. Working with different perspectives is an integral part of this training.

Non-discriminatory practice is essential and to achieve this mediators must be aware of power imbalances, whether on grounds of ethnicity, gender, age, sexuality or any of the other areas of possible discrimination.

After completing introductory training, police checks must be carried out on applicants. Having a police record does not necessarily bar applicants from becoming mediators, if the offences were relatively minor and applicants can show that they have since changed their lifestyle. However, an applicant with convictions for offences against children would not be considered.

Once accredited by the mediation service as mediators, trainees can work on cases with experienced mediators and learn how to do the work. It takes about a year for most mediators to become competent, assuming that they are working on cases every week. Regular case discussion sessions are essential to share problems and solutions, as well as ongoing training, supervision and support.

The mediation process

This begins with a referral from a person or agency. Referrals can be made by social workers, probation officers, police, victim support services, solicitors, courts, citizens advice bureaux and individual victims and offenders. The mediation co-ordinator collects information about the current whereabouts of both victim and offender and details of the offence. Some cases may not be accepted, usually because of adverse safety issues, for example, where it is known that the offender is still using illegal drugs or is an alcoholic.

Pre-court it may be necessary to contact the defendant's lawyer to check whether the defendant is pleading guilty to the offence. Until this point is clear, mediators should not make contact with victims, as it may be considered to be interfering with witnesses if the case goes to a trial.

However, in some areas diversion from court is one of the aims of mediation. Where such diversion schemes operate, victims are contacted first and offered mediation before a decision has been made about their offenders (see p.133).

The choice of mediator is often based on who is available. Mediators may have preferences such as working with young offenders or not working with cases of sexual assault. These preferences can be borne in mind, but all mediators should be able to mediate all types of cases.

Mediators make appointments to see offenders or victims, usually by letter. There are various arguments to support visiting victims or offenders first. In practice the first contact will probably be made with whichever person is more easily available. Mediation UK does not have a policy on who should be visited first. Flexibility is recommended and each case should be taken on its merits. Some mediators feel they need to check out offenders' willingness before contacting victims, in order to prevent re-victimisation. Others prefer to contact victims first as a statement of putting victims first.

Because victims and offenders are visited in their own homes, often in the evening, mediators' safety is an important consideration. It helps to have up-to-date street maps so that venues can be found quickly, to carry personal alarms to deter would-be robbers, and sometimes to carry gadgets which send out high-pitched whines to startle aggressive dogs. Mediators must tell someone where they are going and preferably carry mobile phones with them. Many services insist that mediators work in pairs, for safety reasons as well as good practice. The timing of appointments is important as people do not like to be disturbed late in the evening. Late morning appointments can be offered to retired people and shift workers are best seen in the late afternoon. Mediators say they like to dress tidily but not too formally, as it can be offputting to distressed victims.

The first knock on the door can be quite stressful as mediators do not know what to expect. While offenders have usually been screened by referrers, victims are an unknown quantity and mediators have to be prepared for anything from tears to extreme anger.

At the first visit mediators spend much time listening to what happened, from the victim's or offender's perspective, and soaking up anger or pain expressed. They provide information about the service offered and assess whether there is anything to be gained by mediating.

Case example

Peter and Zack's story

> Peter attacked his partner, Zack, during an argument and beat him up quite badly. Pre-sentence he told his probation officer that he wanted to apologise. He was sentenced to 18 months' imprisonment.
>
> After sentence the mediator saw Peter to check his willingness to continue with mediation. Peter said mediation was no longer necessary. Zack had committed an unconnected offence and was also in the prison, and they had met and shaken hands.
>
> Zack confirmed Peter's story. He said the relationship was over, and they both agreed on this, but they had also patched things up to the point where they could get along in a peaceful manner.

In cases like this, there is no point in bringing the two together as they had resolved the offence themselves.

Participants' safety during the process should continually be assessed. Things to consider include the likelihood of violence, power imbalances between victim and offender, proximity of victim and offender in the community, the type of offence, whether others are involved and fears of retribution. Mediation is only taken as far as willingness and safety considerations allow.

Victims of relatively minor offences such as criminal damage are often more willing to meet face to face as there is less at stake; on the other hand the parties may feel that there is little to gain from a meeting as there is little to resolve. Legal processes may also get in the way of mediation even when both parties are willing.

Case example

Janet and Martin's story

> *Janet was found unconscious with her head stove in. She had substantial memory loss and desperately needed to find out what happened to her. Her victim support worker suggested mediation.*
>
> *The mediator visited Martin (the offender) in prison. He was willing to answer Janet's questions and to meet with her. However, Martin's solicitor was appealing against his seven-year sentence and warned that he would use a meeting with Janet to help Martin's case. (He would argue that the fact the victim wanted to meet Martin again showed that the offence had not damaged her as much as originally suggested in court.) Janet did not want to be used in this way, so mediation was put on hold until the appeal was completed.*

This example demonstrates the tension between the needs of victim and offender for resolution of the offence, and the solicitor's job to do the best he could for his client.

If one of the participants is emotionally unstable or, as occasionally happens with elderly victims, completely confused about mediation, there is no point in taking the case any further. The physical condition of victims or offenders is also important. Mediation may be helpful to those suffering from illness but not if it will put the victim or offender at any risk.

Case example

Dennis and Gavin's story

> *Dennis had his car stolen. He wanted to meet the offender, Gavin, but his Parkinson's disease worsened and he was not well enough to leave his home. The mediator considered it unsafe for the meeting to take place at Dennis's home because of the slight risk that Gavin might use information gained from visiting it to burgle Dennis.*

This case illustrates the tension for the mediator in wanting to show his trust in the offender while ensuring that the victim does not get re-victimised as a result of mediation.

After the first round of visits, the mediator revisits both parties to exchange information, with their permission. During this second visit the mediator challenges the offender about how the offence has affected the victim. Often the information relayed is a shock to the offender and mediators have to talk them through this quite painful stage. Professionals involved with offenders (such as their probation officers) need to be aware of any difficulties offenders may have in receiving this information, so that they can provide support. Offenders in prison are particularly vulnerable after receiving difficult information, and their prison probation officers must be kept fully informed.

Some types of offence are better dealt with through indirect mediation rather than bringing victim and offender face to face. For example, deception cases usually involve victims who are lonely and vulnerable and placed their mistaken trust in offenders. Bringing them together again risks that the situation will be replayed.

Case example

Mary and Lawrence's story

Mary was an elderly woman who lived alone. Her roof needed repairing. Lawrence offered to repair it. He was a personable young man and offered to drive Mary around. She began to depend on him. He disappeared leaving the work unfinished after Mary had lent him a considerable sum of money. He was convicted of deception and placed on probation. He wanted to apologise and Mary wanted to meet with him. On talking it over with the mediator, Mary admitted that if she saw him again she would probably lend him more money. Indirect mediation was carried out.

This example illustrates the necessity for mediators to share their concerns with victims. In this case Mary was able to understand her own vulnerability to being re-victimised and this self-knowledge may help her in the future.

Domestic violence cases should be approached with similar caution. Violent partners may want a face-to-face meeting with their ex-partners to re-establish control. Mediators are aware of power imbalances and protection issues and would not allow mediation to be used for this purpose. In this type of case, again indirect mediation allows both sides to explain their position safely without any risk of further violence. It can also help the abusive partner to accept that the relationship is finally over. Blackmail may require similar treatment.

Case example

Sam and John's story

Sam was short of money and went to a priest, John, who gave him food and drink. Then followed an indecent act. John gave him some money and Sam left, but continued to demand money. John paid up for a while but eventually confessed to his superiors and Sam was charged with blackmail. After sentence the mediator visited Sam in prison. Sam wanted John to know that he wouldn't ask him for money again. The mediator visited John, who had changed his place of work twice to get away from any form of contact with Sam, who was still bombarding him with letters.

The mediator challenged Sam about his continuing to bother John and relayed John's wishes. Sam acknowledged his deceit and confirmed that he would now accept that John did not want any further contact.

These examples demonstrate cases where indirect mediation is most suitable.

However, if the criteria of willingness, safety and admission of guilt are met, the mediator asks both parties if they would like to meet face to face, and then a meeting is arranged. This usually requires two mediators. A neutral venue is booked at a time suitable to both sides, usually in a church hall or community centre, or the mediation service office if appropriate. The mediators drive the parties to the meeting place separately (unless they prefer to make their own way there). This allows for preparation time during the journey. Often the participants are very nervous and may need reassurance and to be reminded of the things they were concerned about and want to say.

Victim and offender are usually seated facing one another as are the two mediators. A square table is ideal. This allows for eye contact between victim and offender. Similarly the mediators may need to communicate with each other through eye contact and body language, to ensure fairness. It is a business meeting, so refreshments are not served until after the conclusion.

The meeting itself follows the standard mediation format of introductions and ground rules, uninterrupted time, exchange of information and negotiation, followed by possible agreement. This is, of course, the ideal. Most meetings do not follow that format exactly and mediators have to be skilled and confident enough to allow variations from the format. Sometimes the meeting might get a little heated and mediators will take the parties out separately to give them 'time out' to cool down. At the end of the meeting, usually one mediator sums up and the second mediator notes down any points of agreement. All present sign their names to these points. If the case takes place pre-court, they are asked if the court can be made aware of this agreement. The co-ordinator of the mediation service prepares the court report and informs the referrer of the outcome, but not of anything which was said as this remains confidential. The co-ordinator or mediator may attend the court hearing and is sometimes asked questions by the sentencer.

Some meetings do not end in agreement and the mediators must not force the parties to agree to something they do not want. It may be more comfortable for the mediators if a formal mediation takes place and a tidy ending is achieved, but the meeting belongs to the victims and offenders, as the following example illustrates.

Case example

Norman and Steven's story

Norman lived in a hostel with other ex-offenders. He borrowed money from another resident, Steven, and got into a fight when Steven asked for it back. Norman went to court and received a probation order. He wanted to apologise, so a meeting was arranged at the hostel. While the mediator discussed final arrangements with the hostel warden, Norman went off to find Steven. By the time the mediator found them, Norman had apologised, Steven had accepted the apology and the money had been paid back. 'They went ahead and did it without me' was the mediator's wry comment.

Reparation

Victims may have a specific request for reparation, such as a sum of money, or for a specific piece of work to be undertaken by the offender. In serious cases reparation is often at a more personal level than financial compensation or practical work. It is important for victims to know that their offenders accept responsibility for their behaviour and its outcome. They want to know that offenders have become aware of the physical and mental pain they have caused. Victims often seek assurance from offenders that they will change their behaviour and not put someone else through the pain they have suffered.

However, in some less serious offences, financial reparation or practical work of even relatively small amounts can be very important to victims. If voluntary financial compensation has been agreed, mediators can collect this and deliver it to victims personally.

If practical work has been agreed, it will need to be supervised. The mediator can only do this if the service is insured for this type of work. Probation mediation units can arrange for work to be supervised by probation community service supervisors, who are covered for insurance purposes. Most services find that practical reparation is carried out in only a small number of cases, for several reasons. Offenders sentenced to community service find extra reparation work difficult to fit in. Some victims do not want offenders to come near their homes and indirect reparation for a third party can be difficult to arrange and supervise, and is very costly for the service in terms of mediator time. Mediators are selected for their personal qualities, not for their ability to supervise practical work, and not all are able or would choose to do this.

For those victims who want their offender to learn a particular lesson, however, reparation can play an important role.

Case example

Lee and Edith's story

> *Lee was walking through the park and passed an old lady. He flicked a heavy coin at her, showing off. This coin hit Edith on the head and she needed medical treatment. Lee was cautioned and referred to mediation. Edith met with Lee and wanted him to respect and understand more about old people, their sense of humour and so on. They agreed that Lee would help serve teas in a local old people's home as reparation.*

Follow-up

When mediation is completed, mediators often carry out a final separate visit to both parties, to ensure nothing has been overlooked. This is a vital procedure because people's perceptions of what has been agreed may change over time, and there are often loose ends to be tied up before the case can be closed. Some cases cannot be closed for a considerable time because victims may want to be kept informed of the offender's progress and behaviour following mediation.

Assessing the quality of the work and participants' satisfaction with outcomes should be done by the service. Satisfaction questionnaires can be useful but independent evaluation should also be carried out at some point.

Mediation throughout the criminal justice process

Diversion

In Northamptonshire the county-wide, multi-agency Diversion Unit diverts suitable cases from juvenile, magistrates or Crown courts. The police refer cases to the Diversion Unit, following which victim and offender are offered mediation. If both parties are willing, the unit produces a mediation action plan. If the action plan is considered acceptable by the police, the offender is diverted from court and mediation takes place.

In Scotland appropriate cases are referred to mediation units by the Procurator Fiscal and victims are then approached. If the victim is willing and mediation takes place, a report is sent to the Procurator Fiscal who takes the mediation into account when deciding whether to divert the case from court. If the case is diverted and the offender does not keep the agreement, the case can be sent back to court later.

Cautions and reprimands

In England, prior to the Crime and Disorder Act 1988, some services operated at the Caution stage, where a decision was taken to caution an offender, but the Cautioning Panel felt it was also appropriate to offer the opportunity to take part in mediation/reparation (subject to the willingness of both offender and victim).

Case example

Robin and Mark's story

The boys (both aged 10) broke into a building site one evening and did some damage to the equipment. The police decided that a caution was appropriate, given the boys' age and previous good behaviour. However, because of the potential seriousness of the offence, mediation also seemed indicated. The site manager was interested in mediation and a face-to-face meeting was arranged. As reparation the boys visited the site during the daytime and the site manager showed them how close they had been to having a dangerous accident.

Under the 1998 Act, police cautions for young people are now replaced by a new system consisting of a reprimand for a first offence and a 'final warning' for a second one. Mediation can be an option at either of these stages (see also p.137).

Pre-sentence mediation

If the case is going to court, mediation can take place before sentence if both parties are willing.

Case example

David and the Browns' story

David (aged 19) started using drugs. He lost his job and ran short of money. His family were friends with neighbours, Mr and Mrs Brown. Mrs Brown had some gold chains. David called at the Browns' house and stole the chains. Mr and Mrs Brown were extremely hurt and angry and David's father could not forgive his son.

A mediator called to see both David and Mr and Mrs Brown, and found they needed to say things to one another. Mr and Mrs Brown wanted to do this quickly as they felt it would ruin Christmas if the families were still estranged. A direct mediation meeting was arranged, unusually, at the victims' house. This was to enable David to feel he could enter their house again. Mr and Mrs Brown expressed their feelings. David apologised and said he had now given up drugs. He wanted to pay back the money. They agreed that he should pay £2 a week until he got employment.

Mr and Mrs Brown wanted the court to be aware of the agreement. David was sentenced to 12 months' probation with a condition of hostel residence. The families were reconciled and his father was finally able to forgive him. Three months later David was still firmly committed to making the reparation payments and was doing well on probation.

Post-sentence

Cases can also be mediated after sentence, irrespective of whether offenders receive a prison or community sentence. In general prison governors are supportive of offenders undertaking mediation with their victims and often allow mediation meetings to be held in prison.

Case example

Allen and Lee's story

Allen was burgled by Lee, who was sentenced to 18 months' imprisonment. As a result of attending a groupwork session on victims' feelings, Lee wanted to try to put things right and asked to be referred to mediation. Allen was contacted and offered mediation. He was interested because the goods stolen were very personal to him and included some religious recordings. A meeting was arranged in prison. Allen challenged Lee and some very meaningful and deep exchanges took place. Allen accepted that Lee wanted to put things right, but said only the return of his property would do that. Lee said he would try to retrieve Allen's property when he returned to the community.

Offence type

Mediatable offences include all crimes which involve clearly identifiable victims and offenders. These offences include arson, assault, burglary, deception, car theft, theft from employer, robbery, kidnapping, violent assaults of all levels of seriousness, sexual assaults and domestic violence.

Offences such as fraud against a government department are not usually considered suitable for mediation. Even here there are exceptions as, for example, where the offender worked in that department and hurt staff members through his or her actions. Offences such as football hooliganism, 'drunk and disorderly' or affray are not usually mediated, as it is difficult to identify specific victims. It is important not to have preconceptions about 'suitable' cases, as it is victims' and offenders' perceptions which determine suitability, not mediators. Shoplifting from a branch of a chain of newsagents' shops may not appear to be suitable, yet in one case, a mediator found a high level of distress among the staff. So much had been stolen that staff felt under suspicion. Similarly, theft from supermarkets may appear unsuitable, yet many services have had successful mediations between store security officers and offenders. Explanations about the effect of shoplifting on the general public can make a surprising impression on offenders.

Fears about upsetting elderly victims could prevent mediation being offered, yet elderly people are very often extremely resilient and more able to cope than younger people.

Offences of sexual assault and rape can be considered, but only with extreme care. There is a consensus of opinion among probation and mediation staff that requests for mediation in rape cases should come from victims. Ideally victims refer themselves or are referred by victim agencies. This then means that the timing is right for the victim and they would not feel that offenders are seeking them out. Sometimes just knowing that they can undertake mediation is sufficient to help victims in the recovery process.

Case example

Amanda's story

Amanda was a young woman living in a flat on her own. A young man living in the same flats knocked on her door one day and asked to use her phone. Once inside her flat he attacked and raped her. The offender was convicted of rape and received a lengthy prison sentence.

Amanda was contacted by probation and offered the victim enquiry service (see p.136). About two years later she contacted the probation victim offender unit and asked if she could meet the offender. She had been working through her feelings with a counsellor and had realised that she needed to confront the offender. She asked if this was possible. The unit offered to send a mediator to visit Amanda and explain the process. Amanda said she would contact the unit again when she was ready. A year later she had not felt it necessary to go any further.

The victim contact worker/mediator involved would like this case to move on but will not do anything until Amanda herself initiates the process. Empowering victims means giving them power and choice over the timing and the process. This victim-sensitive mode of mediation can be difficult to achieve if services are driven by targets set by funders. Ethical practice dictates that mediation should be driven by the best outcome for victims and offenders and not by outcome targets.

Cases involving racial harassment may be unsuitable for mediation. It is essential that victims are not made to feel they should take responsibility for the education of racist offenders. However, a blanket ban on mediating racist offences would exclude those victims from mediation. Victims should be given all the information and allowed to make their own decisions. Indirect mediation may provide the best outcome, but in the end it is the victim's choice.

Is mediation effective?

For mediation to be effective it must have benefits for both victims and offenders. Home Office research on the pilot projects between 1985 and 1987 showed that victims who took part in mediation were less punitive and more satisfied with the outcome, while offenders who took part were less likely to blame the victim in some way and also viewed their offending more seriously (Marshall and Merry 1990).

A cross-national study (UK, USA, Canada) showed that the majority of victims and offenders who took part in mediation were satisfied with the outcome, and more likely to feel they had obtained justice than those who had not taken part in mediation. Victims were also less fearful of being re-victimised (Umbreit and Roberts 1996).

The Leeds Victim–Offender Unit has carried out three reconviction studies of offenders who took part in mediation. In 1989 the service examined the criminal records of the 90 offenders who met their victims during the two-year trial period between 1985 and 1987: 87 per cent had a previous criminal record; 25 per cent of these were persistent offenders who had five or more convictions; 75 per cent had no further convictions after one year and 68 per cent had no further convictions after two years.

A second follow-up study was carried out in 1992 which looked at those offenders who took part in mediation during 1989. This study showed that, of the 69 offenders who were examined, 78 per cent had no further convictions after one year and 58 per cent had no further convictions after two years.

A third study was carried out in 1996 of offenders who undertook indirect or direct mediation between January 1993 and June 1994. This study used the Home Office Offender Group Reconviction Scale, which predicts a reconviction rate for groups of offenders, against which the actual rate can be compared. Using this scale, the predicted rate of reoffending for the 73 offenders was 54.2 per cent whereas the actual rate was 49.3 per cent. When broken down by sentence, offenders on supervision undertaking mediation were 18 per cent less likely than predicted to be reconvicted (Wynne and Brown 1998).

Ongoing debates and issues

In recent years there has been a well-documented rise in the incidence of drug-related crime. Mediators are aware of this and the consequent safety issues not only for themselves but also for victims. Drug addicts are notoriously unreliable. While they may be very sorry for their behaviour and sincere about their apologies, if their addiction takes over again their new-found sense of responsibility can leave them. The risk of re-victimisation is therefore high for victims and services should consider carefully before mediating. It may be necessary to ensure that the offender has a drug support worker or programme, or can show they have tested negative for drugs before being accepted for mediation.

Should mediators be volunteers or paid? The positive outcomes of paying experienced mediators are that they stay with the service, are committed to training and developing practice, are more accountable to management and can be expected to take a variety of cases and work in a more directed manner than volunteers. However, at a time of cash limits and budget cuts for probation services nationally, the expansion of mediation services is difficult to envisage, unless volunteer mediators are used.

Who should be funding mediation services? There is currently a variety of providers, including probation, social services, youth justice centres and independent mediation services. Some people believe that funding should be completely independent of offender agencies, while others think that stable long-term funding can only be provided by government sources, either local or national.

Increasingly probation services around the country are beginning to examine ways of setting up mediation provision in the wake of the Victim's Charter (1990, 1995), which introduced Victim Enquiry work and has raised victims' expectations about the possibility of contact with their offenders.

Under the Victim's Charter, probation services have a duty to contact victims (or their families, if the victim is deceased) of serious violent or sexual offences, within two months of sentence being passed. The point of the contact is to keep victims informed during the progress of sentence, if they wish, and also to receive comments from victims about the eventual release plans of their offender, once these are known. Probation services have discovered that, after contacting victims of serious crime or their families, some victims request mediation with their offender because there are issues which need resolving and questions which need answering (Johnston 1994). The well-established mediation services have been able to undertake this work without any difficulty, but in areas with no mediation service probation staff are having to grapple with the problem of how to mediate without training or experience.

Recent developments

The Crime and Disorder Act 1998 abolishes the police caution, replacing it with a statutory police reprimand for a first offence and a final warning for a second offence. The final warning can be linked with some form of community intervention which may include reparation to the victim. If the case goes to court, a Reparation Order can be imposed directly by the court (subject to the victim's consent) and this could involve the young person carrying out up to 24 hours work for the victim, either directly (if the victim wishes) or indirectly to the community (if the victim does not want any contact). The direct reparation can include a meeting with the victim, a letter of apology and/or other suitable work, as agreed with the victim and offender. Reparation can also be included in the new Action Plan Order (a short intensive programme of intervention, focusing on prevention of further offending) and in the existing Supervision Order.

Conclusion

Although mediation has taken a relatively long time to develop in the UK, the time may now be right for a rapid increase in mediation provision. This may come not only as a spin-off from the Victim's Charter contact described above, but also from the new government proposals for the Youth Justice system, proposing reparation by young offenders for their victims or their community across a range of disposals.

While the government proposals discuss reparation rather than mediation, consultation with the victim must take place before direct reparation can be negotiated. Thus in the near future victim–offender mediation is likely to become a formal part of the justice system, at least for victims of young offenders. Victims of adult offenders may have to wait a little longer.

References

Home Office (1990, 1995) *Victim's Charter*. London: HMSO.

Johnston, P. (1994) *The Victim's Charter (1990) and the Release of Life Sentence Prisoners: Implications for Probation Service Practice, Values and Management*. Wakefield: West Yorkshire Probation Service.

Marshall, T. and Merry, S. (1990) *Crime and Accountability: Victim Offender Mediation in Practice*. London: HMSO.

Mediation UK (1993) *Victim–Offender Mediation: Guidelines for Starting a Service*. Bristol: Mediation UK.

Umbreit, M.S. and Roberts, A.W. (1996) *Mediation of Criminal Conflict in England: An Assessment of Services in Coventry and Leeds*. Minnesota: University of Minnesota.

Wynne, J. and Brown, I. (1998) 'Can mediation cut re-offending?' *Probation Journal 46*, 1.

9

Family Group Conferencing for Victims, Offenders and Communities

Guy Masters and Ann Warner Roberts

Introduction

Family Group Conferencing (FGC) was introduced in New Zealand in 1989 as a radical new process for decision making in child welfare and youth justice settings. FGCs are considered radical because they are designed to enable families, young people and victims (in youth justice settings) to be the key decision makers, rather than professional workers or the courts. In this chapter we concentrate solely on the development of Family Group Conferencing within criminal justice; the use of FGCs in child welfare is covered by Hudson *et al.* (1996a) and Marsh and Crow (1998).

As conferencing in criminal justice settings has spread internationally (to at least Australia, Canada, England and Wales, Republic of Ireland, Israel, Singapore, South Africa and USA), numerous models of practice have emerged, all called 'conferencing'. In fact, many practitioners of victim–offender mediation (VOM) regard conferencing as a variation of the mediation practice they have been developing over two decades. Others who have come to conferencing through the more recent New Zealand or Australian work tend to see mediation and conferencing as unrelated. FGCs differ from victim–offender mediation in considering any action needed to prevent further offending, as well as trying to put things right for the victim. Both are forums in which feelings and issues about criminal offences can be discussed and plans made for the future. Both have shown that successful encounters between victims, offenders and others in the community focus on the emotional needs of the parties rather than exclusively on achieving a settlement. This convergence of good practice suggests that conferencing and mediation may be seen as 'close relations' (McLeod 1998), especially when grounded in restorative justice.

Hence, while the label 'Family Group Conferencing' originated in New Zealand legislation, it has quickly become a generic term for processes that seek to bring together victims, offenders and others. Other names which are also in use for similar processes include: Victim–Offender Conferencing, (Community) Accountability Conferencing, Community Conferencing, Small and Large Group Conferencing, Restorative Conferencing, Diversionary Conferencing, Family Conferencing.

Throughout this chapter we will use the term 'Family Group Conference' when describing the development of New Zealand practice, and thereafter we will use the term 'group conferencing' or simply 'conferencing'.

The growing enthusiasm for conferencing stems from the increasing number of positive outcomes emerging daily from practice: stories of highly meaningful and constructive exchanges and of insight and healing for all involved. This is in contrast to the depressing and destructive outcomes of many mainstream criminal justice systems. The evaluations of conferencing projects are also highly encouraging, and these are detailed later in this chapter.

This chapter first documents the introduction of conferencing in New Zealand as a forum to achieve at the same time offender accountability and family empowerment. Then the practice of conferencing is discussed as a means to accomplish both 'restorative justice' and 'reintegrative shaming' (Braithwaite 1989). The development of conferencing variations follows. Finally, we describe four current conferencing projects in the UK and discuss how conferencing could be applied to implement key aspects of the Crime and Disorder Act 1998 and the Youth Justice and Criminal Evidence Act 1999.

The emergence of Family Group Conferencing in New Zealand

The FGC was introduced in New Zealand through the Children, Young Persons and their Families Act 1989, as the key mechanism to achieve a radical shift in decision making. Young people who came to the attention of the authorities for either care and protection issues, or because of offending behaviour, might take part, with their immediate and extended family, in a meeting in which they would decide what action should be taken. This was intended as an act of empowerment; of returning decision-making powers from professional workers to those who have been or will be most affected. A youth justice co-ordinator employed by the Department of Social Welfare would be responsible for convening the conference and managing its various stages. The key aspect of New Zealand FGCs was a 'private planning time' when the family and the offender were to be left alone, having received relevant information, to produce their own plan. This was intended as a means of empowerment for families and young people to make decisions themselves – with the professionals acting as facilitators rather than decision makers.

The 1989 legislation also greatly encouraged the diversion of young people who had offended away from courts. New Zealand conferences were to be held only when a case could not be dealt with through police diversion, and are best considered as alternatives to court. Conferences concerning offending behaviour also included the victim of the offence who was invited to speak about how they had been affected; and victims and police could also veto any family plan. Though not originally intended as such, this inclusion of victims in an informal process in which they could speak their mind and ask questions soon came to be seen as an example of restorative justice. Thus the introduction of FGCs in New Zealand may be one reason for the recent explosion of interest in restorative justice.

However, the majority of young offenders are not involved in conferences, because 80 per cent are diverted by the police through dedicated 'Youth Aid' officers. When the police decide that diversion is inappropriate, then they may either lay charges in court or refer the case to a youth justice co-ordinator for an FGC. When charges are laid, except for murder or manslaughter, any case against someone between the age of 14 and 17 will be referred automatically to an FGC. In serious cases such as rape and aggravated burglary, this FGC may solely decide the level of court where the case should be heard. Thus conferences are used for almost all the more complicated and serious cases, because they are recognised as a forum for making more informed and appropriate decisions than would be possible in court. Court-ordered FGCs are overseen by the court.

To be eligible for an FGC the young person must have 'declined to deny guilt', which is considered to be very different from accepting legal guilt. Where guilt is denied, the young person is referred to the youth court for a defended hearing; a finding of guilt halts the proceedings and an FGC is then convened to discuss the best course of action.

The ultimate purpose of the FGC, either police or court ordered, is to produce a plan which:

- addresses the behaviour: in practice this means that some element of reparation is expected either directly to the victim or to the community;
- examines and seeks to address underlying causes or concerns.

For example, an FGC in New Zealand observed by one of the authors produced a plan which required a 15 year old to complete 80 hours of community service as reparation to the victim (of assault and intimidation). The young person had been out of mainstream school for over a year, which was identified as a cause of concern for the family. It was agreed that one member of the family would explore all local possibilities for education with the assistance of the local youth aid police officer, who also attended the FGC.

New Zealand practitioners stress the need to bring together extended family as well as immediate family, including anyone who cares for the young person. One way co-ordinators have gathered the right group is by asking the young person who would be likely to attend their wedding or funeral; these are the people you invite to a FGC. Good preparation is essential, as the bulk of the work is done before the conference: informing the participants about the aim of the conference, how it will work and what to expect. Importantly, this preparation gives the co-ordinator an opportunity to build their own relationship with each participant, enabling them to feel safe. Victims feel most dissatisfaction with conferences when they hold unrealistic expectations which are unfulfilled, so they must be realistically informed about what to expect and given the choice whether to attend or not. Likewise, the young person who has offended must be well prepared to talk openly in what is often (initially) a very stressful environment.

There are three distinct phases in a New Zealand FGC (Stewart 1993, 1996):

- information giving;
- private discussion time;
- full conference reconvenes.

Information giving

The YJC introduces everyone and outlines what the FGC is intended to achieve. If culturally appropriate and desired by participants, a prayer or blessing may then be given.

A police officer is invited to read the summary of facts and outline the offence. This is open to discussion and can be altered in the FGC, but the young person must acknowledge responsibility for the FGC to proceed.

The victim(s) are then invited to speak and are encouraged to ask any questions they might have, talk about what they experienced and how they feel about what happened. If no victims attend, then the youth justice co-ordinator or a social worker may present the views of the victims.

The offender can then comment on what has been said. It is at this point that spontaneous apologies are often forthcoming and there is emotional communication between the young person and those harmed. Family members are then asked to make their comments.

Private discussion time

The family is then left alone (although others can be invited by the family to stay) to produce a plan. Plans usually last for three months and include action which is intended to put things right, such as restitution or reparation; and offence-related limitations, such as curfew and non-association, which will make reoffending less likely for the plan's duration. The plan is also expected to include some positive or gainful activity towards the personal growth or development of the young person. The family group is expected to play some role in overseeing the plan's recommendations.

Full conference reconvenes

Everybody then hears the full plan, which can be modified at the request of the police or the victims – who often ask for less reparation or less severe sanctions than the family is offering. The police and victims can veto any plan with which they are unhappy. However, the majority (90–95 per cent) of FGCs do produce plans, of which 80 per cent are approved by the court without modification.

Lessons from New Zealand

Evaluation has shown that over 80 per cent of all FGC participants, except victims, are satisfied with the outcomes. Of victims who attended, 60 per cent found the process beneficial, while 25 per cent said that they felt worse after attending the FGC. What is interesting is that 'negative feelings were linked to dissatisfaction with outcomes and the victims' reasons for attending the FGC in the first instance' and 'not related to the seriousness of the offence' (Maxwell and Morris 1993, p.120). This highlights the importance of sensitive and accurate preparatory work with all participants, as outlined above.

In the first two years of FGCs, victims only attended half of those held. The reasons for non-attendance were primarily poor planning: victims were either not invited, or not told the time of the FGC, or the FGC was scheduled at an unsuitable time for the victim. Less than 4 per cent of victims said they did not attend because they did not want to meet the offender. While the debate still continues on the effect of FGCs on levels of reoffending, a positive and significant effect is noted by Hudson *et al.* (1996b):

> A repeated finding is that family group conferences are able to bring together a number of people who have an interest in resolving a crisis which is real and immediate for them and...this casts a new light on families that have been previously dismissed as 'incapable', 'disinterested' and 'dysfunctional'... Research...fails to identify inadequate family functioning as associated with poor family group conference outcomes...on the contrary, those working in jurisdictions with family group conferences appear to have reconstrued the problem as one of finding appropriate supports and services to strengthen families...a shift in focus has occurred from parent blaming to family support and recognition of family strengths. (Hudson *et al.* 1996b, p.223)

While other countries began to develop their own youth justice conferencing projects (see below), in New Zealand its use expanded to 'Community Group Conferencing' with adult offenders. It is worth noting that other countries which have introduced mediation-type encounters throughout their youth justice systems, such as Austria and Germany (Kilchling 1998), have also evolved in this way, extending practice from young offenders into the adult system after a few years.

Family Group Conferencing and Restorative Justice

There is no room here for a comprehensive review of Restorative Justice theory, but it is important to understand its two key principles; that any justice process should seek:

- to include all affected parties in a meaningful way and leave them feeling fairly treated and stronger;
- to resolve the offence by doing the utmost to enable all those affected to move towards 'closure'.

It is widely considered that the conventional court system cannot achieve this and very often even makes things worse by treating victims as 'pieces of evidence' (Umbreit 1994), under as much suspicion as the offender and open to brutal cross-examination (Rock 1991). Victims' questions and issues have little place in courts. Braithwaite and Mugford (1994) elegantly detail the effect of this:

> Judges…silence the denunciation of victims… Their role in the courtroom is simply as evidentiary fodder for the legal digestive system. They must stick to the facts and suppress their opinions. Consequently, they often emerge from the experience deeply dissatisfied with their day in court. For victims and their supporters, this often means they scream ineffectively for more blood. But it makes no difference when the system responds to such people by giving them more and more blood, because the blood-lust is not the source of the problem; it is an unfocused cry from disempowered citizens who have been denied a voice. (Braithwaite and Mugford 1994, p.148)

FGCs differ from this because they provide all affected parties with time and a 'safe space' for dialogue and questions. It is the emotional focus of conferences which enables them to achieve their success; through genuine emotional dialogue and fair process, truly satisfying and just resolutions can be achieved.

The spread of conferencing to Australia

The most famous implementation of conferencing outside New Zealand was that developed at the caution stage by police in New South Wales, often referred to as the Wagga model. This model uses a standardised (but not rigid) script and has spread to North America (where it is known as the *REAL* JUSTICE model) and also forms the basis for the 'Restorative Conferences' used by Thames Valley Police in the UK. The original Wagga project was developed using the criminological theory 'reintegrative shaming' (Braithwaite 1989), to which we now turn.

Conferencing, shame and shaming

In the same year (1989) that New Zealand introduced FGCs, the Australian criminologist John Braithwaite's *Crime, Shame and Reintegration* was published. Reintegrative shaming rests on the assumption that people are generally far more concerned with what families and friends think of them, than with the penalty meted out by a criminal justice system. What deters people is not harsh and certain punishment, but being aware that they will be regarded less highly by those they care about; and this leads to a sense of shame.

Hence, an effective response to any offence will be to have those persons whom an offender respects shame the offence. However, Braithwaite (1989) highlights the danger that any humiliation or stigmatisation of the person is likely to be counter-productive. To be effective, any action must 'reintegrate', that is, any denunciation must be terminated by gestures of acceptance back into the community. This can be clearly understood from the old teaching of 'hate the sin, but love the sinner'. Initially Braithwaite (1989) did not explicitly link his theory with conferencing and practitioners familiar with Braithwaite's ideas and FGCs developed the Wagga model. The Wagga model differs from the New Zealand model in several ways:

- Facilitators seek to draw together all those who have been affected by an incident (e.g. neighbours of burglary victims may also attend).

- Police facilitate conferences. (This has prompted much discussion about an unacceptable extension of police power, which we will not review here; Alder and Wundersitz 1994; Blagg 1997.)

- The emphasis is on creating 'communities of care' around both offenders and victims, so that all feel safe. (The original New Zealand legislation, now amended, allowed very limited attendance of supporters for victims.)

- There is no private planning time.

- Refreshments are deliberately provided following the conference to enable more informal time for the parties to continue talking.

- The scheme deals mostly with less serious offences, which would have been dealt with informally by police youth aid diversion in New Zealand.

However, the distinctions between the New Zealand and Australian models have become blurred. Some New Zealand youth justice co-ordinators have been trained by Terry O'Connell (originator of the Wagga model) and others in New Zealand describe their practice as the same as Wagga.

A Wagga conference opens with the police officer welcoming and introducing all those present. There is a deliberate effort to concentrate on emotions and each person present is asked very similar (scripted) questions by the co-ordinator: how did they come to be involved in what happened, how they felt and what they thought at the time, and what they have thought about and felt since. This process begins with the young person(s) responsible, moves to the victim(s) and their supporters and then back to the family/supporters of the person responsible.

The Wagga model achieves 'reintegrative shaming' by focusing on emotions. There are no direct attacks on or condemnations of people, but co-ordinators will ask 'How do you feel now about the effects of your actions on Mr Smith?' This concentration on emotion is also considered the key to enabling victims, their supporters and those of the offender to move towards a sense of closure concerning the offence. Supporters are encouraged to talk about the positive aspects of the offender, to establish or maintain a positive identity. Those who have interpreted the Wagga model as one that sets out deliberately to humiliate young people and see it as a modern version of the stocks have misunderstood it. Retzinger and Scheff (1996) point out that there is no need to 'load' FGCs with attempts to shame, because shame is inherent in any conferencing or mediation process. The real challenge posed for practitioners, justice systems and communities is to develop effective reintegration.

Conferencing in England

In England a number of conferencing programmes have been introduced. At least a dozen have been started and many others are in the planning stages. Following are brief descriptions of four areas, with two case studies.

Thames Valley Police

Thames Valley Police have received a great deal of media coverage through their implementation of the Wagga model and they have now trained hundreds of officers and some members of other agencies in conferencing skills. Four levels of police caution are being implemented by Thames Valley Police, including two conferencing options:

1.   *Restorative conferencing* is used in cases where there has been a significant impact on the victim(s) and/or the offender(s), and where both are willing to participate in a meeting.

2.   *Community Conferencing* is used when there has also been a wider impact on the community, or as a problem-solving measure in circumstances without a specific crime.

Although these options may be applied to any offender, most are juveniles and offences dealt with are primarily theft, shoplifting and minor criminal damage. Assessment of potential cases is conducted by a multi-agency youth justice panel, and conferences are currently facilitated by police officers.

Case example 1: Thames Valley Police (Milton Keynes)

A Restorative Conference following an assault

> The offender, Jacob, was a middle-aged company director who had recently been through a difficult time in his personal life. One day Jacob was driving through his village slowly with the car window down. One of two youths, who were standing at the side of the road, spat into the car. The two boys ran off. Jacob stopped the car and found one of the boys standing outside the village shop. In his anger he lashed out, striking the boy across the face and kicking him in the leg. The boy, aged 14, ran off. Jacob was arrested and admitted the assault, showing deep remorse for what he had done.
>
> First a conference co-ordinator (a police officer) attended the home of the victim and spoke to Alex in the presence of his mother, Allison. While admitting the spitting incident, Alex was deeply upset by the assault and Allison, a single parent, was very angry and frightened. She said she and Alex would always be afraid to go out into the community, in case

they bumped into Jacob. She expressed concern that the offender was not being put before the court, but nevertheless agreed to participate in a meeting with Jacob at a Restorative Conference. A week later the co-ordinator met Jacob, who again showed remorse and was particularly keen to meet Alex again, so that he could apologise to him and Allison.

After a further two weeks the Restorative Conference took place at a police station. Jacob apologised immediately to Alex and Allison. He explained the details of his personal life and financial problems that had led to his lack of control on that day. Alex apologised for the spitting and Allison became much more relaxed. Jacob was then issued with a police caution at the conclusion of the conference. Following that, tea was offered, and during this time Jacob and Allison got on so well that they arranged to meet afterwards for a drink at the local pub.

Kent and Hampshire

Both these areas are using FGCs in youth justice in a similar way to New Zealand. Reparation for the victims is still an important feature and their attendance is encouraged. However, the FGC also acts as a focus for various agencies to come together with the young person and their family, to produce a plan that will prevent them reoffending. As in New Zealand, the family is given private planning time.

The Intensive Supervision and Support Programme (ISSP) in Kent and the Hampshire Youth Justice Family Group Conference Project are both examples of this. A criticism which has been levelled at models where victims leave the conference along with the professionals is that victims may perceive this process as overly offender centred and feel exploited. Earlier victim–offender mediation projects in England have also suffered from this criticism. This is a difficult issue as a key strength of this model is that the family are left alone and encouraged (probably for the first time) to produce a plan based on what they think should happen. Facilitators in the Kent scheme come from a local victim–offender mediation scheme; in Hampshire, independent facilitators are contracted.

Case example 2: Kent ISSP

A conference for burglary

Tom, aged 17, has been in and out of trouble for the past three years. His offences were theft from a car, theft from shops and four counts of burglary. He had been subject to two previous supervision orders. From age 15 to 16 he had been looked after by the local authority because of a breakdown in his relationship with his father. A further offence of burglary had led to his being remanded in a Young Offender Institution.

At the time of the conference he was living in the home of one of his friends. The friend's parents and family had decided to help him and the court granted bail to that address, pending an FGC and Youth Offending Team (YOT) recommendation for sentencing. An independent co-ordinator was appointed to convene an FGC within the three weeks prior to Tom's court appearance.

The co-ordinator paid three visits to Tom and the family with whom he was staying, and one visit to his parents to try to get a picture of Tom. Who were the significant people in his life? How did he feel about his offences? What interests/goals in life did he have? In addition the police liaised with Victim Support to see if any of the victims wanted to attend the conference. Based on that information the following people were invited to the conference:

Mother*	Social worker*
Father*	Police officer*
Sister*	Victim Support/victim*
Previous foster mother*	Society of Voluntary Associations*
Friend*	Young Offender Team officer*
Father of friend*	Careers officer
Mother of friend*	Volunteer Bureau manager
Uncle of friend*	Three other friends

(Only those with * actually attended)

The conference followed the pattern of:

1. Talk about the offences and the consequences for the victim.

2. Talk about ISSP reparation and taking responsibility.

3. Talk about opportunities for Tom for personal development, education and work.

4. Development of a plan by Tom and his family.

5. Co-ordinator reviewed the plan.

Although the victim could not come, Tom took on board the statements made by Victim Support about the effects of burglary on victims. Prior to the conference Tom had said that burglary and theft were justified if he had a need and people were 'careless enough to leave goods on display and not protect them'. After listening to Victim Support, Tom said he was sorry and was determined not to commit further offences.

He agreed to get help by visiting the drug and alcohol unit and going on an anger management course. For reparation he would do some work preparing the grounds of the local community centre and try to start a youth club. He also agreed to keep away from friends who had encouraged him to go on drinking binges.

Much of the plan formulated by Tom's family centred around making a home with his surrogate family and getting a job. There was a real sense that he wanted to justify their trust in him. Tom completed the programme without committing further offences and one year on has still managed to keep out of trouble.

Chester

The Barnardo's Restorative and Family Conferencing project in Chester operates two distinct services in an attempt to overcome the issue of providing assistance for offenders while not becoming an essentially offender centred operation. The project believes in fitting the model to the needs of the people and varying it as required. They offer the following services:

- *Restorative Conferencing*, to provide the benefits for victim and offender of meeting in a safe setting. Other participants in the conference are identified by the offender and the victim. The primary goal of this conference is a restorative/peacemaking one; both parties are able to say whatever they wish about what happened and to discuss possible reparation.

- *Family Conferencing*, based on the New Zealand FGC model, featuring private family planning time. There is no victim involvement in this meeting, but the family is encouraged to consider and write into their plan a restorative conference, if the victim indicates that they would like this.

This separation allows the rapid convening of a family conference to produce a plan for the offender, while also providing the option of a restorative conference when and as requested by the victim(s). Except for the time taken by the second conference, there is little additional time needed as most of the participants at the second conference have already been briefed. Where there are no urgent welfare needs, the Restorative Conference could take place first. At present the project is limited to young people. Social workers from the local youth justice team trained in mediation and conferencing skills facilitate the conferences.

London

London Victim Offender Conference Service (VOCS) has been piloted in two inner London areas, Lambeth and Hackney, and extended to several other London boroughs. Created after an extensive two-year planning process, VOCS is a needs-led project offering a multitude of options:

- reparation;
- mediation (both direct/face to face and indirect/shuttle);
- conferencing (with or without the victim present);
- combination of the above.

With this high degree of flexibility, the response to referrals can be tailored to the needs of the individuals involved and the community. VOCS deals with a wide variety and severity of crimes – the bulk being domestic burglary, robbery and assault. Services may be offered at any stage of the criminal justice process (post-caution, post-plea, post-sentence and post-custody). Although some adult referrals are taken, the primary focus is on young offenders. VOCS staff and a core of trained volunteers from the community facilitate the conferences in pairs. A major strength of the project is the strong multi-agency involvement. Both an Operational Group and a Stakeholders Group meet frequently to look at current practice and future strategy.

Evaluations

Several small-scale evaluations have been completed on the Wagga model and its subsequent variations from several countries. All tell the same story of high levels of victim and offender satisfaction, of preferring conferencing to court, and of considering justice to have been effectively done (McCold and Stahr 1996; Moore and Forsyth 1995; Thames Valley Police 1997; Umbreit and Fercello 1997). These results are similar to those attained by victim–offender mediation services (Umbreit 1994; Umbreit and Roberts 1996). Recent research has been conducted in New Zealand examining the long-term impact of FGCs on reoffending (Maxwell and Morris 1999). Using logistic regression, this study shows a clear indication that the FGC process itself influences reoffending rates. In particular, FGCs that were memorable for the young person and their family, which elucidated genuine feelings of remorse in the young person and did not leave the young person and their family feeling humiliated, were most likely to reduce reoffending.

Family Group Conferencing and the Youth Justice system in England and Wales

The White Paper, *No More Excuses*, and various subsequent Home Office statements (Home Office 1997, 1998; Straw 1997) have outlined the government's commitment to introducing restorative justice into the youth justice system. This implementation will take place through the Crime and Disorder Act 1998 and the Youth Justice and Criminal Evidence Act 1999.

Though neither piece of legislation mentions either FGCs or VOM, they introduce several new orders and procedural changes which could use these processes. This is discussed in greater detail in the guidance on restorative practice published by the Youth Justice Board (1999). The new orders are: Final Warning; Child Safety Order and Action Plan Order; Reparation Order; Referral Order.

Final Warning

The system of police cautions is being replaced by a two-stage reaction of *reprimand* for a first offence, followed by a *final warning* for a second offence. At this stage, the young person is referred to the local Youth Offending Team (YOT) which will decide if any work is need to prevent reoffending. An FGC can be convened at this stage to involve and help victims and to design practical and effective measures to support the young person and their family.

Child Safety Order (for children under 10) and Action Plan Order

These both impose short-term conditions on the young person in order to prevent offending, and can be more effective if these conditions are worked out through a conference. Those affected by these orders are far more likely to co-operate with them if they have played a large part in designing them. In New Zealand the vast majority of families have been capable of producing plans that were accepted by the courts.

Reparation Order

Mediation or conferencing are obviously useful here, to decide what would be acceptable as reparation, especially as the Act specifies that victim(s) must be consulted prior to the court making such an order. Research has shown far greater compliance with reparation resulting from mediation than from a court order (Dignan 1992; Umbreit 1994).

Referral Order

This will be a mandatory sentence for the majority of young people pleading guilty in court for the first time and is to be piloted from June 2000. Referral will be made to a Youth Offender Panel made up of the young person, their family and significant others. Victims will also be invited to attend, as well as a YOT officer and two members of the community. The purpose of the panel will be to discuss the offence informally, why it occurred and what the impact on the victim was. The panel will then agree a contract that may contain reparation for the victim, and conditions or activities to prevent any further offending. The purpose of these panels is identical to that of FGCs, so the lessons learned from FGC practice will be very useful. The FGC model itself could also be used here.

Conclusion

If done well, group conferencing represents a new way of people working together to deal with an issue: one of support, co-operation and empowerment. It is proving invaluable in enabling everyone affected by an offence to move on constructively. Furthermore, the conferencing process, whether FGC or any of the other models, is proving so flexible and robust that it is spreading rapidly from its original application in child welfare and youth justice, to being used throughout the criminal justice system, in schools and in the workplace (public, private and voluntary organisations).

However, to achieve this, we must stress the critical importance of basing practice on the principles of Restorative Justice. All responses to crime and conflict must seek to serve the needs of people and communities, and attempt to strengthen and include rather than weaken and exclude. At every level, criminal justice systems should work towards transforming conflict, repairing harm and promoting 'right relationships' to strengthen communities. The community must also be pivotal in responding to problems, facilitated by government and the criminal justice system; 'community' is both a means and an end.

Acknowledgements

The authors wish to give special thanks to the practitioners involved in the programmes for providing abundant material. Also, much gratitude to the editor Marian Liebmann, Stephanie Braithwaite, Judy Doherty, Chris Stevens, Barbara Tudor, Mark Umbreit, Karen Wright and Sue Wright, who each provided unique guidance and support.

References

Alder, C. and Wundersitz, J. (1994) *Family Conferencing and Juvenile Justice: The Way Forward or Misplaced Optimism?* Canberra: Australian Institute of Criminology.

Blagg, H. (1997) 'A just measure of shame? Aboriginal youth and conferencing in Australia.' *British Journal of Criminology 37*, 481–501.

Braithwaite, J. (1989) *Crime, Shame and Reintegration.* Cambridge: Cambridge University Press.

Braithwaite, J. and Mugford, S. (1994) 'Conditions of successful reintegration ceremonies: dealing with juvenile offenders.' *British Journal of Criminology 34*, 2, 139–171.

Dignan, J. (1992) *Repairing the Damage.* Sheffield: University of Sheffield.

Home Office (1997) *No More Excuses.* London: HMSO.

Home Office (1998) *Proceedings from the Criminal Justice Conference: Youth Justice held at Shifnal, 18–20 February.* Liverpool: Home Office Special Conferences Unit.

Hudson, J., Morris, A., Maxwell, G. and Galaway, B. (1996a) *Family Group Conferences: Perspectives on Policy and Practice.* Annandale NSW: Federation Press.

Hudson, J., Morris, A., Maxwell, G. and Galaway, B. (1996b) 'Concluding thoughts.' In J. Hudson, A. Morris, G. Maxwell and B. Galaway (eds) *Family Group Conferences: Perspectives on Policy and Practice.* Annandale NSW: Federation Press.

Kilchling, M. (1998) 'Victim–offender mediation in Germany and Austria.' Paper presented to the Justice seminar 'Youth Justice Futures' at the Law Society, London, 8 May.

McCold, P. and Stahr, J. (1996) 'Bethlehem police family group conferencing project.' Paper presented to the American Society of Criminology, November.

McLeod, C. (1998) Personal communication.

Marsh, P. and Crow, G. (1998) *Family Group Conferences in Child Welfare.* Oxford: Blackwell.

Maxwell, G. and Morris, A. (1993) *Family, Victims and Culture: Youth Justice in New Zealand.* Wellington: Department of Social Welfare.

Maxwell, G. and Morris, A. (1999) *Understanding Re-offending.* Wellington: University of Victoria.

Moore, D. and Forsyth, L. (1995) *A New Approach to Juvenile Justice: An Evaluation of Family Conferencing in Wagga Wagga.* Wagga Wagga NSW: Centre for Rural Social Research.

Retzinger, S. and Scheff, T. (1996) 'Strategy for community conferences: emotions and social bonds.' In B. Galaway and J. Hudson (eds) *Restorative Justice: International Perspectives.* Amsterdam: Kluger.

Rock, P. (1991) 'Witness and space in a Crown Court.' *British Journal of Criminology 31*, 266–279.

Stewart, T. (1993) 'The youth justice co-ordinator's role: a personal perspective on the new legislation in action.' In B. Brown and F. McElrea (eds) *The Youth Court in New Zealand: A New Model of Justice.* Auckland: Legal Research Foundation.

Stewart, T. (1996) 'Family group conferences with young offenders in New Zealand.' In J. Hudson, A. Morris, G. Maxwell and B. Galaway (eds) *Family Group Conferences: Perspectives on Policy and Practice.* Annandale NSW: Federation Press.

Straw, J. (1997) Paper presented to the conference Calling Young Offenders to Account: UK Applications of Restorative Justice, London, 29 October.

Thames Valley Police (1997) *An Evaluation of the Aylesbury Restorative Cautioning Unit.* Aylesbury: Thames Valley Police.

Umbreit, M. (1994) *Victim Meets Offender.* New York: Willow Tree Press.

Umbreit, M. and Fercello, C. (1997) *Woodbury Police Department's Restorative Justice Community Conferencing Program 'An Initial Assessment of Client Satisfaction'.* Minneapolis: Centre for Restorative Justice and Mediation.

Umbreit, M. and Roberts, A. (1996) *Mediation of Criminal Conflict in England: An Assessment of Services in Coventry and Leeds.* Minneapolis: Centre for Restorative Justice and Mediation.

Youth Justice Board (1999) *Guidance for the Effective Development of Restorative Practice with Young Offenders.* London: Youth Justice Board.

Further reading

Moore, D. and O'Connell, T. (1994) 'Family conferencing in Wagga Wagga: a communitarian model of justice.' In C. Alder and J. Wundersitz (eds) *Family Conferencing and Juvenile Justice: The Way Forward or Misplaced Optimism?* Canberra: Australian Institute of Criminology.

Roberts, A. and Masters, G. (1998) *Group Conferencing: Restorative Justice in Practice.* Minneapolis: Centre for Restorative Justice.

Van Ness, D. and Strong, K. (1997) *Restoring Justice.* Cincinatti: Anderson.

Wright, M. (1996) *Justice for Victims and Offenders,* 2nd edn. Winchester: Waterside Press.

Zehr, H. (1995) *Changing Lenses,* 2nd edn. Waterloo: Herald Press.

10

The ACAS Approach to Employment Dispute Resolution

Francis Noonan

Introduction

The starting point for describing the present-day approach to employment dispute resolution in Great Britain lies in the latter part of the nineteenth century. During that time employers and trade unions voluntarily set up neutral conciliation committees to help resolve disputes which they could not resolve on their own. This approach was adopted by the 1891 Royal Commission on Labour report, which proposed a system of collective bargaining in a voluntary framework. The Conciliation Act 1896 gave effect to this and repealed all the earlier provisions for compulsory and binding arbitration.

The Board of Trade was charged with administering the Act and, wherever an industrial dispute occurred, the Board was given the power to inquire into the causes and to take steps to encourage the parties to meet together under an independent conciliator, board of conciliation or mediator. The Board was empowered to conciliate and also to appoint an arbitrator 'with a view to the amicable settlement' of differences.

These provisions remain the essence of the British system of dispute resolution and underlie the statutory basis for the Advisory, Conciliation and Arbitration Service (ACAS) which was set up in 1974.

The purpose of ACAS is to improve the performance and effectiveness of organisations by providing an independent and impartial service to prevent and resolve disputes and to build harmonious relationships at work. The rest of this chapter describes how ACAS gives effect to this statement. This involves ACAS in more than conciliation in industrial disputes. ACAS also provides advisory mediation, arbitration and dispute mediation in collective matters and conciliates in cases involving individual statutory rights.

Definitions

Collective conciliation is conciliation in what are legally known as 'trade disputes', which usually involve a trade union but occasionally some other staff body or just an ad hoc group of employees.

Individual conciliation is conciliation between employers and individual applicants who have claimed that a statutory employment right has been infringed. Essentially conciliation is a process of assisted negotiation. The parties control their own positions.

Arbitration is a process where an arbitrator appointed by ACAS makes a decision which is binding on the parties. *Dispute mediation* is a similar process, but the outcome is a recommendation rather than an award.

ACAS arbitration and dispute mediation are both reserved for trade disputes, although the Employment Rights (Dispute Resolution) Act 1998 allows ACAS to set up a scheme to provide arbitration for unfair dismissal cases. At the time of writing ACAS is preparing such a scheme for the Secretary of State's approval.

Advisory mediation is essentially a preventive process and involves ACAS in facilitation of problem solving rather than dispute resolution.

Collective disputes

Advisory mediation

Employment disputes are very costly both to employers and employees, so it makes sense to resolve workplace problems before they develop into disputes. ACAS believes that disputes can best be prevented if employers and employees work together jointly. Such a joint approach can help:

- to provide better thought-out solutions;
- to encourage acceptance of change;
- to foster a more constructive long-term working relationship between employer and employees.

In helping organisations to avoid costly disputes, ACAS employs two principal operating methods:

- workshops;
- joint working parties.

WORKSHOPS

An ACAS workshop is a non-negotiating forum in which employer and employee representatives can discuss and agree on potential barriers to the achievement of long-term organisational goals. Workshops are particularly useful for exploring problems where the underlying causes are not clearly known. As a result of carrying out this sort of analysis, problems holding back the organisation can be identified and new courses of action devised to rectify the problems.

ACAS was asked by management and unions at a prison to assist in developing a strategy to achieve shared organisational goals. A one-day workshop was set up with a cross-section of members and the outcome was a report and action agenda leading to further meetings and a jointly agreed strategy encompassing:

- commitment to the purpose, vision and values of the prison and the delivery of its goals as described in the business and strategic plans;
- commitment to the training and development of all staff and to their secure future;
- commitment to open and honest dialogue and the provision by both sides of information, communication, consultation and involvement;
- recognition of the roles of management and unions and consideration of actions upon all staff.

Since the introduction of the new strategy, joint groups have successfully addressed many issues.

JOINT WORKING PARTIES

A joint working party (JWP) is not a negotiating body but a group of employer and employee representatives working together to devise and implement practical solutions to specific problems. A JWP will:

- adopt a structured problem-solving approach;
- define the problem(s) to be tackled;
- collect and analyse information;
- evaluate options;
- select and implement agreed solutions.

ACAS staff, who often chair the working party, enable members to identify and clarify the issues to be considered, examine the various options for resolving the problem(s) and help develop constructive solutions.

Although prevention is better than cure, employment disputes inevitably occur. When this happens, ACAS can help by offering conciliation, arbitration or dispute mediation.

Conciliation

Requests for conciliation normally come from trade unions or employers, separately or jointly, but occasionally ACAS itself may offer conciliation to parties in dispute. Before agreeing to conciliate, ACAS will check to see that the parties have exhausted any internal dispute resolution procedures they may have. The important issue here is that ACAS expects the parties to use every means at their disposal to resolve the problem themselves, as there is likely to be more commitment to a solution that is arrived at mutually.

In coming to conciliation, no prior commitment is required from the parties, only a willingness to discuss the problems at issue. Conciliation is an entirely voluntary process and it is open to either party to bring discussions to an end at any time.

ROLE OF THE CONCILIATOR

ACAS conciliators aim to help employers and unions settle their differences by agreement, if possible in a long-term way. In handling disputes, ACAS conciliation staff:

- remain impartial and independent at all times;
- seek to understand both the dispute and the attitude of the parties to it;
- try to gain the trust and confidence of both parties so that a sound working relationship can be developed;
- make constructive suggestions to facilitate negotiations where appropriate;
- provide information (e.g. about legislation) at the request of the parties.

ENTRY INTO A DISPUTE

ACAS can be invited to conciliate by an employer, a union or both jointly. Sometimes ACAS is specifically mentioned as a final stage in procedures for the avoidance of disputes. On occasion, almost always when industrial action is either threatened or taking place, ACAS will invite the parties to a conciliation meeting. Timing is a crucial factor here. Before an invitation is issued, ACAS will usually have held discussions with both sides separately. In order for an invitation to a joint meeting to be worthwhile, there has to be a reasonable prospect that some progress might be made. In its initial discussions, ACAS will be trying to judge whether sufficient common ground exists for a joint meeting to be useful. To hold meetings for the sake of them can actually be counterproductive. Where insufficient common ground is perceived, ACAS will continue with separate contacts.

THE PROCESS OF CONCILIATION

Many disputes involve what one side or the other regards as matters of principle and can therefore look intractable. However, the experience of ACAS is that acceptable solutions can be found in most cases.

The first step in tackling any dispute is for the ACAS conciliator to find out what the dispute is about and the attitude of the parties to the dispute. This fact-finding stage usually involves the conciliator meeting both sides separately, but occasionally this information may be obtained at joint meetings.

Conciliation is assisted collective bargaining. The parties do not lose control of their positions. Because the process has negotiation as its basis, it is not surprising that it tends loosely to follow the pattern of negotiations. Initially it is not uncommon for the process to confine itself to the factual position, with the conciliator asking questions for clarification. As the discussions develop and the process enters a phase where positions are being examined, the conciliator, as well as relaying the parties' questions and comments, will begin to develop his/her own questioning. The conciliator then begins to take a more active role. When bargaining proper begins, the conciliator may introduce some ideas for settlement. These ideas will be no more than suggestions for discussion. In some disputes the forms of words are important and those produced by the conciliator may attract less opposition than those produced by either of the parties.

The detailed process of conciliation will inevitably vary from case to case. However, almost all conciliations involve a mixture of side meetings (where the conciliator explores issues separately with the parties) and joint meetings (where the parties can explain their positions face to face). Occasionally the conciliator might feel that a caucus meeting (where the conciliator talks only to the leaders of both sides together) might be useful. This option can be helpful to agree the process that discussions might take, or to cover technical points, or if deadlock is reached, as a belt-and-braces meeting to check that there really is no prospect of progress being made. The exact mix of side, joint and caucus meetings is determined by the conciliator in discussion with the parties. Where it is clear that a settlement might be achieved, the conciliator will look to secure a joint agreement, usually in the form of a signed document, which will finalise the terms of the settlement.

Any agreements reached in conciliation are the responsibility of the parties involved. While conciliators may suggest possible ideas for settlement, ACAS has no power to impose or formally recommend settlements.

There is no time limit for the conciliation process and ACAS will continue to help the parties as long as they wish and there seems a chance of reaching an agreed settlement.

PUBLICITY

Some industrial disputes attract a measure of media interest. ACAS never comments on the merits or demerits of parties' positions. Parties come to conciliation because it offers confidentiality and impartiality. Public statements would threaten them both. ACAS confines its public announcements to factual statements on such things as the dates and times of meetings, whether agreement was reached and whether any further meetings are planned. It is for the parties to put their positions to the media if they so wish. However, during conciliation talks, parties tend to confine their observations to relatively neutral matters, accepting that negotiating through the media is not helpful to the delicate issue of trying to find an agreed solution.

Conciliation is ACAS' preferred option in settling employment disputes. If, however, a settlement is not reached through conciliation, ACAS can arrange for the issue to be resolved through arbitration or mediation.

Arbitration

Normally a single arbitrator is appointed by ACAS to consider a dispute and to make a decision to resolve it. Occasionally ACAS appoints a board of arbitration with an independent chair and two side members drawn from employer and trade union representatives. ACAS maintains a panel of arbitrators who are mostly industrial relations academics with some labour lawyers. ACAS will set up a separate panel to deal with unfair dismissal disputes under the scheme envisaged by the Employment Rights (Dispute Resolution Act 1998). ACAS officials do not themselves arbitrate.

The process of arbitration involves each side setting out its case in writing, followed by a hearing at which the two sides present in person their evidence and arguments. Hearings are usually held at ACAS offices or at the premises of the employer or trade union.

Before ACAS will arrange arbitration, both parties must agree the terms of reference – that is, the question that the arbitrator is to answer. The terms of reference must be clear and unambiguous. Conciliation assistance is sometimes needed for the parties to reach agreement on the wording of the question to be put. On occasion ACAS-suggested wording is more readily accepted than one party or the other's draft. There is sometimes the suspicion that a draft produced by one party might be an attempt to bias the possibility of an award in their favour. The parties must also agree to accept the arbitrator's decision as a binding settlement of the dispute. This is a long-established principle and, in practice, arbitration awards are invariably accepted and implemented. Any weakening of this principle would render the process pointless.

Arbitration can be used to very good effect when reaching agreement proves impossible by any other means. On the other hand, it takes decision-making power out of the hands of the parties themselves, and there can be winners and losers. If the latter applies, while the immediate problem may be resolved, some resentment on the part of the losing party can linger on and may fuel future conflict.

Arbitrators tend to be drawn from the ranks of those perceived to be neutral, largely industrial relations academics with some law academics. Arbitrators are selected for their knowledge of industrial relations, as well as for their expertise and experience. From time to time arbitrators have to make stark choices, particularly with so-called 'pendulum' arbitration, where the arbitrator is required to decide wholly in favour of one party and therefore against the other. The advantage claimed for mandatory pendulum arbitration is that it forces the parties to adopt more realistic stances, and this in itself encourages negotiation rather than the use of arbitration. A disadvantage is that, if the dispute goes to arbitration, neither position might be wholly right from an industrial relations point of view.

Dispute mediation

Mediation is a sort of halfway house between conciliation and arbitration. The essential difference between conciliation and mediation in ACAS terms is that the conciliator acts as a catalyst, attempting to bring the respective positions of the parties closer together, to the extent that they can eventually be bridged. In the course of his or her work, the conciliator will discuss with the parties a whole range of possible solutions, until one is found which is acceptable to all concerned.

By contrast, mediation is more formal. As with arbitration, terms of reference need to be agreed and the process results in formal recommendations. While these recommendations are not binding, ACAS expects the parties to give them full weight. The process of mediation can follow a number of paths. Some are similar to conciliation with discussions with the parties separately and jointly. Some are more akin to arbitration with all the proceedings taking place in a single hearing. The process is determined largely by the parties' expectations.

The British model of dispute resolution, exemplified by the approach adopted by ACAS, places great emphasis on speed of reaction and ready access to assistance. It is this rapidity of response and informality, in terms of obtaining the involvement of a third party, which has made the system very effective. The parties in dispute can contact any ACAS office either individually or jointly, simply by making a telephone call. They can then expect the conciliation process to commence within a few days or even more quickly if all the necessary people are available. Providing a conciliator within 24 hours would not normally cause ACAS a problem.

Because of this ease of access and because the process of conciliation has proven itself to be a very effective means by which the parties can reach an agreement acceptable to themselves within a short period of time, conciliation through ACAS has become the preferred method of employment dispute resolution within Great Britain. Arbitration is seen very much as a last resort.

In Great Britain the decisions as to whether, when or how to seek outside assistance rest solely with the parties in dispute. It is their choice – and both parties have to agree – as to whether they will:

(a) involve a third party;

(b) opt for conciliation, mediation or arbitration.

It is also up to them to agree at what point in time they will elect to involve the third party.

ACAS can also take the initiative and offer conciliation itself and it is entirely up to the parties whether they accept the offer. This ability to offer conciliation rather than await an approach from the parties can often hold the key to unlocking a difficult situation where meaningful communication between the parties has broken down.

Case examples

Shipping industry

ACAS invited the management and union to conciliation, the parties having failed to settle their differences themselves. The meeting took place against a background of threatened industrial action following a ballot. The dispute concerned a proposal from the union to change shift patterns. They wanted to alter the existing pattern of three weeks on and two weeks off duty to 'even time' shift working (two weeks on and two weeks off).

It became clear in the early stages of conciliation that the cost of introducing the changed shift pattern was – in management's view – prohibitive, as it would involve employing five additional ratings. The union considered the change to be so important to their members that this, rather than any increase in wages, had been put forward as the basis of their annual pay claim for two successive years. Following exhaustive discussions, the industrial action (which would have come at a critical point in the tourist season) was suspended. Instead, the parties accepted a suggestion by ACAS that a joint working party (JWP) be set up to consider the feasibility of such a change. Terms of reference for the JWP were also agreed.

The JWP was set a difficult task in trying to achieve a solution which would involve no extra cost to management, but would also meet the union's objectives. Importantly, it also sought not to disturb existing agreements with two other unions. A number of meetings were held and ACAS facilitation techniques enabled the group to move from an atmosphere of mistrust and suspicion to a process of freely exploring a number of different options until an acceptable solution emerged. The JWP devised a new shift rota alternating between two weeks on and two weeks off, and two weeks on and one week off. This met management's need to avoid a rise in current costs while at the same time eliminating the requirement for crew to work three consecutive weeks, which the union saw as the most undesirable feature of the existing pattern. The dispute was satisfactorily resolved.

A port authority

For some twelve months, management had been attempting to introduce a radical re-organisation within the docks via a process of consultation and negotiation with union representatives. The proposed changes sparked fierce resistance from the unions and discussions had reached an impasse. In hopes of avoiding management imposition of changes, it was agreed by all parties that ACAS be requested to provide conciliation.

By the time ACAS involvement commenced, the parties had taken up entrenched positions. The proposed changes to working practices included a new payments system, annualised hours, a fully flexible workforce, team working, revised shop steward representation and consequential redundancies.

Following a protracted and fairly difficult conciliation, a 'Fully Flexible Labour Force Agreement' was agreed by all parties and endorsed by the workforce, with the 'annual hours' concept and 'multi-skilled crew working' being uncommon for an organisation owned by a local authority. Significant improvements in pay were also made. By accepting this agreement, the trade unions acknowledged that 11 employees would be made redundant. In the aftermath of such a difficult dispute, all parties recognised the potential for further problems during the redundancy handling exercise. Management and unions therefore both approached ACAS with a request to facilitate these discussions using advisory mediation techniques.

The exercise took place at a local hotel over two full days. Neither side had softened their stance (even with the new agreement), so a variety of techniques were required, including collective conciliation.

Despite these difficulties, two days of intensive discussions provided a series of 'agreed principles' for the redundancy exercise. These principles provided a firm base for the handling of a highly emotive redundancy programme and laid the foundations for working with further issues.

While it may take some time for relationships to settle back down, the ACAS assistance provided a catalyst for the change process within the organisation to take place in the most constructive way possible.

A manufacturing company

The company had sought to make changes in employees' terms and conditions of employment, and also to change the culture of the business. It gave the union three months' notice of the termination of its recognition agreement. The union received a mandate for industrial action from its membership and planned a series of one and two day strikes.

Following reports in the media, ACAS contacted both sides in the dispute and offered conciliation in an attempt to resolve the dispute. The offer was accepted although the company said it was not prepared to reverse its decision on recognition, and the union was not prepared to cancel the strikes unless the recognition issue was settled to its satisfaction. A conciliation meeting was therefore arranged.

In conciliation, the trade union said that the dispute centred on two main issues, changes to terms and conditions of employment and the decision to de-recognise. It was willing to enter into negotiations on the former, but only if management agreed to recognise the union for collective bargaining purposes. Management, on its part, stated that the decision to de-recognise was the result of the failure of past collective bargaining. In its view, the union had not played an active role locally and there had been no sense of partnership with the company. The company believed it had an open management style encouraging good communications, and it did not feel that there was a need for a trade union.

In these preliminary discussions, ACAS asked management to outline the principal items which it thought were important for the future, in terms of personnel and industrial relations matters. Several items were identified, including encouraging employee involvement, good communications, empowering employees, rewarding effort and results, and providing a secure future. ACAS invited the union to comment on this list with the result that it confirmed that it would actively support 80 per cent of the items. The trade union also acknowledged that there had not been a 'partnership' locally when the site had been owned by a different company, neither side making enough effort in this respect. These initial exchanges illustrated the common ground between the two sides, and this proved to be a breakthrough in the dispute.

By the end of the first day, the parties had agreed that a new procedure agreement should be negotiated urgently between them, providing the framework for a new relationship. They also agreed to negotiate on terms and conditions of employment. On the basis of this agreement, the trade union was prepared to recommend to its members that the industrial action (planned for the following day) should be called off. Later that evening members agreed to cancel the strike.

Conciliation in individual cases

ACAS provides conciliation in cases which are, or could be, the subject of complaints by individuals to employment tribunals about alleged infringement of statutory employment rights. Conciliation is undertaken independently of the tribunal process. This aspect of ACAS' work is where the largest part, some two-thirds, of its budget goes.

Copies of all the application forms making claims under most jurisdictions to employment tribunals are sent to ACAS offices and allocated to a conciliation officer. On receiving details of the complaint, the conciliation officer contacts the parties or their nominated representatives to explain the ACAS role and to offer conciliation. Where there is a relevant grievance or appeals procedure, the conciliation officer encourages its use to settle the complaint.

If both parties are willing to accept conciliation, the conciliation officer will help in a neutral and independent way. This involves helping both parties to become aware of the options open to them and thus to enable them to reach informed decisions on how best to proceed. The conciliator makes it clear that he or she cannot act as a representative for either party. Information given to a conciliation officer in connection with conciliation is not admissible in evidence before a tribunal without the consent of the person who gave it.

There are a number of differences between this type of individual conciliation and conciliation in collective disputes. It is high-volume work and each full-time conciliator handles over 300 cases a year. Unlike conciliation in collective disputes, much of the work is done not with the parties directly but with their representatives. Another difference is that a high proportion of cases are dealt with on the telephone. A further difference in the cases where applicants and respondents are unrepresented is that often conciliators are dealing with parties who are unused to the process of conciliation and negotiation, at least in this field. Nevertheless, the underlying process is the same. The facts are established, strengths and weaknesses are explored, and some bargaining takes place.

Like collective conciliation, any resulting agreement is the property of the parties and is freely entered into, rather than something imposed on them by ACAS. The effect of an agreement is to withdraw the application from the industrial tribunal and thus obviate the need for a hearing.

Not all tribunal cases are capable of settlement, and conciliators recognise that some parties may wish to have their cases heard in a legal setting. However, in our experience, time and circumstances often cause views to change, and conciliation officers therefore try to remain in touch with parties until a tribunal hearing.

One example where this proved beneficial occurred in a case of unfair dismissal where the applicant initially sought the maximum he might gain from a tribunal award. The employer was only willing to countenance a payment at the bottom end of the scale and the conciliator was unable to make progress towards a settlement. The circumstances of the case changed when the applicant found another job, and the conciliation officer renewed her efforts to settle the case. Following a series of telephone calls, the conciliator narrowed the differences between the parties but the settlement was not achieved until the applicant was on the point of leaving the airport departure lounge to board a flight to the tribunal hearing.

Conclusion

ACAS has a number of approaches to its role of preventing and resolving disputes and building harmonious relationships at work. They are successful in these aims. Around 88 per cent of collective conciliation cases are settled in conciliation, or sufficient progress is made for the parties to settle the dispute themselves through negotiation. In individual rights conciliation, more than a third of cases are settled without a tribunal hearing. In arbitration and advisory mediation, which have less measurable outcomes, our research has shown that there are high levels of customer satisfaction.

11

Workplace Mediation

Carl Reynolds

All great civilisation has been in a certain measure a Civilisation of the Dialogue. The life substance of them all was not, as one customarily thinks, the presence of significant individuals, but the genuine intercourse with one another. The future of mankind depends upon a rebirth of dialogue...and most especially of genuine dialogue between people of different kinds and convictions. (Buber 1957)

Introduction

Workplace mediation is an idea whose time has come. The last two decades have seen mediation services setting up all over the country to deal with a variety of disputes including community, commercial and family disputes. The Woolf Report (1996) into the legal system made wide-ranging suggestions for the extension of mediation into other areas of the law, such as civil disputes and legal disputes with local authorities. Since then, several government reports and consultation papers have been circulated to establish how mediation can be used, and legislation has been passed to introduce alternative dispute resolution (ADR) methods into employment law. The first formalised approaches to mediation in the workplace were developed in 1996 in Lewisham Council's Housing Department and the Department of Health. These are the subject of a more detailed study later on in this chapter.

Because of my personal involvement in developing workplace mediation, this chapter is based on direct experience and feedback from participants in mediation sessions and people who have been trained as mediators and conciliators.

It is apparent that mediation has at least three meanings in the UK:

1. Mediation and conciliation are used to mean the same thing by some organisations.

2. In some NHS trust complaints procedures, it is used to mean the intervention of a third party who is both an expert in the context of the dispute and can offer advice and solutions to help parties resolve their differences. ACAS (see Chapter 10) also uses the term mediation in this sense.

3. In this chapter mediation is used to mean the intervention by an impartial third party. Mediators do not offer advice or solutions; their skill is in

facilitating parties to come to their own solutions. A mediator in this sense is concerned with the process, not the content, of the dispute.

Pure impartiality is, in my opinion, unachievable. Our conscious and unconscious engagement with the world make it impossible for us to be unresponsive to what we perceive. On a conscious level we can inhibit our prejudices, but our subconscious responses to events weave their way into all our interactions. A mediator has to bear this perspective in mind when working with people in dispute, using their responses as a reminder to resume an impartial state of mind. If an organisation decides to use in-house mediators, the issue of impartiality becomes critical because of the informal knowledge that employees will have of one another.

In many of the places I have worked, managers and employees are demanding more autonomy and control over their working lives. This inevitably creates new tensions. The reluctance of organisations to replace 'command and control' methods of management with 'adhocracies' and complex work teams, often results in workers being given responsibility, but not power. My own experience of being a middle manager in a local authority led me to believe that mediation was the appropriate way for consenting adults to resolve their differences; and that mediation skills are a critical skill for managers in the new millennium. This 'zeitgeist' feel to mediation manifests itself in the reactions of people who have received mediation training. They report an improvement in their relationships at home, at work and while socialising. These in turn allow a greater understanding of the human spirit and its potential for growth. So workplace mediation has a significance, not just as a way of resolving conflicts between people in an organisation, but also as a paradigm for successful personal and team management.

Emergence of mediation in the workplace

The public sector has been maligned for being bureaucratic and inflexible. This generalisation masks the verve with which many people in the public sector produce initiatives that improve the quality of life for the users of their services. The equalities framework used by most public sector organisations allows them to see the potential in difference and diversity. This breaking away from the dominant cultural paradigm (that only white males can be successful) allows the space for unusual ideas to flourish and be adopted. Mediation is one of these ideas. Many local authorities now fund local community mediation services. They do this for two main reasons: first, to resolve neighbourhood disputes in a cost-effective way; second, because they recognise that mediation demonstrates a more productive way for people to communicate with each other.

Lewisham Housing had supported a local community mediation service for a year when the first workplace mediators were trained at the end of 1996. I was at the time a volunteer with the community mediation service and had, until a couple of years before, been an active trade unionist representing people in a variety of settings. Growing tired of unconstructive grievance and disciplinary hearings, I conducted research with people who had been through these procedures and those who had acted as arbitrators in the disputes. Overwhelmingly they expressed a desire for a less confrontational way of dealing with disputes. I set about convincing both my departmental management team and local trade union officials to allow a pilot mediation project to be run.

At this time I had already mediated one dispute in a local office between two housing benefit officers, one of whom was on the verge of taking out a grievance against her manager for 'failing to deal with' the other officer. Using the face-to-face model I had used in community mediation, I helped both of them to resolve their dispute and agree about how they could work together and minimise their differences. The effectiveness of this intervention and the desire for a less confrontational approach to resolving conflict in the organisation created the space for the emergence of mediation as a viable alternative.

Towards the end of 1997 the Local Government Management Board (LGMB) ran a seminar on the use of mediation in local government. Recognising mediation as an emergent idea, the seminar introduced the concept of mediation to a range of service providers from across the country. The participants identified a plethora of uses for mediation, including complaints procedures and employee disputes. The cost benefits of mediation and its ability to effect cultural transformation were high on the agenda. Since the seminar several local authorities, such as Bradford City Council and Kent County Council, have developed workplace mediation schemes to deal with employee disputes.

Limitations of traditional grievance and disciplinary processes

Traditionally, organisations use grievance and disciplinary procedures to settle disputes, but they often remain unresolved. Mediation is a process that recognises the parties in a dispute as the experts. A mediator acts as a neutral third party, facilitating employees creatively to solve difficulties and create a win–win solution to their problems. In my years as an active trade unionist, I represented over a hundred people in a variety of disputes. I won many of these cases, but it was rare for the relationship between the parties in dispute to be reaffirmed. The aftermath of many cases was that one or other of the parties would ask for a transfer, leave the organisation or maintain a resentment which inevitably developed into a new dispute. Mediation is useful in the workplace because it has both interpersonal and cost benefits.

Interpersonal relationships improve because mediation is explicit about openness. The parties in a dispute are encouraged to express their feelings about what has happened to them and are expected to work together to find a mutually beneficial solution. Because it is rare in an employee–management relationship to have this openness, mediation acts as a metaphor for a better way of working. Participants in workplace mediation report an improved working environment, not just between themselves, but between other members of the team as well.

The cost benefits arise out of an increasing recognition that qualitative costs are as important as quantitative costs. Managers are willing to look at the cost of unresolved disputes on the effectiveness of their teams, on the service to internal and external customers and the messages that transfer to other parts of the organisation. There is also a benefit in 'hard' costs. My own research (Findlay and Reynolds 1997) shows that the resolution cost of a dispute in local government using mediation is one-third of the cost of using a traditional grievance procedure.

Some local authorities recognise that grievance and disciplinary hearings are counterproductive because they result in winners and losers. In local authorities a senior manager sits in on a case and acts as an arbitrator. Both parties present evidence and cross-examine witnesses, and the chair of the hearing is expected to make a ruling that will settle the matter. By contrast, mediation assumes that the people in dispute should be coming to an agreement with each other. The mediator's role is to facilitate this process. Unlike the chair of a grievance or disciplinary hearing, mediators do not give advice or make decisions about the outcome. This is essentially where the appropriateness of mediation lies, because it focuses on resolution from the disputing parties', not the third party's, perspective.

An ongoing issue in any dispute in the workplace is how people will communicate with each other after a dispute is settled. Grievance and disciplinary hearings concentrate on deciding the degree to which people are right or wrong, so communication issues rarely get discussed; nor do they get discussed in the normal day-to-day life of organisations. The concept of dialogue will, I predict, gain currency in the next few years, as mediation becomes more accepted and as organisations realise that no amount of restructuring will work without people learning how to speak to one another.

Grievance and disciplinary hearings also have another flaw – the limitations imposed on people who want disputes resolved. Both processes perpetuate conflict because they are essentially about imposing sanctions. For example, an employee may want to speak to the manager about why her ideas seem to be marginalised and dismissed. In a private meeting, usually held in the manager's office, my experience shows that the manager is defensive and the employee does not feel either that she has been heard or that the issue is resolved. Resorting to a complaints procedure, even one that has an initial informal stage, is unlikely to resolve the issue satisfactorily. So employees are left with a stark choice – to direct their ideas elsewhere in their life or move to another job where they feel more valued. This is a 'lose–lose' outcome for the individuals concerned, the team they work in and their organisation. Mediation would provide the opportunity for people to come together with an impartial third party, and would be more likely to lead to a positive outcome.

The barriers to mediation being implemented are, in my view, conceptual. First, there are misunderstandings about the differences between mediation and conciliation. Second, it is difficult for managers to conceptualise a scheme working when adversarial approaches to conflict resolution are so entrenched in organisational consciousness. But mediation will save money and will model ways to be creative about problem solving.

How mediation works in organisations

In the USA and Australia workplace mediation is common. In the UK independent consultants are called on to deal with senior management conflicts; ACAS (see Chapter 10) conciliates and arbitrates in industrial disputes; and organisations such as the Centre for Dispute Resolution (CEDR) intervene on a more commercial level.

The peer mediation scheme in Lewisham Housing

The Lewisham Housing scheme works on the principle that the mediation procedure should be separate from both the grievance and disciplinary procedures, and that one's peers in the organisation are the appropriate people to act as mediators in disputes. The advantage of having a separate mediation procedure is that it enables employees to use mediation for disputes which might otherwise fall outside the grievance or disciplinary procedures. For example, mediators can be used to help teams sort out unspecific disputes (such as mistrust, absenteeism or high staff turnover). Employees in dispute with each other can resolve the matter using mediation, rather than having to take out a grievance against their manager for failing to deal with a situation. One of the principles of mediation is that it is voluntary. If it is a required step in a grievance procedure its effectiveness is compromised. Employees will feel obliged to be conciliatory and so the voluntary nature of mediation will be compromised.

How the scheme works

1. To access the Lewisham Housing mediation service, a member of staff with a complaint approaches the personnel department, which offers them two mediators to resolve their case.

2. The mediators ring both parties in the dispute, talk to them about their problem, explain mediation to them, tell them that all the information disclosed in the mediation is confidential, and check that the parties have the power to arrive at their desired outcomes. If both parties agree to mediation, a session is set up in a neutral venue.

3. Both parties can reject the mediators if they feel that they could not be impartial. This may be because the parties have a prejudice against a particular mediator, or because one or both of the mediators have worked with them in the past and they do not feel confident about them. Personnel would then offer fresh mediators to the parties.

4. The mediators are also obliged to declare an interest. They may, for example, have prior knowledge of the case, not uncommon in an

organisation, which would prejudice them against one or other of the parties. However, knowing the parties may not in itself be a barrier to their effectiveness as mediators. Peer mediators in organisations have to balance their personal opinions with the interests of the parties. This is similar to the dynamic in community mediation, where before a mediation session the mediators interview both parties and form opinions about the case. The key here is the ability to remain impartial and to suspend judgement.

5. If the parties come to an agreement, they are asked if they want to have this written down. They are also asked if they want a copy of their agreement to be placed on their Personnel file. If one of the parties expresses a wish not to have the agreement lodged with Personnel, the mediators will ask why, and if the party is adamant the agreement is not passed to Personnel. In these cases the mediators will inform Personnel that an agreement has been made and that is all.

6. After a month, the mediators will contact both parties and ask them whether the agreement is holding. Personnel will also make calls to check how the parties felt about the mediation process and the mediators' ability to help them to resolve their dispute.

A critical feature of the scheme is that the parties agree that the content of the mediation is confidential, and that the mediators cannot be called as witnesses in any subsequent hearing outside the mediation scheme. If one party decides to take the case through another procedure and discloses information from the mediation, the chair of that hearing should rule the information out of order; in any case the information will remain unsubstantiated because the mediators cannot be called to verify it.

The Department of Health (DH) scheme

The DH scheme is designed to change the emphasis of disputes from win–lose to win–win by getting managers who would have previously adopted an arbiter's role to use a conciliation approach. The difference from a mediation scheme is that the degree of voluntarism is smaller. To progress their grievance, an employee has to go through conciliation. The DH scheme does not cover cases of alleged harassment or discrimination, which are dealt with by a different procedure.

How it works

1. An employee in the DH with a complaint is initially required to raise their grievance with their line manager.

2. If the dispute is not resolved, the senior line manager listens to evidence from both parties and then makes a recommendation to settle the dispute. In this role they are acting as an arbitrator, but their recommendation has the

status of a non-binding arbitration because the employee can appeal against it.

3. If the employee exercises this right, the case is assigned to a trained conciliator. They will speak to both parties, identify the issues, clarify what they have both done to try and settle the matter, and check that they both have a desire to resolve it.

4. If an employee chooses not to use conciliation, they have to drop their case, and there is then no other avenue for them to pursue it. The manager who is being complained about, on the other hand, may not decline conciliation.

5. The conciliator will attempt to bring the parties together in a face-to-face meeting on neutral ground, and try to help them to come to their own agreement. As a conciliator they also have the discretion to offer their own advice and solutions. Most of the conciliators in the DH scheme are middle or senior managers. If the parties fail to come to an agreement, the conciliator will produce a report that suggests a way to resolve the dispute. Only the employee can appeal against this recommendation.

Considering all the options

In addition to such schemes, there are now an increasing number of independent facilitators who also have mediation training and are willing to offer this type of service. This model could be adopted by organisations reluctant to train in-house mediators or who want to have more options at their disposal.

The differences between all these schemes may be explained by looking at the different mediation models which are taught in this country. In the main, commercial and ACAS models of mediation work with the disputing parties in separate rooms for most of the mediation. Family mediators mostly mediate by bringing parties together in the same space. Community mediators do this where they can, but also work with parties separately if they are not willing to meet. My experience shows that, in the majority of workplace disputes, it is more effective to bring the parties together. Separating them reinforces the dispute and overlooks the need for both parties to establish how they will work together in the future, as inevitably they will have to do. This debate (indirect vs. direct mediation) continues, but both approaches have elements of the other in them and a skilled mediator will be open to the potential of both.

Given the different styles of mediation, what approach should an organisation take? This depends on the culture of the organisation and where the demand for mediation comes from. As the use of mediation in the workplace is still quite new, mediation is likely to be introduced by enterprising organisational development staff, or in organisations where there is already an existing culture of mediation or conciliation for dealing with customer complaints. As mediation evolves as an everyday practice, different models will emerge and the whole field of employment law will change to accommodate this.

Obstacles to implementation

Although mediation is seen as the appropriate way to resolve disputes, for many trade unionists and managers it poses a threat, because it shifts the balance of power from those with organisational authority to employees. Mediation requires a shift of perception; a successful mediator has to learn how to be neutral and impartial about the outcome of a mediation session, but remain committed to the process. Most people in organisations are required to give advice and provide support on a daily basis; breaking the habits of a working lifetime can be difficult. Mediation is one element in creating positive change in an organisation. Given the low cost of mediation (a peer mediation scheme can be set up for as little as £5000), even processing two or three cases through mediation can save organisations a lot of money.

The widening use of mediation

Many interpersonal disputes are resolved informally in organisations, but there is a growing recognition that alternative formal procedures can be useful for resolving disputes. Several large UK companies, including Shell and NatWest, now have anti-bullying and anti-harassment procedures. These procedures use a third party to offer counselling to the victims of bullying and harassment, and provide support to those who take their cases through grievance or disciplinary procedures. These developments will create the space for mediation and conciliation methods to become attractive to human resource and organisational development managers, because the inevitable next step is to recognise the parties in a dispute as adult and able to reconcile differences themselves, with the help of a neutral third party.

Other organisational initiatives such as Open Space conferences and agenda-less meetings, where the participants create discussion using brainstorming and Post-It notes, have similar principles to mediation, because they too believe that participation should be voluntary, that the facilitator is impartial and there is a focus on ongoing communication, collaborative problem solving and achievable action points.

The Employment Rights (Dispute Resolution) Act 1999 provides another impetus for organisations to consider mediation. From April 2000 it changed the way cases are processed by employment tribunals (formerly called industrial tribunals). The two changes relevant to this chapter are:

- the introduction of a voluntary binding arbitration procedure;
- new powers for the chair of an employment tribunal to refer the case back to the employer.

ACAS has been given powers to develop a new national arbitration service. Rather than going to an employment tribunal, employees will be able to opt (with the agreement of their employer) to refer their case to binding arbitration. The arbitrators in these cases do not have to be lawyers, but will be expected to act in a way that settles the dispute. The new powers given to the chair of an employment tribunal to refer a case back to an organisation's disciplinary or grievance procedure should prompt a series of reviews in organisations about the effectiveness of their procedures in resolving disputes, rather than establishing who is right or wrong.

Case examples

The names and details of the people involved in these cases have been altered to ensure that they remain anonymous and that their cases remain confidential.

Local authority

Robert is a service unit manager whose unit is subject to Compulsory Competitive Tendering (CCT). The tendering process was nerve-racking for many people in the local authority because of the uncertainty around jobs and the future provision of services. Tenders were submitted centrally to the director of the organisation and were then to be put formally to a Tenant Evaluation Panel for consideration. Once the tender documents were opened, it was immediately clear that the in-house bid would win, both in terms of price and quality. This news was passed to various people in the organisation and within a few days everyone working in the organisation knew about it. Before the documents were presented to the Tenant Evaluation Panel, Robert published the news in a newsletter to the tenants to whom he provided a service. The director of the organisation was extremely angry about this and suggested that Robert look for another job. Robert reacted badly and became very stressed about his future; so much so that his doctor signed him off sick for a month. Robert approached his union with a view to taking out a grievance against the director for breach of employment practice and for operating double standards. The union pointed out that, given the power structures, he was unlikely to win and the organisation could sack him for misconduct. They suggested mediation around a return to work. Robert and the director agreed. Over the next couple of weeks the mediator held separate meetings with both parties and an agreement was reached safeguarding Robert's position in the organisation.

International charity

A team of six information workers had been in dispute among themselves for several months. Factions had formed and one individual in particular was feeling vulnerable and excluded. She was the only part-time worker on the team. There was also a feeling that the work they were doing was overwhelming. The team worked generically. The manager of the team approached a mediator who agreed to work with the team over a period of a few weeks. The mediator initially interviewed all the team members to establish their concerns and explain the mediation process to them. At the end of the interviews the team agreed to try to resolve their differences and that it was desirable to do so. They also requested that the manager be present at the mediation session, because they felt that she too was part of the problem. The day was structured so that each person could speak about how they had been feeling up to now, how they were feeling in the session and what they wanted for the future. Following these presentations, which were conducted without interruption and subsequent commentary, the team split into smaller groups to look at the different areas of work in which they were involved. These groups came back to the larger group and the mediator helped the team to divide the work into specialisms. The team went on to identify different members who would specialise and the manager's doubts were listened to and resolved. The issue of personal differences had remained fairly dormant during the day, so the mediator then raised this issue. Each person was allowed uninterrupted time to say what effect the actions of others had had on them. After each person had spoken, the mediator invited people to ask questions of one another, summarising key points as they were made. These formed the agenda for discussion. By the end of the session, some apologies had been made and several people said they felt better.

The change in working practices proved a success and made the team more effective and raised morale. Unfortunately one personal dispute lingered on and one of the team left a few months later for another job.

How to set up a workplace mediation scheme

1. The first step is to test for demand and to consider the cost and cultural benefits that might accrue to your organisation. One way of doing this is to conduct some qualitative research with people who have been through an employee complaints procedure, as well as talking to top management teams and human resources managers.

2. In addition, an analysis of the costs of current dispute procedures, in terms of salary costs and lost productivity, will prove useful in making an economic decision about introducing mediation. If you opt for a mediation procedure that stands alone, you may need to consider whether employees who were reluctant to take up complaints may now do so because it will appear less onerous to use mediation.

3. Local terms and conditions of employment may also need to be changed. If you have a collective bargaining agreement with local trade unions, any changes will need to be formally agreed with them. If this is the case, the consequence will be a change to the statements of particulars which need to be issued with a contract to any new employees within 13 weeks of starting employment.

4. Once the need for mediation has been established and it seems economic, the next step is to decide whether to opt for in-house or external mediators or a combination of the two. For in-house mediators there are two main options – peer mediators or middle and senior managers. If you opt for the former, you will need to trawl for mediators at all levels of your organisation. The advantage of this is that you will realise the potential of a much wider range of people and your pool of mediators will be more likely to reflect the diversity within your organisation. The disadvantage will be that, in terms of status, some mediators will not be welcomed. I prefer the peer mediator approach because it enables employees' peers to help them

resolve disputes. In school mediation projects, children as young as five are involved in resolving playground disputes. One of the characteristics of mediation is to recognise the potential in people for creativity and problem solving; by insisting that mediators are senior managers the scheme is still tied to a past where the same people sat as arbitrators.

5. After agreeing on the potential pool of mediators, the next step is to recruit them and identify their training needs. Unless you have an experienced mediator working for you, who is also a seasoned facilitator, you will need to have mediators trained by someone with experience of organisational life and as a mediator and facilitator. To develop your mediators further, a mediation NVQ at level 4 is available and Mediation UK has an accredited mediator scheme.

Conclusion

Mediation is not a panacea for employee disputes, but it is beginning to be used as one of a range of processes that may transform organisational culture. It is also being used to save money. Of US companies 21 per cent now have some form of alternative dispute resolution procedure. These usually include the option of mediation. In the UK, the number of cases going to employment tribunal has risen from 60,605 in 1991 to 113,636 in 1998 (ACAS 1999). Mediation can provide both a cost-effective way to resolve employee disputes and a transformational effect on human relationships in organisations.

References

ACAS (1999) *Annual Report 1998*. London: ACAS.

Buber, M. (1957) 'Hope for this hour.' In *Pointing the Way*. New York.

Findlay, Z. and Reynolds, C. (1997) *The Workplace Mediation Manual*. London: Hilltop.

Lord Woolf (1996) *Access to Justice: Final Report to the Lord Chancellor on the Civil Justice System in England and Wales*. London: HMSO.

Further reading

Battram, A. (1998) *Navigating Complexity*. London: Industrial Society.

Ellinor, E. and Gerard, G. (1998) *Dialogue*. New York: Wiley.

Mindell, A. (1995) *Sitting in the Fire*. Portland: Lao Tse Press.

12

Commercial Alternative Dispute Resolution (ADR)

Paul Newman

A slow beginning

The perceived failure of litigation and arbitration, seen as costly and damaging, first in the USA and then elsewhere, has encouraged the rise of alternative dispute resolution (ADR). The main processes of commercial ADR will be described: early neutral evaluation, mediation, med-arb and mini-trial.

Since the late 1980s and early 1990s, ADR has been promoted in the UK by a number of bodies. It remains, for its advocates, an idea whose day has frustratingly not quite arrived. Even in the construction sector, one of the more prominent sectors to use ADR, data suggests that ADR is used in only 5 per cent of disputes (*The Lawyer* 1995). This may be changing with the effect of the Civil Procedure Rules on 26 April 1999 (the Woolf reforms).

The three most prominent promoters of commercial ADR in the UK are the Academy of Experts (formerly the British Academy of Experts), the Centre for Dispute Resolution (CEDR) and the lawyer-led ADR Group. Other groups, such as the Chartered Institute of Arbitrators, have remained ambivalent.

The Academy of Experts, which was formed in 1987, is prominent in providing mediation training services to existing and potential third party neutrals. Its members' handbook includes a description of mediation and how the Academy can assist in setting up mediation hearings.

CEDR, the most well-known ADR provider, started in 1990 with backing from the Confederation of British Industry (CBI). It has member organisations drawn from commerce, industry and law firms. Like the Academy, CEDR is an important training organisation and appointer of mediators. In addition, CEDR has set up specialist working groups, such as the Construction Industry Working Group which brings together construction lawyers, professionals and representatives drawn from contracting and client organisations. CEDR has also been active in providing seminars and presentations throughout the UK, often in conjunction with the CBI, to increase the general level of awareness of ADR among businesses.

The ADR Group is an alliance of legal firms who promote and offer ADR throughout the UK.

Although the Chartered Institute of Arbitrators is primarily concerned with the promulgation of arbitration, nevertheless when ADR began to develop momentum after 1990, the Chartered Institute produced several initiatives of its own. However, the Chartered Institute is not currently a prime promoter of ADR in the UK.

The value of ADR processes may not be apparent until litigation is well under way, at which point it is often difficult to stop the legal process. It is sometimes useful for one party to contact an ADR organisation, which can then suggest the possibility of ADR to the other party.

Lawyers and dispute resolution

So why do so many clients use lawyers to resolve their commercial disputes? Most disputes result in a negotiated settlement, either before or after the start of formal legal proceedings. However, clients use litigation lawyers for a number of purposes. First, the litigation process can be cynically manipulated if one party sees advantage in delay (particularly in a money claim), where there is always the possibility that the creditor will either run out of steam and go away or simply become insolvent. Second, there are those clients who have not made a realistic assessment of their own position or who have decided that a realistic assessment is best avoided. They may have a position to protect within their organisation, hoping to cover up their mistakes with the litigation process.

Lawyers often assist the client's inability to face reality. Most lawyers wish to be helpful and to highlight the positive features in their clients' cases. Traditionally, many lawyers have taken the course of easy resistance – issue a writ and see what happens. The overwhelming majority of cases do settle before trial, but not before high legal costs have been incurred and the scope for creative negotiation lessened. The substantial fees incurred to lawyers and expert witnesses can become real bones of contention. Lawyers also ignore the mental stress that litigation places on clients. When litigation starts, clients never consider the unnatural and unfair exercise of giving evidence in court. Courts are a hostile environment where lawyers play at home.

People do win legal trials but often only after a long and bloody battle; conversely legal trials also produce heavy losers. To litigate is to play a lottery: ultimately each party has to possess the capacity to lose. Litigation does have a serious role to play where there are clear legal issues, particularly if they favour one party, but if the dispute is centred on fact litigation is not the best means to resolve it.

So what is the role of lawyers in dispute resolution? A former US Chief Justice, the late Warren Burger, once said:

The obligation of our profession is...to serve as healers of human conflict. To fulfil our traditional obligation means that we should provide mechanisms that can produce an acceptable result in the shortest possible time, with the least possible expense and with the minimum of stress on the participants. That is what justice is all about. (Coulson 1984, pp.6–7)

Dispute resolution is a service industry and must recognise client needs. This theme was the cornerstone of Lord Woolf's interim and final reviews of civil litigation, *Access to Justice* (Woolf 1995, s. I para. 18; 1996, s. II para. 16c).

All too often the effects of litigation and arbitration are:

- polarised positions;
- a drain on the client's managerial time;
- clients who feel out of touch with their own dispute and victims of a legal takeover;
- damaged commercial relationships;
- expensive and long drawn-out proceedings;
- use of deliberate delaying tactics by a defendant who knows how to play the system;
- a pyrrhic victory for the successful litigant with monies recovered representing a mere fraction of actual expenditure;
- a judgment that is impossible to enforce.

However, litigation and arbitration may occasionally be in a client's best interests, for instance, in dealing with an unprincipled opponent who has no intention of negotiating sensibly, or where legal principles are involved.

Alternative dispute resolution

In the context of High Court litigation, lawyers have been forced at least to pay lip service to ADR for a number of years. An important change before the Woolf reforms was the *Practice Note (Civil Litigation: Case Management) [1995] 1 All ER 385*. This mirrored the earlier *Practice Statement (Commercial Court: Alternative Dispute Resolution) [1994] 1 WLR 14* in emphasising the value of ADR.

On 7 June 1996, the Commercial Court under Justice Waller issued an endorsement of ADR in its *Practice Statement (Commercial Cases: Alternative Dispute Resolution) (No 2) [1996] 1 WLR 1024*:

The Judges of the Commercial Court, in conjunction with the Commercial Court Committee, have recently considered whether it is now desirable that any further steps should be taken to encourage the wider use of ADR as a means of settling disputes pending before the Court.

The Commercial Court identified five factors which might encourage the use of ADR:

- a significant reduction in cost;
- a reduction in delays;

- the preservation of existing commercial relationships and market reputation;
- a greater range of settlement solutions than those offered by litigation;
- more efficient use of judicial resources.

Judges of the Commercial Court would positively encourage parties to adopt alternative dispute resolution techniques, adjourning proceedings for a specified time to enable parties to take such steps.

Early neutral evaluation

A further radical departure in the *Practice Statement* was the endorsement of the principle of early neutral evaluation, so that lengthy trials might be curtailed. The assigned judge of the Commercial Court could provide the evaluation, or arrange for another judge to do so. The judge could not impose early neutral evaluation upon the parties unless the parties agreed. If early neutral evaluation did not result in settlement, that particular judge would not take any further part in the proceedings.

The new post-Woolf Civil Procedure Rules (1999) encourage ADR. Lord Woolf endorsed ADR in his reports on civil justice reform (Woolf 1995, 1996), and parties to a dispute can agree that their case be transferred to ADR for an attempted settlement, or alternatively judges can actively suggest this. The court then allows enough time for ADR to take place.

Mediation

Mediation is a process in which an independent third party, the mediator, assists the parties through individual meetings (caucuses) and joint sessions, to focus on their real interests and strengths, as opposed to their emotions, in an attempt to draw them together towards possible settlement. The independent third party does not make recommendations regarding an appropriate settlement, but assists the parties to find their own agreement. Mediation is likely to be suitable under the following circumstances:

1.   The parties have and want to maintain a commercial relationship.
2.   Both parties have a mutual interest in a quick resolution of the dispute.
3.   Both parties recognise that litigation will provide an unacceptable drain on their managerial time, be expensive, long drawn out and unpredictable.
4.   Neither party wishes to have the publicity that litigation may bring them.
5.   The parties have come to understand that mediation may provide them with the best option to have their day in court, a form of catharsis, yet carried out in the most cost-effective way possible.

6. The parties have already experienced litigation and mediation in other disputes and have learnt the value of mediation and the drawbacks of litigation.

7. There may be problems with witness availability or quality and the full intensity of a possible trial is best avoided.

Mediation may not work under the following circumstances:

1. The dispute is centred more on law than fact and established precedent strongly favours one party over the other.

2. One party wishes to delay the resolution of the dispute for as long as possible.

3. One or both of the parties are not acting in good faith.

4. One of the parties believes that litigation will be a complete vindication of their position.

5. There is inequality of bargaining position between the parties.

6. One of the parties lacks the resources or the money to face its responsibilities under a particular contract.

7. The dispute is one where the creation of legal precedent is desirable.

So do lawyers have a role in mediation?

1. They can advise their clients on their legal rights.

2. They can advise their clients on the choice of a suitable dispute resolution procedure.

3. They can assist clients in the preparation of cases for ADR sessions.

4. They can represent their clients during mediation meetings and mini-trials.

5. They can assist clients to prepare and complete appropriate settlement agreements which are legally enforceable.

6. They can assess what documentation should be prepared and possibly exchanged prior to the mediation sessions.

7. They can carry out a risk assessment of the likely outcome if the matter were to be pursued via litigation or arbitration.

8. They can consider any general policy considerations, or the requirement for legal precedent, which render litigation in the High Court more advantageous to the client.

9. They can assess whether, if litigation or arbitration is pursued, there are likely to be witness problems.

10. They can decide whether the documents are so confused or incomplete as to render recourse to litigation or arbitration undesirable.

The use of ADR is not a means of avoiding proper case preparation. Presenting a case effectively at a mediation session requires a full understanding of all the issues.

Mediation and principled negotiation

Presentation of any case at a mediation session requires awareness of what a party wishes to achieve. The approach has much in common with principled negotiations, as popularised by Fisher and Ury (1990) in *Getting to Yes – Negotiating Agreements Without Giving In*. The use of principled negotiations involves deciding issues by an agreed objective standard, rather than by resort to positional bargaining. The latter encourages each side to take a position and hold to it stubbornly, rather than focus on their underlying concerns and needs. There are four fundamentals of principled negotiations:

- *People*: separate the people from the problem.
- *Interests*: focus on interests, not positions.
- *Options*: generate a variety of possibilities before deciding what to do.
- *Criteria*: insist that the result be based on some objective standard.

One of the great values of mediation is its ability to promote a realistic understanding by each party of the other's interests. A good mediator should put the parties at their ease and encourage them to consider issues rather than dwell on personalities, adopting a co-operative negotiating strategy. First, and this is to be distinguished from weak bargaining, the common ground and shared values need to be identified and confirmed. This strikes a positive note, may immediately reduce the areas in dispute, and provides each of the parties with a feeling that the process is beneficial.

The mediation session

Before the formal mediation sessions begin, the seating plan for the parties needs to be arranged. The seating must not create the feeling that a particular party is being advantaged. Ideally, representatives of the various parties should be equidistant from the mediator at the opening session, so that eye contact can be engaged with anyone. Depending on the number of parties, the preferred options may be a round table, a rectangle or an H configuration (two long tables with a short table in between; the parties sit at the long tables, the mediator at the short one between the parties). Both arrangements place the parties' representatives equidistant from the mediator, thereby allowing him or her to engage either side in dialogue without antagonising the other.

Once the mediator has convened the parties, he or she will make some opening remarks, indicating to the parties what it is hoped to achieve, and confirming that mediation is non-binding and will not impose any solutions on them. If the parties' position papers have been submitted in advance, the mediator will indicate that he or she has read them. Next the mediator will ask each side to make a short opening statement, lasting not more than 10–15 minutes, to explain their position. This statement should be as neutral as possible, set out the issues and draw attention to the interpretations and conclusions of each party.

If position papers are submitted to the mediator, they should be no more than twenty pages of double-spaced A4 typescript. Position papers should be meticulously prepared to strike the right note and contain the appropriate information. Flowcharts, diagrams, photographs and plans may all be useful to include. Although the precise format of position papers will depend on the nature of the dispute, they might include the following:

- a positive indication that the client wishes to work towards settlement;
- a resumé of the facts of the case as seen by the client, but highlighting any agreements or disagreements that are believed to exist in regard to particular facts;
- an analysis of responsibility and monetary value.

In preparing and making oral submissions, those involved must be realistic and honest. Although a litigator might emphasise strengths and ignore weaknesses, this is unacceptable in mediation, except as a starting point. Position papers and oral submissions should avoid specific settlement figures and emotive language. It would be futile to commence a mediation session with 'I'll settle for £50,000 and not a penny less', as the second party will then spend the time thinking up opposing arguments, rather than listening to the first party presenting its case.

Throughout the mediation session, the mediator must remain aware that the parties do not wish to be cajoled or coaxed into a settlement, and that mediation is not simply about splitting the difference. It is about trying to achieve win–win situations. Methods of case presentation can be flexible. It is legitimate for the parties to use all the presentational aids they can muster, such as photographs, site diaries, works records, plans, and so on.

Qualities of a mediator

An ideal mediator will have the following virtues, alongside general experience of the industry in which the dispute occurs:

- *Empathy*: the ability to get on with the parties, understand their position, even if he or she does not agree with them, and the ability to deflect parties from fixed views gently and without causing them irritation. Any change of position must be genuinely the party's own shift, so that feelings of having been bullied are absent. The mediator must be seen to be a good listener.
- *Patience*: the ability to wait for the parties to make movements in their own time.

- *Self-assurance:* the ability to inspire confidence in the parties, with a game plan of what is to be achieved without obviously leading the parties.

- *Clarity of thought:* the ability to ask questions which are intelligent and result in new information and perspectives.

- *Ingenuity:* the capacity to bring in new ideas when the discussion appears to be flagging or on the point of failing, including the power to think laterally and propose novel solutions for the parties to think about and promote as their own ideas.

- *Stamina:* the mediation sessions may take place over an extended period of time, and there may be less scope for breaks as momentum increases towards possible agreement.

Case examples

Central London County Court

In May 1996 the Central London County Court began a pilot scheme (made permanent in 1998) to allow mediation of civil disputes in the £3000–£10,000 range. Parties who opted for mediation did so without prejudice to their court-based rights, and had a single three-hour session with a trained mediator from one of five ADR providers, outside court hours 4.30 pm to 7.30 pm. Each side paid £25 towards the mediator's costs. The mediation was arranged within 28 days. The Patents County Court ran a similar two-year scheme. Professor Hazel Genn carried out detailed research to evaluate the scheme (Genn 1998). Although a disappointingly low number, 5 per cent, accepted the invitation to mediation (Genn 1998, p.40), the 200 cases going to mediation were successful: 80 per cent settled at the mediation session or soon after, and 85 per cent said they would use the process again (Genn 1999, p.35).

Medical negligence

Mrs Brown was a 40-year-old mother of two children aged 13 and 15. She had a sterilisation operation which failed and she became pregnant. There were problems with the pregnancy and the birth, but after some time in the special care unit, the baby was found to be healthy. The NHS Trust accepted that they were negligent, and the argument was about the amount of damages.

Mrs Brown's case was concerned with the traumatic birth of the child and the disruption to her career, for which she had been undertaking training before becoming pregnant unintentionally. She claimed damages for pain and suffering, loss of earnings, layette and equipment expenses, costs of bringing up a child till age 22, child-minding costs till age 12, transport costs and investment advice costs for any lump sum awarded. Her total claim was £143,500.

The Trust was prepared to admit negligence for the purpose of the mediation but not provide an open admission. They argued that it was invidious to put a value for damages on an unwanted life, but accepted that Mrs Brown was entitled to compensation for the trauma of the birth and some of the continuing costs. They had made an offer of £50,000, which was rejected.

Both parties and their solicitors came together for the mediation session and the process was explained. The Trust's solicitors had sent a letter referring to two previous terminations, inferring that Mrs Brown could have avoided the expense by terminating the pregnancy, and had only continued with it to gain financial compensation. Mrs Brown was very upset at this allegation. She had also received no explanation of why the sterilisation operation had failed. The Trust apologised for these things. The mediation then continued in separate sessions with Mrs Brown and the Trust. In these meetings, the Trust offered an interview with the consultant to explain why the operation had failed, and Mrs Brown accepted. The negotiation concerning the money proceeded using 'shuttle mediation', with each side making concessions until they agreed a sum of £80,000. The parties came back together to draft the agreement. The whole process had taken five hours, far less than a court case would have done – and both parties were very pleased with the result.

Mediation-Arbitration (Med-Arb)

Generally ADR techniques are not felt to encompass the adjudicative. For this reason, arbitration, for some the original ADR method, is not considered to form part of the ADR family. However, it is occasionally used in conjunction with mediation.

The hybrid technique of Med-Arb attempts to address the concerns of those lawyers who see mediation and other non-binding ADR techniques as weak. Its purpose is to commit the parties, usually through a clause in their contract, to continue the ADR process in a manner which will ensure resolution of the dispute. It is a way of having the best of both worlds.

Med-Arb recognises that mediation may not resolve all the issues between the parties, and limits arbitration to the intractable ones, thereby bringing a cost and time saving. The disputants first attempt to negotiate a settlement. If that fails they try mediation and if no agreement (or only partial agreement) is reached the mediator changes roles and becomes an arbitrator empowered to impose a binding decision on them.

Med-Arb has not been greatly used in the UK. However, there are some recorded successes of Med-Arb in the USA, including an environmental clean-up dispute between Conoco and Browning Ferris Industries over removal of hazardous chemicals. Three years of litigation gave way to nine months of mediation. This resolved most of the issues but did not finally settle liability. The mediator then became an arbitrator, resolving the remaining issues (Elliott 1996, p.176).

If mediation fails, the mediator's subsequent appointment as arbitrator of the same dispute is superficially attractive. Anything that may lessen ultimate costs must seem a good idea to the parties. An arbitrator already well acquainted with the facts does not have the same learning curve as a fresh arbitrator, and may simply need to clarify the outstanding issues before drafting a final award. However, many doubts have been expressed about Med-Arb:

- It may be difficult to assess when mediation should give way to arbitration. An inexperienced neutral might move prematurely to arbitration whenever there is an apparent impasse in the mediation.

- A busy arbitrator might coerce the parties during the mediation stage into a settlement which the parties might not desire.

- Knowing that the mediator might subsequently act as their arbitrator, the parties may be less forthcoming.

- The arbitrator's award might owe more to knowledge gained during the mediation (communicated by one party during the caucus sessions and unknown to the other party) than to that gained in the arbitration under the rules of evidence.

On the other hand, mediation succeeds because it is based on communication and trust. A mediator is not constrained to accept one party's case at the expense of rejecting the other. Mediation, founded on a lack of coercion, allows the parties to agree without judicial imposition.

The mini-trial (executive tribunal)

Another ADR option is the mini-trial or executive tribunal. Its aim is to involve the real decision makers at an early stage in the dispute resolution process, before relationships sour and costs escalate to such a level that neither side feels able to back down.

Each party presents the issues to senior executives of both parties, who are often assisted by a neutral chairman. The parties may be, but not necessarily, represented by lawyers. The chairman, again not necessarily a lawyer, may advise on the likely outcome of litigation but without any binding authority on the parties. After presentation of the issues, the executives try to negotiate a settlement. If successful, the settlement is often set out in a legally enforceable written document. The mini-trial is not really a trial at all (e.g. the legal rules of evidence are usually dispensed with), but a settlement procedure designed to convert a legal dispute back into a business problem. It aims to bring business people on each side of the fence directly into the resolution process, in the hope that compromises can be reached. To date the technique has been little used in the UK. Advantages of a mini-trial include:

- A lengthy hearing is eliminated.

- Each party's case is professionally presented but without any formal rules of procedure or evidence.

- Those who ultimately decide whether the dispute should be settled (and, if so, on what terms) have the opportunity to be guided by a person with some degree of prestige and outside objectivity.

- The presentations are made to and the ultimate decision made by persons with the requisite authority in their organisations.

- It brings a fresh mind to the process.

Disadvantages of a mini-trial include:

- Complicated technical and legal issues may be over-simplified.

- The senior management time needed for a mini-trial may not be cost effective for smaller disputes.

One of the first mini-trials took place between TRW and Telecredit Inc in the USA to resolve a dispute concerning infringement of a computer terminal patent in 1977. The parties had already spent over $500,000 each. Faced with the enormous costs of continued litigation and the potential futility of such a process to the loser, the parties' representatives decided to follow the format of the mini-trial. This included four-hour presentations by both sides, with answering statements and question-and-answer sessions after both presentations. This took two days. The presentations were mostly made by lawyers, but once the mini-trial was at an end, senior management personnel undertook the negotiations and only took 30 minutes to reach agreement.

Although it is often better for the parties to devise their own mini-trial procedure, in the USA both the Center for Public Resources and the American Arbitration Association have published mini-trial procedures. In the UK the Chartered Institute of Arbitrators has had a mini-trial procedure since 1990.

Achieving certainty in ADR

One of the constant criticisms made of ADR is that, even if successful, any agreement is difficult to enforce if a party later goes back on their word. However, the agreement can be written in such a way that, if necessary, the courts can be asked later to enforce it. Enforcement will also be possible if the agreement is deemed to have the same effect as an arbitration award to which the Arbitration Act 1996 applied. Then, if necessary, enforcement of the 'award' can be made under s. 66 Arbitration Act 1996.

Privilege and confidentiality

If a mediation fails and the parties return to the courts or to arbitration, what is the status of documentation prepared for the (failed) mediation? It is important to be reassured that documentation is secure and that mediators cannot be called to give evidence in legal proceedings.

Parties often state that non-binding mediation will be carried out on a *without prejudice* basis, but even if this is not expressly stated, it would be characterised as such by lawyers. Non-binding mediation has much in common with ordinary settlement talks that parties to litigation might attempt. The phrase without prejudice simply means that, in the event that settlement talks are unsuccessful, any statements made will be privileged; no reference can be made to them in any subsequent litigation or arbitration hearing. The privilege in statements made on a without prejudice basis is the joint one of the parties and extends to their solicitors: *La Roche* v. *Armstrong* [1922] 1 KB 485. It can only be waived with the consent of each party.

The question of privilege arising out of a mediation hearing has been addressed in the USA and Australia. For instance, the Southern District Court of New York has ruled that documents from an ADR proceeding are protected from discovery and subsequent court proceedings *North River Insurance Co.* v. *Columbia Casualty Co, Dispute Resolution Times*, New York, June 1995.

The confidentiality of the mediation process was considered in Australia in the long-running proceedings, *AWA Limited* v. *Daniels and Others* (Unreported, 2 May 1992). In this case Chief Justice Rogers said:

> It is of the essence of successful mediation that parties should be able to reveal all relevant matters without an apprehension that the disclosure may subsequently be used against them…were the position otherwise, unscrupulous parties could use and abuse the mediation process by treating it as a gigantic, penalty free discovery process.

The law in the UK has not developed on this point in the commercial and civil sector, although in the family sector the Court of Appeal decided that admissions or conciliatory gestures made during mediation are not admissible if the mediation is unsuccessful and comes to court, except in the rare case where someone indicated that he had caused, or was likely the cause of, severe harm to a child. *Re D (minors)* Court of Appeal, 11 February 1993.

Cultural perspectives

Certain religious and ethnic groups may have a cultural bias in favour of particular methods of dispute resolution. Perhaps the Anglo-Saxon mindset is traditionally adversarial. Even if the Christian message is one of reconciliation, this has not been very evident in legal methods of dispute resolution. Enquiries suggest (Newman 1995/6) that the Beth Din (Court of the Chief Rabbi), which includes dispute arbitration and mediation, is now sometimes asked to mediate in disputes involving non-Jews. In some cultures, e.g. those on the Asia/Pacific Rim, there is a cultural preference in favour of mediation, as opposed to adjudicative methods of dispute resolution:

> In various Asian Countries, there is a profound societal philosophical preference for agreed-upon solutions. Rather than a cultural bias towards 'equality' in relationships, there exists an intellectual and social predisposition towards a natural hierarchy which governs conduct in interpersonal relations. Asian cultures frequently seek a 'harmonious' solution, one which tends to preserve the relationship, rather than one which, while arguably, factually and legally 'correct' may severely damage the relationship of the parties involved. (Donahey 1995, p.279)

Donahey (1995, p.280) also identified the Chinese approach as being in keeping with traditional Confucianism:

> Within traditional Confucianism, going back thousands of years, there is a concept known as *li* which concerns the social norms of behaviours within the five natural status relationships: emperor and subject, father and son, husband and wife, brother and brother, or friend and friend. *Li* is intended to be persuasive, not compulsive and legalistic, a concept which governs good conduct and is above legal concepts in societal importance. The governing legal concept, *fa* is compulsive and punitive. While having the advantage of legal enforceability, *fa* is traditionally below *li* in importance. The Chinese have always considered the resort to litigation as the last step, signifying that the relationship between the disputing parties can no longer be harmonized. Resort to litigation results in loss of face, and discussion and compromise are always to be preferred. Over time the concept of *fa* and *li* have become confused and the concept of maintaining the relationship and, therefore, face, has become part of the Chinese legal system.

While it is not suggested that Christian or Confucian/Taoist principles will permeate business relationships (although they might, with increasingly global trade), ADR does require changed attitudes. However, the more cynical must be given something tangible – most obviously the saving of time and money.

Conclusion

Currently, the capacity of ADR (including mediation) to assist the resolution of commercial disputes is an unrealised potential. The hard-talking commercial client, with a lawyer to match, remains an everyday reality. These are not people who look for win–win solutions, taking as their maxim 'Successful people do not compromise.'

There are two ways out of this impasse. There is a natural reluctance to promote ADR through diktat of the state. In its purest form ADR should be consensual; coercing people to mediate militates against its inherent effectiveness. However, it is quite appropriate for the state to draw attention to the existence of an alternative to litigation or arbitration.

Second, and ultimately more compelling, is a willing adherence to ADR principles. The way lawyers are trained in the UK is based on adversarial assumptions and sees dispute resolution as a purely legal exercise. There needs to be a greater emphasis on ADR in professional courses in colleges and universities and, however difficult, a turning away from the 'mediation equals weakness' mentality. This is the challenge facing ADR.

References

Coulson, R. (1984) *Professional Mediation of Civil Disputes*. New York: American Arbitration Association.

Donahey, M.S. (1995) 'Seeking harmony.' *Journal of the Chartered Institute of Arbitrators 61*, 4, 279–283.

Elliott, D.C. (1996) 'Med/arb: fraught with danger or ripe with opportunity?' *Journal of the Chartered Institute of Arbitrators 62*, 3, 175–183.

Fisher, R. and Ury, W. (1990) *Getting to Yes – Negotiating Agreements Without Giving In*. London: Business Books.

Genn, H. (1998) *The Central London County Court Pilot Mediation Scheme: Evaluation Report*. London: Lord Chancellor's Department.

Genn, H. (1999) *Mediation in Action*. London: Calouste Gulbenkian Foundation.

The Lawyer (1995) News item. 13 June, 15.

Newman, P. (1995–6) Enquiry data, unpublished.

Lord Woolf (1995) *Access to Justice: Interim Report to the Lord Chancellor on the Civil Justice System in England and Wales*. London: HMSO.

Lord Woolf (1996) *Access to Justice: Final Report to the Lord Chancellor on the Civil Justice System in England and Wales*. London: HMSO.

13

Medical Mediation

Marion Wells

Introduction

As the reader will have noticed, in every field of conflict there are common factors. For medical mediation I would highlight three: difficulties of communicating when under stress; the need to find someone to blame when things go wrong; and a divisive feeling of self (here it is the lay person) against others (in this case, the professionals).

The National Health Service (NHS) introduced a new complaints procedure in April 1996. The NHS directions to health authorities require them to provide a conciliation service which may be used by patients and family health service practitioners in primary care – doctors in general practice (GPs), dentists, pharmacists and ophthalmologists. There is no similar expectation of NHS trusts which manage hospitals (secondary care) and community services. However, their complaints procedure is under review. There is also some movement towards exploring the scope for mediation as an alternative to litigation, to resolve claims of clinical negligence against NHS trusts or health authorities.

Within the field of primary care, the words conciliation and conciliator are more often used than mediation and mediator. People have different views on whether these words are synonymous. Mediation is certainly becoming the more universal term. I have to describe my role as a conciliator in this context though the work I do is equivalent to being a mediator in other fields.

The new complaints procedure guidance for general practices states:

There will be no direct connection between complaint procedures and disciplinary action. It is possible however, that some complaints will reveal information about serious matters which indicate a possible need for disciplinary investigation. Where it proves necessary, disciplinary action will continue to be linked to the terms of service. A health authority will consider whether informal action might be helpful before invoking disciplinary procedures. For example, the health authority might suggest to the doctor that he or she undergoes training in a specific area or finds help to improve practice procedures. (NHS Executive 1996)

If a complainant starts legal action against a practitioner the complaints procedure is abandoned. Health authorities will halt a complaints procedure if there is a disciplinary procedure to be dealt with.

The complaints procedure in primary healthcare

The complaints procedure is described as 'practice based and practice owned'. Its aim is to try to resolve complaints at practice level by someone within the practice, usually the practice manager, meeting the complainant somewhere private as soon as possible, to talk through what has happened to cause distress. This is described as local resolution. A complaint may be about any aspect of the service provided by anyone working in the practice and is not restricted to the general practitioner. Health authorities can contribute to the local resolution process by offering advice on the procedures and access to conciliators.

The word 'complaint' may cover general as well as specific dissatisfaction and could be confined to an offer of comment or suggestion. A complaint could be described as an expression of dissatisfaction that requires a response. Patients do not always use the word 'complaint'.

If a complaint cannot be resolved at local level, the complainant is told that the health authority can look into the complaint further. This is done by someone appointed as convenor by the health authority. The convenor is a non-executive director of the health authority who is empowered to carry out an independent review. There are several options open to the convenor:

1. Refer the complaint back to the practice, if insufficient effort has been made to resolve the matter – perhaps recommending conciliation.

2. Set up an independent review panel to investigate the complaint.

3. Take no further action, where it is clear that everything has been done that could be done.

The convenor also informs the complainant of the right to approach the Ombudsman.

Readers interested in full details of the complaints procedures should ask their local health authority for further information and for their annual report. However, as health authorities can only ask practices for the number of complaints received, not their nature or resolution, the statistics on complaints are not very revealing. The separation between primary care and hospital care can be confusing and unsatisfactory for complainants, if their complaint is about both. Advice and support from the community health council may be invaluable in these circumstances.

The procedure in practice

During the first 18 months of the new complaints procedure, the number of cases in different health authorities involving a conciliator varied from 10 to 50. I will take as an example one health authority which has four conciliators who worked on 29 cases. Of these cases, 20 were medical, eight dental and one opthalmic. In 19 cases the request for a conciliator came from the complainant. In five of these cases the complainants had initially asked for an independent review, but the convenor had requested them to go back to the practice for local resolution, suggesting the use of a conciliator. The remaining ten requests were received from practices.

There is, as yet, no published statistical information available on outcomes of conciliated meetings. In 11 cases the complainants requested an independent review following conciliation meetings. At these meetings there may have been no resolution and so the complainant remained unsatisfied, or a partial resolution in which some issues had been addressed to the complainant's satisfaction while others had not. The convenor may ask the conciliator if all issues have been explored thoroughly before deciding whether to call a review panel.

The nature and purpose of patient complaints

A patient, or relative when the patient has died, may decide there is cause for complaining about the attention, diagnosis or treatment they have received. They may want an explanation for what has happened. They may want to ask about something they have not understood. They want answers, perhaps different answers, or to challenge the doctor's judgement. The moment of crisis has passed and the complainant is now able to express concerns. These are frequently about perceived delay in diagnosing, treating or referring to hospital. A lay person may not realise how suddenly a condition can deteriorate.

Advice from others who have views or their own experiences of similar situations may prod a complaint: 'It ought never to have happened.' 'It didn't happen to me like that.' Maybe the complainant just wants an apology for something the doctor said or did not say, or did or did not do. There may be a desire to restore the relationship or to become more involved in decision making. Patients may simply want to feel that their illnesses are being taken seriously, that they have been heard and their anxieties noticed.

A relative may have any of these concerns. In addition there may be a strong urge to blame the doctor, particularly if the patient has died. Something must have gone wrong: we do not expect people we know and love to die. If the patient was a child it is even more unacceptable. Anger and blaming are often part of the grieving process.

So when do people deliver a complaint and how? It may be immediately after the event which gave rise to the complaint. It may be later or very much later. GP practices are now required to have available an information leaflet explaining how to make a complaint. This leaflet should make it clear that it is helpful for everyone involved if the complaint is made as soon as possible after the event, within days or, at the most, weeks. Practices may set a time limit but they are encouraged to be flexible. If a patient is refused or not offered a practice-based complaints investigation, he or she may ask the health authority to investigate. Health authorities will also encourage the complainant to bring a complaint as soon as possible and will not normally take on a complaint later than six months after the incident which gave rise to it, or six months after the problem became apparent.

A complainant may go straight to the health authority. It is not always easy to walk into the surgery or telephone the receptionist. Practices are encouraged to train their staff to respond to complaints sensitively and find somewhere private to discuss them. Minor matters of misunderstanding, misinformation or a simple administrative error, can be dealt with satisfactorily on the spot. Maybe an explanation, an apology or an assurance that it will not happen again is all that is expected or required. This may come from the reception staff, the practice manager, a designated complaints manager, a nurse or a doctor.

Where conciliation can help

Other complaints have a longer journey and this is where the conciliator may be brought in.

When a practice receives a complaint in writing, it should be acknowledged immediately. Doctors are advised by their defence societies to take advice from them at this point. Their staff are experienced and skilled in dealing with complaints and may help a member by talking the matter through on the phone, as well as by giving written advice. They will comment on a doctor's draft response to the complainant in terms of both content and tone. They may remind the doctor that an offer of a face-to-face meeting with or without a conciliator might be helpful. They also point out that the doctor must inform the complainant of the right to request an independent review if not satisfied.

This stage may take some time. It will take longer if the patient has left the practice, as the medical records will have been transferred to another practice and will need to be retrieved. There are two exacerbating factors here: the doctor's delay in replying to the complainant and an assumption by the complainant that the doctor will be able to remember the events which gave rise to the complaint without referring to the patient's records. As in other disputes, both perception and remembered detail will differ between the parties.

If the complainant is not satisfied with the doctor's response and asks for or agrees to try conciliation, a conciliator appointed by the health authority is asked to take on the case. The conciliator will check the names involved to make sure the parties are not personally known to him or her and then contact the complainant and the practice to arrange a convenient meeting date, time and place. The time allocated for the meeting is usually an hour but may be longer. The place is usually the surgery but should not be a consulting room. The practice manager is often invited to take short notes as the practitioner is required to write a letter to the complainant after the meeting summarising the outcome of the meeting. A copy of the correspondence relating to the complaint is sent to the conciliator in advance. A conciliator may need some explanation of any relevant medical details. There are professional advisers available, one of whom can be consulted and may be invited to attend the meeting (with the parties' permission).

How does the doctor regard a conciliated meeting? I asked one for his views:

The doctor's reaction to the conciliator will depend on the ability of the conciliator to distance him or herself from any position of judge or representative of the health authority. The doctor will inevitably feel vulnerable and must be certain that the conciliator will listen with an open mind and not be prejudiced. The doctor will be concerned that the conciliator may be ignorant about medical matters and not fully aware of the medical issues in the case. He may also construe conciliation as being two lay people (conciliator and complainant) arrayed against a professional person.

Doctors usually find confrontation of any kind difficult, as the traditional relationship between doctor and patient is paternalistic. The recent emphasis on patient-centred consultations is difficult for some doctors to accept and in complaints where an authoritarian doctor is involved, the conciliator is likely to have considerable difficulty in getting understanding between the parties.

Some conciliators arrange to visit each party beforehand and others talk over the phone. It is usual to meet each party separately just before the meeting starts. The purpose is to establish contact, clarify the conciliator's role and credentials, and to explain how the meeting will be managed. The complainant may want to say something more about the complaint. Feelings and desired outcomes may have changed since the original letter of complaint. The doctor may need to express some feelings and views. The conciliator clearly demonstrates an impartial stance.

The complainant may want to bring someone, a relative or friend for support, or someone from the community health council. This is particularly helpful when the complainant has difficulty in communicating. The doctor may also ask for a colleague to attend. A conciliator sometimes has to balance the wishes of the parties to bring along other people with the benefits of having a small meeting which allows those who are there to speak more freely. It might be unwise to arrange a meeting with four doctors present even if the complainant is angry with the entire practice. Usually there is one conciliator at the meeting, though some conciliation services provide two.

What do complainants expect and what do they want?

Before I try to answer these questions, I want to explore the basis of the relationship between doctor and patient. Most of us are patients at some time and some are doctors as well. We may meet in moments of crisis, such as emergency admission to hospital, diagnosis of a serious condition or major life events such as childbirth or death: we have unspoken and unconscious expectations of each other. The doctor expects the patient to give clear, accurate information and to be receptive to instructions or advice. If he or she is an optimistic sort of doctor, there will be an expectation that the patient will do what is suggested. The patient expects the doctor to find out what is wrong, communicate it and treat it immediately, or at least make arrangements for treatment. The patient may want sympathy and a full understanding of the family situation and past medical history. It can be a tall order.

It is probably a rare practice where the expectations of the relationship are discussed and agreed when a patient chooses a doctor (or is allocated to one after removal from another's list, following a breakdown of the doctor–patient relationship). So, if these expectations are not arrived at through mutual agreement, where do they come from? They are based on past experience, other people's experience, information gathered from various sources – and hope. There is plenty of scope for mismatches.

I sometimes discover where the difficulties lie when I meet the parties. In one case they were incompatible people and there was a personality clash. If the patient is

---

Box 13.1 The conciliated meeting

- This is an informal meeting, part of the local resolution procedure, to try to resolve a complaint.

- The conciliator assures parties that s/he acts confidentially.

- The conciliator will manage the meeting and ensure that parties are able to put their points and ask their questions.

- Ground rules are laid down about name-calling, interrupting or other unhelpful behaviour.

- The complainant has five to ten minutes uninterrupted time to speak.

- The doctor is asked to respond.

- The conciliator facilitates communication between them, using the skills of a mediator, looking for positive statements and summarising where the meeting has got to.

- If the going gets difficult, a short break may be taken and/or separate meetings held. Ground rules may need to be reinforced.

- The conciliator summarises the outcomes at the end of the meeting and subsequently writes a summary and sends it to both parties.

- The practice has an obligation to inform complainants of their right to ask for an independent review within a time limit of 28 days from the date of the meeting.

strident and well informed and the doctor is self-effacing and reticent, the relationship breaks down when a complaint is made. In another case, at a superficial level there were differences of opinion and assumptions to be worked through. At a deeper level we uncovered a mismatch around values and beliefs; strong prejudices got in the way.

In a crisis there is neither the time nor the capacity to invest in developing a better relationship. To take a transactional analysis approach, a set-up which is in a 'parent–child' communication state does not switch easily to 'adult–adult' communication, particularly if there is no precedent for such communication.

The conciliated meeting

The meeting is based on the same principles and follows a similar process to that used in family or community mediation meetings. The conciliator brings everyone into the room together, seats them, makes any necessary introductions and outlines the purpose and process (Box 13.1).

Possible outcomes of conciliation

A conciliation can result in several outcomes. From the complainant's point of view, the outcome could be:

- a better understanding of the medical aspects of the complaint;
- a better understanding of what happened and what the doctor was thinking at the time;
- an opportunity to talk to the doctor with the help of an impartial third party about dissatisfactions and distress;
- if appropriate, an apology;
- a chance to get the doctor or the practice to change something so that others will not suffer in the same way in the future.

If the complainant achieves whichever outcome s/he needs, there is rarely any 'call for blood'. The conciliation meeting may resolve some issues but leave others which the complainant will take further by asking for an independent review. The meeting may occasionally fail to achieve anything positive. When this happens it is very disappointing for all concerned, and the matter may or may not be taken further. There are also some patients who (for whatever reason) will never be satisfied and move from doctor to doctor, either by self-referral or by being taken off the doctor's list.

From the doctor's point of view the outcome could be:

- a chance to talk matters through, and explain medical aspects of examination, diagnosis and treatment, with the help of the conciliator;

- an opportunity, if appropriate, to apologise, to admit mistakes or agree that things could have been handled better. Medical defence societies will advise their members that it is all right to say 'I am sorry that you have been unhappy with the care you have received', or 'I am sorry this has happened';

- an opportunity to review their own practice, including knowledge, manner and attitudes, and to make changes if necessary.

- a chance to improve the relationship for the future, if the patient is still registered with the practitioner.

Conciliators do not make a judgement about who is right or wrong, or about disciplinary action or financial compensation. There is an interesting contrast here with other kinds of mediation. Where others are 'future focused', looking for some forward movement or a change in behaviour in a relationship in the future, in medical mediation the focus is mostly on understanding past events. Bearing in mind that one cannot change the past, medical mediation has a particularly challenging remit. However, understanding past events can lead to a new view of the present and the future.

Case examples

Bereavement

In this case the patient had died and his widow brought the complaint. She came to the conciliation meeting accompanied by her sister-in-law. There were three doctors involved and all came to the meeting held in a small conference room at the surgery.

After making the introductions and explaining the process for the meeting, the conciliator asked the complainant to talk about what had happened, and asked the doctors to listen to her without interruption. They would each be given an opportunity to speak.

The complainant described her husband's distress, leading to depression as he discovered that his business partner had been cheating him. The business was failing. His anxiety about that and the strong feelings against his partner became totally preoccupying. She encouraged him to see one of the doctors, who prescribed some tablets. Things got worse; he sometimes lost control and cried or shouted. She became more and more frightened. Another doctor saw him and had different views about suitable medication. There was a mix-up over the number of tablets prescribed over a bank holiday weekend. He may have taken too many. Anyway, his supply ran out.

There was an urgent call to the surgery and a third doctor became involved. Then, after a particularly bad night, her husband said he was feeling much better and was going out to get a paper. He came back looking calm and his wife did not try to dissuade him when he said he wanted to go out again for a short walk.

He never returned. His body was found at the bottom of a cliff near their home.

The complainant and her sister-in-law were very upset and very angry with the doctors for 'letting him kill himself', for not liaising with each other, for going on holiday at the wrong moment and for not believing her when she tried to describe how her husband was behaving when they were not there.

The doctors listened. They were restrained from interrupting when she said accusatory things. One doctor had a tear in his eye. She noticed it and softened her tone. When she faltered in her story the conciliator prompted her or summarised what she had said, so that she could continue.

Then each of the doctors was invited to speak. They were sorry her husband had died. They apologised for specific things that might have been done differently and noted others which, with hindsight, could have been dealt with better. The conciliator kept the complainant and her sister-in-law from interrupting here.

Gradually the atmosphere changed. Both parties began to ask questions for clarification and further knowledge. The conciliator facilitated these exchanges and fielded the sister-in-law's retrogressive interventions. The others moved to rebuilding a composite 'story' of what they were going to remember. Then came the moment when the complainant said she didn't blame them any more – she blamed herself for letting her husband go out that last morning. One of the doctors took this up and assured her that she could not have known what was going on in her husband's head, nor minded him like a child.

The meeting ended with a new understanding between the complainant and the three doctors, and with the complainant beginning to persuade her hard-line sister-in-law that she had received a full response and her husband's death was nobody's fault.

A case where correspondence failed to resolve what mattered

A man in his early forties made an appointment with his doctor because he was experiencing blurred vision. The doctor examined him and told him he had 'perfect eyesight'. Two days later he suffered a detached retina. He had two operations and was left with restricted vision and was unable to return to his usual work. When he made a complaint, the doctor wrote that, as far as she could tell, his eyes were normal at the time of her examination; a retinal tear could happen very suddenly and must have occurred some time later. He was not willing to accept this explanation and took his complaint to the health authority. The convenor referred it back for a further attempt at resolution at practice level, this time with a conciliator.

At the meeting the complainant was able to show his distress and describe his loss to the doctor. Several concerns were addressed. It emerged that what he particularly wanted and, with assistance from the conciliator, eventually got from the doctor, was a sincere apology for using the expression 'perfect eyesight' when 'normal at examination' would have been more acceptable. This resolution shows how a face-to-face exchange can reach subtle levels of communication that most written correspondence between complainants and doctors fails to achieve.

Appointment of conciliators and their terms of reference

The directions to health authorities state that every health authority shall make arrangements to provide conciliation services and, after consultation with the relevant local representative committee of practitioners, appoint conciliators. Family health service practitioners and nurses, midwives and health visitors past or present are excluded from being appointed as conciliators for reasons of confidentiality. There appears to be a wide variation concerning who is appointed and what, or whether, they are paid. Likewise there are differences in provision of training, support and supervision. People are selected because they already have relevant skills, and mediators trained in another field are increasingly showing an interest in medical mediation. Each authority has drawn up its own terms of reference for contracting its conciliators.

Complaints within NHS trusts

While the government's directions oblige health authorities to provide a conciliation service for primary healthcare complaints, there is no such requirement for NHS trusts, which run the hospitals and community services. Those responsible for managing complaints within secondary healthcare are mostly resistant to the idea of involving a neutral outsider trained in conciliation. Traditionally, patients have always had greater direct access to GPs and involvement in treatment questions at primary level. One viewpoint was explained to me as follows.

> I am not in favour of conciliation. In our hospital we offer the patient who has a complaint a face-to-face meeting with the consultant. A written summary of the meeting is sent to the patient as people remember only 20 per cent of what is said to them. A member of staff may be brought in to facilitate a second meeting if the first one doesn't resolve the matter.
>
> The most frequent problem is excessively high expectations patients have been led to have of a consultation that lasts 5–10 minutes. Patients are naïve in not realising some treatments fail and are ignorant of the percentage success rates.

He assured me that complaints are quite adequately dealt with in this way and people are usually satisfied. He knew of other hospital trusts which did not offer face-to-face meetings and these, in his view, provided a less satisfactory procedure. I have doubts both about some consultants' ability to communicate effectively in such meetings and patients being able to express their concerns adequately. Another person told me:

> There is no real opportunity for conciliation as most complaints about hospital-based treatment are clinical matters, and dealt with by clinicians internally or, if that fails, externally by involving a consultant from another region.

I find this a rather restricted view of the nature of complaints.

Mediation in clinical negligence cases

Over the last few years, mediation has been introduced to help resolve cases of clinical negligence, where there are insurance claims for such things as operations that have gone wrong. Mediation in these cases can cut down the time and expense of long drawn-out legal proceedings.

In the High Court in London, parties involved in clinical negligence claims must now state whether alternative dispute resolution (ADR) has been considered and if not, why not; and if ADR has been considered but rejected, why this is so. ADR is not a panacea for the ills of increasing medico-legal claims, but it is a true alternative. ADR may also expand as more clients begin to ask for it.

Conclusion

It has not yet been possible to achieve a meaningful assessment of the use and effectiveness of conciliation in the practice-based complaints procedure. Health authorities could encourage take-up by offering opportunities for exploring how conciliation works, such as by arranging meetings with conciliators for practice managers and practitioners, community health councils and patient associations. Practices where conciliation has been tried and found to be effective are the best advocates. If, as it seems to many doctors and dentists, their patients are criticising them more frequently and more vocally than in the past, there will be greater scope for using conciliation, but it needs to be seen to be quick, effective and unbiased. Complainants will accept conciliation for the same reasons if it also achieves the outcomes they want. As its scope covers relationships, emotions, expectations and needs, it can be said to be an holistic approach. There seems no justifiable reason why access to conciliation services should not be extended to NHS trusts and secondary healthcare.

We may confidently expect mediation to play an increasing part in the field of medical disputes.

Reference

NHS Executive (1996) *Practice-based Complaints Procedures*. London: Department of Health.

14

The Multicultural Elder Mediation Project (EMP)

EMPowerment for Older, Disabled and Mentally Frail Persons

Yvonne Craig

Introduction

This chapter is in three parts, with a brief introduction and conclusion. The first part describes the social context of the conflicts which can affect older, disabled and mentally frail persons, where mediation can be a positive process promoting helpful healing in relationships and situations.

The second section discusses the development of the multicultural Elder Mediation Project (EMP) as a self-help group providing relevant services, its origin in the social context of the national voluntary organisation, Mediation UK, and its wider diffusion through networking with multidisciplinary agencies.

The third part has vignettes illustrating some of the different kinds of cases and diverse mediation processes with which EMP is concerned. The conclusion suggests that elder mediation has the potential for making a valuable contribution to the welfare of those who suffer from social conflicts associated with their ageing, disabilities and mental frailties.

The social context

Old people are living longer. Soon we shall be 25 per cent of the population. This is why I, in my seventies, and other older members of Mediation UK, felt that we should start EMP. There will be increasing numbers of very old people, more reaching 100 years, and a greater number of physically and mentally disabled persons, many being dependent on others. Although the values of this chapter subscribe to the view that every individual is unique, as are the special needs of different groups, so that stereotyping is wrong, nevertheless they share common problems.

Older people are vulnerable to negative discrimination in the form of ageism, and what is awkwardly called disablism and mentalism. This is because, like culturally diverse communities facing racism, the majority are poor, marginalised and suffer from inequitably shared resources of the competitive infrastructure. However, no groups are homogeneous, and there are rich and middle-class people among us.

Through struggling, many people overcome disadvantages, affirm rights and responsibilities and develop potential in positive, inspiring ways which enrich personal lives and society. Mediation can empower people in achieving self-realisation and in coping with social conflicts.

Although, increasingly, older and disabled people live independent, active and often separate lives, many are looked after by families or in institutions. Social conflicts arise in all these situations.

When living alone, we are vulnerable to community conflicts arising from problems with neighbours, especially in small flats of crowded tenements, where well-meaning social and housing workers sandwich us between families with young children or people with alcohol problems. Ironically, they hope that elderly people can be wise old mediators (which we often are), although some call in community mediation service volunteers when midnight raves prevent sleep.

Older people can also cause conflict. We may irritably impose our opinions on younger generations and make life a misery for them by constant complaints. As we lose control of our physical senses, we bolster our sense of self by trying to control others.

Living with our families can be a blessing or a burden to them. Conflict is likely when there is inadequate privacy; poor families suffering especially in crowded rooms. If we are incontinent or incompetent, carers often dispute about whether we should go into institutions. Families may break up through carer conflicts.

Institutions are generally staffed by devoted workers who make residents feel valued. Yet too often staff are overworked, underpaid and inadequately trained for demanding duties. Residents resent and react negatively if they suspect neglect. Some fight depressing powerlessness by tyrannising everyone. Conflicts occur with staff and relatives. In such sensitive situations, blaming and judgement is inappropriate. All involved need to improve relationships and issues in practical, problem-solving ways before conflicts escalate into abuse or breakdown, from which residents or staff can suffer.

However, older, disabled and mentally frail people have special rights to protection from negative discrimination and abuse, as do children, sick and other vulnerable people. Hence it is important that everyone is aware of rights of access to the authorities, law and police, if conflicts become uncontrollably harmful.

Nevertheless, mediation enables people to confront conflict constructively and early, thus developing its healing potential. It was through awareness of the social context of conflicts involving older, disabled and mentally frail persons that the multicultural Elder Mediation Project (EMP) was formed in 1991.

EMP's work

Some committee members of Mediation UK were older persons. Its secretary was a retiring senior probation officer, who had pioneered victim–offender mediation, and was also an Anglican priest and chaplain to an old people's home, often mediating there. Another committee member, a lawyer in his seventies, with disabilities, had written the constitution for his local community mediation service. A Barbadian elder and a Karachi Muslim also wanted to start EMP.

As a retired social worker, counsellor and magistrate, I knew that mediation could fill gaps for inadequate relevant social services, so I offered to co-ordinate EMP voluntarily. One aim was to be a special interest area of Mediation UK, becoming financially self-supporting while offering free training to its members and other organisations interested in developing similar services.

Our workshops for Mediation UK's community mediation services were always co-designed with them to fit their needs, and our role-play scenarios focused on situations which they met in their work. We always began by asking the circle of participants to share their hopes and fears of ageing, and then went on to sensory exercises which enabled them to simulate experiences of being blind, deaf, dizzy, disabled, and so on. One of our volunteers was experienced in photography and video work, so he made a video of the whole or part of the workshop for group evaluation, and then gave it to the co-ordinator of the service to use for further training. He would also offer to photograph participants for their own personal or publicity purposes. Needless to say, their permission was given for both these processes, as the videos were never shown publicly. We also had available an excellent video from the USA of three cases of mediation, one in a sheltered housing complex, another in a hospital and the third in a community mediation service room.

EMP's acronym was chosen to show that we sought to empower others, not empire-build our own project, by freely sharing our knowledge and experience with other mediators and professionals from many disciplines. EMP was academically termed a 'social diffusion project', spreading understanding and skills widely, without acquiring separate status. We gave presentations and workshops to national and international conferences, publishing books and articles and networking information. We gave workshops to old people's clubs, including Afro-Caribbean and Asian ones, encouraging people in managing their own conflicts, while describing conflicts where community mediation services or EMP could help. We reminded people of their rights to protection from abuse and violence, through contacting the authorities, lawyers or police.

EMP also responded to cries for help from individuals without nearby community mediation services, although we always checked to see if these were available for referral. Sometimes community mediation service co-ordinators consulted with us about their difficult cases involving older people, or asked if we could supply a volunteer to act as a co-mediator with one of their members. At the same time, we were all members of our own local mediation services, where we were often asked to work on cases involving older people, although we also mediated in general cases.

We raised £4000 of charitable funding between 1991 and 1998, holding many workshops for old and disabled people and for community mediation services, while hundreds of workers from various disciplines attended other workshops and presentations.

Practical experience encouraged me to develop theories about the possibility that early resolution of conflict could contribute to the prevention of elder abuse, from which 4 per cent of elders suffered. I was given university and additional grants for my doctorate on this.

EMP's ideas diffused into Age Concern's Advisory, Information and Mediation Service for retirement housing (AIMS), managed by a legally trained enthusiast for mediation who affiliated to Mediation UK. I became their voluntary consultant and mediator. I also mediated small and large group conflicts involving older people, but failed to impact the disability movement whose younger members understandably preferred advocacy: fighting for rights which the 1996 Disability Discrimination Act had not made enforceable. It appears to be the older disabled people, who cannot be as active as the young, who prefer the gentler processes of mediation. However, it is to be hoped that the activists will see the advantage of increasing their negotiation skills through mediation, as it was on these that we laid emphasis when offering disability groups a suggested workshop programme.

EMP's work, on tiny budgets, was possible only because it was run from my home, with volunteers paid minimal expenses, although Mediation UK gave moral support. In five years, we gave over 30 workshops, presentations and contributions to conferences, with many articles in publications, chapters in books (two of which I edited) and a book of my own, all listed in the references. I also mediated about 50 cases involving older people; the work of our other volunteers is recorded by their own community mediation services. EMP's future is uncharted, as volunteers are ageing, with disabilities increasing. We always stress that we shall be delighted to transfer the work to any group sympathetic to EMP's aims, who will incorporate them into its own. This chapter now turns to the case studies (anonymised) of EMP's work.

Case examples

It should be stressed that mediation is not the perfect process solving all problems. Mediation, like advocacy and counselling, can fail. It can be refused, tried in-appropriately or provide only short-term remedies while long-term difficulties remain. It is a human social process, involving ordinary individuals at different stages of personal and professional development.

Nevertheless, mediation, often the last social process tried, at least begins to help people to respect each other, communicate together and realise that they share problems which seldom go away unless some kind of mutual readjustment is made. Mediation enables them to begin what may be lifetime learning experiences in developing interpersonal relationships.

Miss Molly and Ms Sue

This case was referred from a community mediation service. Many conflicts arise because of noise and this case is an example of the kind often dealt with by community mediation services, although untypical in that it concerns two people living in an expensive mansion block, in adjacent flats. The rooms were spacious, but the soundproofing was poor.

Miss Molly was a retired teacher in her eighties who had lived there for 15 years. Ms Sue was a young single woman who had just arrived. At first the two neighbours exchanged daily welcoming greetings as educated people, both having university degrees, but then Ms Sue began to put letters through Miss Molly's door complaining of her TV noise.

Miss Molly responded courteously saying that never in 15 years had any previous tenants next door or elsewhere in the block complained. She admitted that she wore a hearing aid and added that, due to her age and increasing physical disabilities, she was going out less and watching more TV. However, she said she would try to lessen the sound.

Later Sue agitatedly said she was trying to run a small business from her flat, insisting on more peace and quiet. What about mediation? Molly agreed. Mediation brought out the shock and hurt that Molly felt as a respected resident, now experiencing first-ever complaints. She expressed anxieties about her future lifestyle being challenged: she would feel guilty if she turned up the TV because she couldn't hear it properly. She relied on it for contact with world events.

Mediation equally encouraged Sue to share her anxieties about making daytime difficult for phone calls, and getting early night sleep. She admitted she was sensitive to sound, with insomnia problems.

Mediation acknowledged that both neighbours had rights as well as responsibilities in maintaining good relations and explored practical options. Could Sue, newly arrived, change her bedroom, which was next to Molly's TV wall? Sue would not agree, and Molly's TV furniture fitted nowhere else. Sue suggested ear-muffs for Molly, but Molly had an old TV and video without sockets. Then mediation encouraged both to discuss possibilities of fixing hours and levels of sound as a compromise.

Sue said she should not have to put up with any work disturbance. Molly responded that the property was only residential, and no businesses should be there. She had not complained about Sue breaching her contract, out of sympathy for young career people, but felt that because Sue was not out at an office, like other young residents, her demands for perfect peace were unfair. Molly felt no responsibility for enabling Sue to conduct her business next door in sterile conditions.

Molly added that she had never complained about anyone else in the block, over the years, despite the fact that there had been noisy children, late-night parties and loud quarrelling. Sue should try practising neighbourly tolerance too. Sue was silent, re-evaluating her position. Molly then made the practical offer that she would only watch TV for two to three hours after lunch, and then between 8 pm and 11 pm at night, a maximum of four to six hours per day. She would use teletext screen subtitles, when available, turn the sound as low as possible, and certainly not watch late-night TV.

In return, would Sue stop complaining? Sue readily agreed, and apologised for any unintentional effects her business had on Molly, hoping eventually to move it elsewhere.

Molly replied that she valued Sue as a hard-working young neighbour and hoped they would become real friends. Sue smiled happily as they shook hands.

This is a good example of intergenerational face-to-face mediation succeeding in helping people with different lifestyles to readjust problem situations, and reconcile diverse needs. Had the conflict not been addressed at an early stage by mediation, it could have escalated into a more painful public row in which the landlords, caretakers and other residents became involved in situations jeopardising the neighbours' reputations.

This happened in the next case described, involving shuttle mediation, which required acting as a go-between with people who did not want face-to-face mediation.

Mrs Smith and Mrs Brown

In this case, one of Mediation UK's affiliated community mediation services asked EMP to work with them on a sheltered housing conflict referred by their local authority which owned it. It was agreed that the EMP volunteer and their co-mediator should consult with the relevant staff at a local authority case conference.

The sheltered housing warden said she was on the verge of a nervous breakdown resulting from the recent arrival of Mrs Smith, an 85-year-old resident who was terrorising everyone. The co-mediators listened for over an hour while the warden and her line managers described the situation. The warden cried as she related that she had a child with learning disabilities who was verbally abused and ridiculed by Mrs Smith, who also made unpleasant remarks about the warden's partner who lived with her there. She added that sometimes Mrs Smith went to the other extreme and tried to fondle her intimately and unacceptably.

The warden then focused on the main issue for which she wanted mediation: Mrs Smith's abuse of Mrs Brown, a wheelchair-bound, 75-year-old resident who was chair of the residents' association. The warden added that she did not want to be included in the mediation, and her line managers stressed that their urgent concern was to deal with the conflict between their two old residents, which had spoilt the peace of everyone else and could potentially erupt into a public scandal.

The co-mediators and their co-ordinator responded by feeding back what they had heard to check on the accuracy of their understanding, and then explained the process and possibilities of mediation, as well as its limitations. As both old ladies had already agreed to the mediation, it was arranged that the co-mediators should start by visiting each in turn as soon as possible.

They visited Mrs Brown first, as it was she who had complained about Mrs Smith's attacks. Mrs Brown tearfully described her wheelchair restrictions, but said that she had always put her concern for others first, and had tried to forget her troubles through all the work she did over the years for the residents' association. As a result, residents came to her with their own troubles and were grateful for all the activities she organised for them.

However, she said Mrs Smith was jealous of all this and verbally abused her in front of everyone, calling her a busybody, an interferer, a 'bossy boots', and 'a pain in the arse'. On more than one occasion she said Mrs Smith had pushed her shoulder painfully, while shoving her wheelchair out of the way.

Mrs Brown felt her role was threatened by this newcomer. Just as Mrs Brown had lost her husband years earlier, now she felt she was losing the work that filled the rest of her life. She only wanted to help people, not be a source of conflict and misery.

The co-mediators then visited Mrs Smith, who was also distressed at being labelled a troublemaker. She explained that she understood it was the warden's job to arrange all the social activities for residents. She thought there was corruption and connivance going on, with Mrs. Brown being given the power to do this, so that the warden could spend time with her child and partner.

Mediators do not advise, but can correct misinformation. They explained to Mrs Smith that modern good management of sheltered housing encouraged residents rather than staff to arrange their own activities where possible. So, as Mrs Brown had been democratically elected, neither she nor the warden had done anything wrong which could merit complaint.

Mrs Smith became quiet, and then spoke about her own troubles. Her son had committed suicide and she had also made an attempt, which resulted in her being admitted to a psychiatric hospital. There she had been told she suffered from chronic depression and was given assertiveness training. When she was eventually transferred to the sheltered housing flat, she decided that she would start as she meant to go on by being assertive. She was not going to let anyone boss her around.

The co-mediators listened empathically to this now rather sad and isolated old lady, who obviously had suffered great loneliness and whose behaviour, ironically, was now contributing to her problems. They asked her if she would 'put on Mrs Brown's shoes' to understand her feelings about this assertiveness. Mrs Smith acknowledged that Mrs Brown probably didn't like it. Mrs Smith was then helped to develop insight into realising that assertiveness can sometimes be perceived as aggression. She gradually accepted that this was what had probably happened with Mrs Brown.

Mrs Smith then said she was worried that she might be transferred elsewhere, as a result of Mrs Brown's complaints, and asked if these would be withdrawn if she kept out of Mrs Brown's way. However, she adamantly refused to meet face to face with Mrs Brown, apologise, or shake her hand. In view of Mrs Smith's history of mental ill health, we felt it would be ethically wrong for us to spell out the advantages of a meeting, as we might have done in less sensitive circumstances. We said we would call again on Mrs Brown, if we had Mrs Smith's permission to pass on her offer of reconciliation.

This was given and we visited Mrs Brown, who was relieved to hear of Mrs. Smith's promise and readily agreed to sign an agreement withdrawing her complaints. In turn, she asked us to deliver a message to Mrs Smith, assuring her that she was always ready to be friendly and helpful, which we then relayed.

The local authority and its warden were pleased with the agreement. Although the co-mediators wondered whether the conflict might erupt again in the 'complaint culture' atmosphere that even the most amiable sheltered housing residents can sometimes generate in their cloistered and close dwellings, the only report received by their co-ordinator three months later was that peace and serenity still reigned.

Mrs Jones, her relatives and the matron

Sometimes telephone mediation is the only immediate help EMP can offer when people live in distant rural areas inadequately resourced by all services.

The matron of a nursing home in rural Wales telephoned EMP about a 99-year-old patient in great distress because her relatives wanted to move her elsewhere. The matron suspected that financial abuse could be involved, as she thought the relatives might want to find a cheaper nursing home and that this, not Mrs Jones's welfare, was their only consideration.

The matron asked if she could be helped to mediate in the situation. It was pointed out that she could not be regarded as impartial or independent as, understandably, she had a commercial interest in keeping Mrs Jones as a patient.

However EMP could offer telephone mediation if the relatives and Mrs Jones consented, provided she had the mental capacity to cope with it. Matron responded that Mrs Jones was mentally active, although she had voluntarily given her relatives Enduring Powers of Attorney (EPA) so that they could be responsible for paying her nursing home bills.

Those involved agreed to the offer and telephone contact was immediately made with Mrs Jones, explaining mediation simply, and then listening to her wishes about staying in her present nursing home. She was quite firm that she was very happy and wished to end her days there.

The relatives were represented by a nephew who said that the reason why they wanted to move Mrs Jones was so that she could be nearer them and they could visit more often. They found the present travelling long and expensive. They also felt that, as they had EPA powers, this gave them the authority to make any necessary transfer decisions.

They were surprised to be given information about their responsibilities not to go against Mrs Jones's decisions while she was competent to make them and while she had sufficient money in her accounts. It was also mentioned that she had the right to legal advice if she felt she was being wrongly pressurised. However, it was agreed to make Mrs Jones aware of the cost and inconvenience to her relatives that resulted from the present arrangements.

Mrs Jones considered this and then offered to pay their travel costs and possibly overnight hotel accommodation out of her account, so as to remove the cause of their problems. The wise old lady added that, in future, she wanted to see her annual accounts, so that she herself could be the judge of her future arrangements.

The relatives agreed to this offer and Mrs Jones remained happily where she was. The matron later reported to EMP that mediation had provided a valuable third party presence, however invisible, in a situation where her patient's interests needed protecting. Nevertheless, mediation had also benefited the relatives, while reminding them of their legal accountability.

Conclusion

This chapter has shown that in the context of contemporary social conflicts, which can be particularly painful for older, disabled and mentally frail people, mediation can be an appropriate, gentle and healing process. EMP's work has provided another social resource for hard-pressed and inadequate statutory and voluntary agencies and, although it is very limited, its principles and practices can be diffused and absorbed by others. EMP also shows symbolically and practically the value of self-help activities in addressing the problems of peer groups.

The three case examples illustrate some of the processes which EMP uses in its work and how it co-operates with others. There is a basic focus on its educational aspect, which is to encourage people to develop their natural abilities in peacemaking, empower them to manage their conflicts themselves if possible, and to seek mediation or legal help when necessary.

A valedictory comment from a community mediation service co-ordinator closes this chapter: 'The good work that EMP did with us has been publicised by our local authorities, and we have since had a 40 per cent increase of relevant referrals resulting from this.'

Further reading

Acland, A. (1990) *A Sudden Outburst of Common Sense*. London: Hutchinson.

Biggs, S. (1993) *Understanding Ageing*. Milton Keynes: Open University Press.

Blakemore, K. and Boneham, M. (1994) *Age, Race and Ethnicity*. Milton Keynes: Open University Press.

Craig, Y. (1997) *Elder Abuse and Mediation*. Aldershot: Avebury.

Craig, Y. (ed.) (1997) *Changes and Challenges in Later Life*. London: Third Age Press.

Craig, Y. (ed.) (1998) *Advocacy, Counselling and Mediation in Casework*. London: Jessica Kingsley Publishers.

Goldsmith, M. (1996) *Hearing the Voice of People with Dementia*. London: Jessica Kingsley Publishers.

Greengross, S. (1986) *The Law and Vulnerable Elderly People*. London: Age Concern.

Hoggett, B. (1993) *Mentally Incapacitated and Other Vulnerable Adults*. London: HMSO.

Oliver, M. (1990) *The Politics of Disablement*. London: Macmillan.

Phillipson, C. and Walker, A. (eds) (1986) *Ageing and Social Policy*. Aldershot: Gower.

Tinker, A. (1992) *Elderly People in Modern Society*. London: Longman.

15

Consensus Building
and Environmental Decision Making
Roger Sidaway and Hally Ingram

Problems in environmental decision making

Environmental decision making contains the classic ingredients of conflict: misunderstanding through lack of information or poor communication; competing interests of development and conservation; and diametrically opposed beliefs and value systems. The complexity of environmental issues has long been recognised, but the main emphasis in decision making has been on a rational scientific approach, which stresses the importance of marshalling information and neglects the human dimension. Communication problems are exacerbated by the adversarial style usually adopted when presenting evidence at public inquiries, to discredit witnesses and dismiss a rival case. These formal statutory procedures may protect the legal rights of interested parties, but access to them may be limited by lack of expertise or financial resources. Such procedures also tend to arbitrate in favour of one party at the expense of others, without concern for future relationships. Arguably they do not actually resolve conflicts.

The other major weakness in traditional environmental decision making concerns the inadequacy of consultation procedures – commonly 'too little and too late' – which at best appear tokenistic and at worst lead to mounting public frustration and political protests over road building or waste disposal schemes. All too often public officials present only one option, their preferred solution, leaving little opportunity for genuine public participation. The main elements which distinguish environmental from interpersonal disputes are:

- their *multi-party* nature: even though the interested parties may be organised into representative groups, it is quite common for 50 or more groups to be interested at varying levels of involvement;

- their *complexity*: frequently a range of public policy issues are in contention, compounded by differences in national and local perspectives within each interest, together with related issues of power.

Approaches to conflict resolution

Although there are marked differences in the legal, political and administrative systems in Britain and the USA, the North American approach to alternative dispute resolution (ADR) has attracted considerable British interest. One of the main ADR processes is mediation, which is negotiation assisted by a neutral third party. The attraction of mediation lies in its ability to identify and recognise the interests of disputing parties, offering them greater control over the outcome (and hence less risk) than the generally more costly option, legal action in the courts.

Mediation depends on consensus-building principles and, as illustrated in other chapters, has been used to resolve disputes over business contracts, between neighbours, in divorce proceedings and labour relations. The use of mediation in actually resolving environmental disputes in Britain is still fairly limited, although consensus-building principles are being applied to prevent environmental disputes. This chapter will describe how these principles are being used, before considering the barriers to their wider application and ways to develop better practice.

The concepts of consensus building

Most people are familiar with voting to reach a group decision. But voting favours the greater number or the strongest grouping, while a compromise reached by one or both sides making concessions suggests a midway position that satisfies nobody. Both methods can be used to break a deadlock but, inevitably in an adversarial situation, one side gains while the other loses and is likely to feel aggrieved.

A consensus decision is reached by open discussion and is in effect a negotiation in which the parties devise a solution from which they all benefit (a win–win solution), rather than compromise and lose part of their interest to others. Consensus building has been described as 'a collaborative approach to making a decision in which the interested parties identify common ground and work voluntarily towards finding a mutually acceptable solution to a contentious problem' (Environment Council 1995).

The crucial distinctions between consensus building and other approaches concern:

- *the way in which decisions are reached*: decisions are reached by consent and each party holds the power of veto;

- *who is involved*: everyone with an interest, who is prepared to participate, is involved;

- *whether the process of decision making is deliberately constructed to achieve and maintain consensus*: this means in practice that the parties agree, in advance, procedures which build trust and secure fairness and openness in expression. The way in which they reach a decision becomes almost as important as the decision itself.

While the conventional British procedures of committee working depend on the roles of the chair (most often a male authority figure given a casting vote to break deadlock) and a secretary (often a 'fixer'), consensus building relies on equal contributions from the partners. This process is often aided by a neutral, independent party,[1] who concentrates on helping the group reach a decision. Although the differences in procedure may appear to be slight, they constitute a major shift in attitudes away from 'committee culture' to shared responsibility and the equalisation of power. It is only recently that the need has been recognised in Britain to design more inclusive processes of decision making.

However, consensus building is not a universal panacea. It has major advantages (as can be seen from Table 15.1), while most of its limitations can normally be overcome by a carefully designed process tailored to the specific situation.

Table 15.1 The pros and cons of consensus building

Advantages

- Increased understanding of the issues involved.
- The voluntary and less formal procedures allow the parties to explore the problem and consider a range of possible solutions.
- Improved relationships between the interested parties make it more likely that they trust each other and less likely that they disagree in the future.
- The interested parties have greater commitment to and control of the outcome.
- There are savings in time and money, over the longer term.

Limitations and constraints

- Deeply held beliefs are non-negotiable and may make consensus difficult to obtain.
- The interests of the less powerful may need to be safeguarded.
- Lack of formal organisation may preclude some interests from being represented in negotiations.
- Reaching consensus is time consuming and may be difficult to sustain over time.

Source: Sidaway (1998b)

---

1   The distinction is often made between a *facilitator* (who assists by suggesting procedures to establish and conduct a dialogue) and a *mediator* (who facilitates but also, with the agreement of the disputing parties, takes a more active role in brokering negotiations), but the boundaries between these roles are frequently blurred. Facilitator is used to cover both roles in this chapter as it is the term most commonly used in this context in Britain.

In summary, if consensus building is to be effective, decision making must be seen as legitimate, balanced and open. This means that:

- the interested parties must participate directly or decision makers must be accountable;
- involvement must be early, with all parties having a say in the terms of reference and agenda;
- statutory responsibilities must be recognised, yet discussions must have real influence on official decisions;
- information must be freely available to all parties.

Table 15.2 Conditions for consensus in decision making

Terms of reference and agenda
- Is there agreement on the purpose and form of the exercise?

Communities and representation
- Are all the relevant communities of interest represented?
- Is the representation of interests evenly balanced at each level of decision making?

Accountability of representatives
- How accountable are the representatives to their interest groups?

Authority and power in decision making
- Who holds the power to determine and/or execute decisions and do they welcome participation?
- Has authority been delegated to the group to influence or determine policy?
- What is the relative power between the partners? Is power perceived to be evenly balanced between them?

Information
- Is information freely available to all interests?
- Has information been gathered by independent sources?
- Is the information coverage of issues evenly balanced?

Openness of and involvement in decision making
- Are all phases of the process open to all interest groups?
- What is their degree of involvement in each phase?
- Is the agenda balanced to cover the full range of issues or is it pre-empted by a policy or proposition made by powerful interests?

Sources: Bryden *et al.* 1997; Sidaway and van der Voet 1993.

These key points form a set of conditions (set out in Table 15.2) which can be used to evaluate whether a process of decision making encourages and permits consensus building.

How consensus building works in practice

All too often traditional decision making displays the following flaws:

- The stages of decision making are improvised rather than being set out and agreed in advance.
- Public involvement is not integrated into each stage of decision making.
- There are no clear objectives for involvement at each stage.
- Individual techniques are used, virtually at random, rather than systematically selecting a combination of techniques at each stage that are most appropriate to the situation.

These problems can be overcome by a carefully designed consensus-building process, preferably using the skills of an experienced facilitator who works openly with all the parties involved. The process needs to take into account the conditions set out in Table 15.2 as these apply to both conflict prevention and conflict resolution. Perhaps the main distinction between these two situations is that planning exercises, at least in the early stages, tend to be more creative and positive, with the potential to prevent conflict. Active conflicts, on the other hand, frequently carry a history of events which has soured relations, making direct discussions about resolution difficult to initiate. The role of 'honest broker' is crucial when there is a high degree of conflict, and that role requires experience of how to make a careful and dispassionate assessment of the situation, how to maintain neutrality and how to gain trust. Complex environmental problems usually require a major commitment of time and expertise on the part of a facilitator (or team of facilitators) and it is unlikely that this can be done on a voluntary basis. Ideally, the cost of the exercise is borne by all the parties to emphasise the facilitator's neutrality. Whether the process is applied to conflict prevention or resolution, it follows three stages:

1. *Preparation* – to establish the form participation should take.

2. *Participation* – to obtain agreement.

3. *Implementation* – to implement a plan or agreement and review progress.

As in many other walks of life the importance of thorough preparation cannot be over-emphasised. To ensure that participation leads to consensus, careful thought has to be given in the preparation stage to:

- having clear *aims* for the exercise;
- identifying the *level of involvement* desired by the interested parties, e.g. discovering who wants to know about, influence or be party to a development decision;

- the *timing* of their involvement throughout the entire process from the initial stages to implementation;
- using the most *effective techniques* to secure their involvement.

Clarifying the aims of participation

In a consensus-building exercise, the initiating organisation needs to be clear about its intentions, exactly why it is seeking participation and how this links into existing responsibilities for decision making. It needs to establish the extent to which participation will influence the final decision. Agencies with statutory responsibilities may be restricted in this respect, in which case the other parties need to understand why the agency is seeking participation.

Assessing who wants be involved

A successful consensus-building exercise depends on the accurate identification of stakeholders; their issues and concerns and why their participation is desirable or even essential. Some interest groups may appear to be peripheral, but they may be able to stop things happening (i.e. they may have 'veto power'). One of the facilitator's tasks is to ensure, early in the process, that no significant interests or stakeholders are isolated and ignored. The number of stakeholders may be relatively small in a conflict resolution exercise but a wider range of community interests is likely to be concerned in conflict prevention. While many communities have activists, it is not always clear whom they represent. They may be well qualified to articulate the views of their interest group but there are often other viewpoints that are not heard. A consensus-building exercise needs to identify these views and find ways of representing them. Criteria for identifying stakeholders are set out in Figure 15.1.

Stakeholders have an interest in what happens, because they will be affected by the outcome or can have some influence over it. Stakeholders should be identified by asking:

- Who will benefit from the proposals?
- Who may be adversely affected?
- Who may help, or may delay and hinder the initiative?
- Who has skills, money or resources they can contribute?
- Who ultimately is in a position to decide if this goes ahead or not?

Source: Wilcox (1994)

Figure 15.1 Stakeholder analysis

The size of a negotiating group can be another crucial consideration. There is a tendency for the major players to press for a small group on the grounds that this eases negotiation. While this is true, there is always the danger that someone – an individual or organisation – who is excluded from the negotiations may exercise veto power at a later stage, e.g. initiate legal proceedings to overturn an agreement. One option is to establish a large inclusive forum, which then agrees that separate aspects of the dispute or its solution are negotiated by subgroups and referred back to the forum for ratification.

Identifying the desired level and timing of involvement

The other assessment that can clarify both the desired level and timing of involvement is to locate the stakeholders on a 'ladder of participation'. The 'ladder' (shown in simplified form in column 1 of Table 15.3) helps to understand who may want to be involved at each stage, remembering that the 'rungs of the ladder' probably overlap rather than form discrete steps. Some people may be content to be informed about what is happening rather than become more fully involved. They may want to contribute to a greater degree at specific stages but not at others. That should be their decision. Others may wish to play a more central role throughout. It is vital that stakeholders play a consistent role and there is continuity of representation throughout the process.

How to select the most effective techniques to secure appropriate involvement

Once the appropriate level of involvement has been identified for the various stakeholders, careful consideration should be given to the selection of appropriate techniques to obtain their involvement. A wide range of techniques is available to inform, obtain the views of, consult with and involve interested parties. A brief indication of the techniques that may be considered for different purposes is set out in Table 15.3. Generally speaking, techniques that encourage direct contact are more effective at higher levels of participation.[2] Where the resources are available, a combination of techniques is more likely to be effective than one technique used on its own, in encouraging participation by different types of stakeholder and ensuring that particular groups are not excluded from the process.

---

2   More sophisticated versions of the ladder of participation, together with more detailed assessments of participatory techniques, are to be found in a number of handbooks, such as Agyeman (1996); Department of the Environment, Transport and the Regions (1997); World Bank (1996).

Table 15.3 The range of participatory techniques

Purpose of involvement (level of participation)	Techniques to consider
Acting together: deciding on and forming partnerships to carry out strategies	Joint working groups Advisory groups Facilitated workshops
Developing advice: providing ideas before a joint decision is made	Facilitated workshops Participatory appraisal Face-to-face meetings, interviews
Consultation: offering options and requesting feedback	Face-to-face meetings and interviews Facilitated workshops Staffed exhibits Reports Social surveys

Source: Sidaway (1998b)

The participation and implementation stages

Ground rules for participation, agreed in advance, are necessary to ensure that:

- everyone's views are respected;
- everyone has equal access to information;
- rules for confidentiality or disclosure are established;
- representatives' obligations are clearly understood.

Indeed, representatives need to feed back information to their parent organisation and to make its views known. Otherwise there is a risk that the representative agrees to a course of action without consulting the organisation, which is then not committed to the agreement.

As well as providing procedural assistance, the role of the facilitator is to convene discussions which will improve communication between the parties and help them build a constructive relationship. Inaugural meetings are concerned with exchanging information, understanding respective interests, building trust and agreeing a common goal, recognising that any group also has to agree the nature of the underlying or potential problem before attempting to develop a range of alternative solutions.

Information should be treated as a common resource at the outset. Much time can be wasted disputing the validity and relevance of data. The limitations of existing information should be revealed, and joint responsibility taken to fill essential gaps. As with the choice of facilitator, any technical expert brought in to assist has to be acceptable to the group as a whole.

In due course, the group has to agree the type and form its recommendations should take, and how they are to be implemented. When an agreement has been ratified by all the parties and possibly put in a legally binding form, it is important to have a system of monitoring to keep the agreement under review. This helps to maintain trust between the parties.

The range of potential consensus-building approaches: Case examples of current practice in Britain

As suggested earlier, the number of conscious attempts at environmental mediation have been limited in Britain, although many recent initiatives have moved towards collaborative decision making to prevent disputes. We have chosen three recent British case studies which include developing best practice. These cover the development of good practice guidelines for the renewable energy industry; the deliberate use of a participative approach in the decommissioning of the Brent Spar oil rig; and a mediated negotiation in the dispute over public access to privately owned moorlands in the Peak District National Park.

Good practice guidelines for the renewable energy industry

Although wind energy developers were not expecting that their plans to build wind farms would meet a lot of opposition, they were proved wrong. A number of conflicts arose between developers and local communities, with the latter drawing support from national environmental groups concerned about the potential impacts of this new industry. The developers were surprised and even a little hurt, because they expected support from environmentalists who had been advocating the development of renewable energy resources for years. The problem lay in the limited opportunities for people to have a meaningful say in the process of change. Too often public consultation had taken place long after the project had taken shape and appeared to have gained an unstoppable momentum.

Through this experience, renewable energy developers became aware of the scrutiny under which this new 'green' industry operated and the need to be particularly sensitive in how it developed. As a result, wind energy developers, including the British Wind Energy Association, decided that good practice guidelines would help counteract their increasingly poor image, and would demonstrate their commitment to responsible and sensitive development. Despite initial misgivings on all sides, the guidelines were successfully produced with the input of a broad range of stakeholders, including opposition groups. As a result of this successful process, a series of good practice guidelines for a number of renewable energy technologies were produced, including wind energy, short rotation coppice and anaerobic digestion of farm, food processing and forestry residues for energy.

Each set of guidelines took nine months to produce and followed a similar innovative approach. The process was independently facilitated throughout and involved preparatory interviews with a wide range of stakeholders with an interest in the industry. An initial workshop was held to define the audience and framework for the guidelines, and to develop criteria for what they should include. The ground rules were agreed and it was made clear that participation did not necessarily lead to the endorsement of the guidelines. However, participants agreed to express their support for the process.

The initial workshop was followed by a series of small subgroup meetings to draft the various sections of the document. The key stakeholders who attended the first workshops then came back together for a final workshop to discuss, develop and finalise the final draft produced by the subgroups. Throughout the eight-month process draft material was written up by an editor, circulated for comment and amended by agreement.

A series of documents has been published since 1994 by the Energy Technology Support Unit (ETSU) on behalf of the Department of Trade and Industry. This official backing is very valuable, but even more important is the fact that the guidelines are 'owned' by all those who contributed. The logos of all organisations involved are printed inside the front cover of each book (over 30 organisations for each document). It is believed that the guidelines will play an important role in the development of an economically and environmentally sustainable renewable energy industry, which does not suffer from the conflicts and problems associated with the more well-established wind energy industry.

The decommissioning of the Brent Spar

The Brent Spar case provides a powerful example, as it shows how stakeholder involvement can help a company in its decision-making process when there has been intense public interest in its operations.

The Brent Spar is a floating storage buoy, which was based for many years in the Brent oilfields off Norway. When the buoy went out of service, Shell UK Exploration and Production (Shell Expro), which is responsible for its decommissioning, made a recommendation to the UK government on deep-sea disposal, based on thorough scientific analysis. There was limited consultation in making the decision, as it was not expected to generate a high level of public interest, and in 1995 the UK government approved the company's recommendation.

Greenpeace then waged a campaign that resulted in wide media coverage across Europe. Following the campaign and the resulting public outcry (particularly in Germany), Shell Expro decided to halt the deep-sea disposal plan and consider new options. The decision not to sink the Brent Spar in the summer of 1995 left the company with a problem that had to be resolved in an extremely transparent and open way.

This time Shell Expro wanted to be sure they made a widely acceptable decision. Learning of the process expertise of the Environment Council, they engaged the Council to design a dialogue which would ensure that Shell Expro heard the concerns of and suggestions from a wide variety of stakeholders. The process was designed to ensure it coincided with the technical decision-making process occurring in parallel within Shell Expro.

Following telephone interviews with many stakeholders, a launch workshop was planned for November 1996. Before the workshop Shell Expro invited tenders for the disposal of the

Brent Spar, resulting in 30 proposed solutions which were presented at the workshop. The aim was to present clear, concise information about the 30 options to a largely non-technical audience, and then maximise the opportunities for all participants to feed back their views.

The workshop was attended by over 60 people, including Greenpeace UK and Germany, Friends of the Earth Europe, the Institute of Marine Engineers and many other engineers, academics, environmentalists and consumer interests from around Europe. The facilitators set out to select a balanced group from the range of interested parties.

Following the launch workshop, Shell Expro took all the participants' comments, issues and suggestions, and used them to inform their short-listing process. Eleven proposals were short-listed and the relevant contractors were invited to work up detailed proposals. The short-listed proposals included: a training centre for personnel working offshore, a quay, a coastal defence scheme and disposal on-shore.

The dialogue process continued in 1997 in parallel with the technical decision-making process. Like many long-term projects, the dialogue process evolved and changed over time, in response to the needs of the participants. A series of facilitated workshops was held in the UK, Netherlands, Germany and Denmark, to hear the concerns and views of the stakeholders both within and outside the UK.

During the process Shell Expro heard many views, concerns and recommendations, which helped them inform their final recommendation to the UK government on the disposal of the Brent Spar. In January 1998, Shell announced their recommendation to the UK government, namely to reuse the Brent Spar to build a new quarry extension at Mekjarvik near Stavanger in Norway. Shell described in a press release the main lesson they had learnt:

We have learned that we must change the ways we identify and address issues, and interact with the societies we serve. Our way forward for the Brent Spar has helped to promote a different approach in Shell to making decisions, and has stimulated us in developing new ways of being more open and accountable.

Access management in the Peak District National Park by local consensus[3]

The dispute concerned the possible effects of public access to open country on grouse shooting and the breeding populations of upland waders. However, the Ramblers' Association contested whether the effects of recreational disturbance were seriously damaging, and has continued to press for further public access in the national park, while at the same time seeking national legislation for public access to uncultivated land (the so-called 'freedom to roam'). The dispute is further complicated by the expiry of the existing access agreements and their renegotiation, and the designation of the Dark Peak Moorlands as a Special Protection Area under EU environmental directives. In 1992, the Peak Park Joint Planning Board suggested the establishment of an Access Consultative Group (ACG) upon which the principal interests would be represented.

3   Based on Sidaway (1998a).

THE ESTABLISHMENT OF THE ACCESS CONSULTATIVE GROUP

The feasibility of establishing the ACG was investigated in a series of pre-negotiation meetings between an independent researcher and the individual stakeholders. The meetings considered whether the ACG should be established, what work it might undertake, its size and composition and the procedures under which it might operate. This phase of work concluded that there was support for establishing the group. Its remit would be to advise the Board on the mechanisms by which access might be managed. The preference was for the establishment of a small task force of nine members balanced so that three 'representatives' were drawn from each of the landowning, access and conservation interests. The group would be led by a neutral facilitator, and would hold monthly meetings over a period of six months, under a set of agreed procedures.

THE OPERATION OF THE ACCESS CONSULTATIVE GROUP

The ACG met on six occasions between September 1993 and June 1994. The later meetings of the group were concerned with preparing a report that could be agreed and submitted to the Board. The report set out the case for access management planning based on a series of underlying principles:

- *landowners', farmers' and occupiers' rights to manage the land were to be respected;*

- *a strategy should be developed to maintain critical wildlife populations;*

- *opportunities should be maximised to experience freedom on the moors;*

- *the relationships between access, moorland management and wildlife conservation were recognised;*

- *the interests of others were to be understood and respected.*

The key elements of the management strategy were:

- *a commitment to the preparation of local access management plans using a voluntary and collaborative approach;*

- *the agreement of a programme for the preparation of access management plans, linked to the renegotiation of access agreements and the search for voluntary agreements on new areas.*

REVIEW AND ASSESSMENT

The facilitator was required to assess the exercise and undertook a series of telephone interviews with members of the ACG in November 1994. Most members of the group felt that they had a better understanding of others' points of view and that a workable document had been prepared, which provided a basic framework for further negotiations. There were some reservations about whether basic conflicts had been addressed; whether trust had been established; and whether the management approach was sufficiently detailed.

Consensus building with an independent facilitator appears to have succeeded where conventional committee working might not have done. The strengths of the consensus-building approach were considered by the participants to be its inclusiveness, that it had been fair and that it had enabled personal relationships to develop. The main weakness was the apparently long time scale.

The size and composition of the group was seen to be appropriate, but there needed to be clearer arrangements about how other interested organisations could become involved. With hindsight, reporting back to member organisations was seen to be a crucial issue, particularly when the group's work took place over such a long period.

Although the process was undoubtedly time consuming, it is worth remembering that this was the first occasion in which representatives of all three interests had met and worked together. The ACG largely achieved the task that had been defined in the Access Strategy two years earlier. However, the recommendations have yet to be acted upon, as the Board subsequently concentrated on separate negotiations to reach agreement with landowners on the terms of new access agreements, while the Ramblers' Association has continued to press for access legislation. Such legislation is likely to include provision for local access forums, which could build on the experience of the ACG (DETR 1999).

Lessons from the case examples

The case examples illustrate many of the issues to be resolved before consensus can be obtained: the importance of neutrality and careful preparation to build trust; the difficulty of overcoming non-participatory traditions; and the need to consider alternative decision-making cultures. Indeed, to move from conflict to co-operation requires a change from an adversarial to a consensus-based form of decision making, and this requires a degree of trust between decision makers which takes time to develop. Agencies entering into a partnership or a negotiation have to be confident that their autonomy is not threatened. Those most lacking in such confidence seek to maintain control and exclude others. Public involvement in decision making is not an abdication but a sharing of responsibilities, with all the advantages that this brings. It has to be recognised that organisations have different yet equally legitimate agendas, and that they tend to be unequal in power and resources. The inhibitions of many organisations may be understandable, particularly if their efficiency is judged by the achievement of targets and performance indicators rather than the development of relationships and processes. There may be cases when, because of statutory responsibilities, some issues are not negotiable. There may be others where there is much more flexibility in interpreting an organisation's remit.

Some of these problems can be overcome by more carefully designed decision-making processes, bearing in mind the conditions of balance and openness identified earlier in this chapter (see Table 15.2). In some cases, the limitations of consensus building have to be recognised – it is not appropriate to every situation. Even the most carefully designed processes may fail, if the parties do not have sufficient incentive to work together or if there is a lack of senior commitment (Ingram 1997).

The way forward

Thus, there are many barriers to be overcome and techniques to be further developed, if consensus building is to be more widely applied in environmental decision making. There is considerable scope for the consolidation and dissemination of expertise and for ensuring that this is gained by officials through training and first-hand experience of initiating and sustaining collaborative processes. If consensus building is to be adopted as a more general practice on environmental issues, government and its agencies will need to offer leadership and guidance by disseminating good practice. The publication of advice by the Department of the Environment, Transport and the Regions (DETR 1997) and the Scottish Office (Sidaway 1998b) mark the first vital steps. The core areas for development are:

- undertaking research into those situations where current procedures act as barriers to consensus building;

- rigorously evaluating current projects to demonstrate good and bad practice, and disseminating the results widely;

- providing training and educational materials which raise understanding of the process and lead to the acquisition of key skills, and extending training opportunities.

References

Agyeman, J. (1996) *Involving Communities in Forestry through Community Participation*. Forestry Practice Guide 10. Edinburgh: Forestry Commission.

Bryden, J., Watson, D., Storey, C. and van Alphen, J. (1997) *Community Involvement and Rural Policy*. Edinburgh: Scottish Office Central Research Unit.

Department of the Environment, Transport and the Regions (DETR) (1997) *Involving Communities in Urban and Rural Regeneration – a Guide for Practitioners*. London: DETR.

Department of the Environment, Transport and the Regions (DETR) (1999) *Access to the Countryside in England and Wales: The Government's Framework for Action*. London: DETR.

Environment Council (1995) Memorandum to House of Commons Environment Committee. *Session 1994–5 Fourth Report: The Environmental Impact of Leisure Activities*, volume 3, Appendices. London: HMSO, pp.92–93.

Ingram, H. (1997) 'Experience in the United States of using collaborative processes to resolve environmental problems: a briefing for central government and agencies in the United Kingdom.' Winston Churchill Fellowship Working Paper. Unpublished.

Sidaway, R. (1998a) 'Access management by local consensus.' *Rights of Way Law Review 13*, 1, 7–12.

Sidaway, R. (1998b) *Good Practice in Rural Development No 5: Consensus Building*. Edinburgh: Scottish Office Central Research Unit.

Sidaway, R. and van der Voet, H. (1993) *Getting on Speaking Terms: Resolving Conflicts between Recreation and Nature in Coastal Zone Areas of the Netherlands, Literature Study and Case Study Analysis*. Centre for Recreation Report no. 23. Wageningen: Wageningen Agricultural University.

Wilcox, D. (1994) *The Guide to Effective Participation*. Brighton: Partnership Books.

World Bank (1996) *The World Bank Participation Sourcebook*. Washington DC: World Bank.

16

Mediation in Situations of Large-scale Violence

Adam Curle

Introduction

There was a time when simple-minded people like me believed that every type of malady could be cured by antibiotics. A few years ago I (and they) tended to think the same of mediation. In 1992 I attended a conference in Bratislava where a number of people from Eastern Europe approached me, stating that what was needed in that part of the world was mediation (I had written on that topic); how could more people be trained in mediation and sort things out, in what had recently been Yugoslavia and in other troubled or potentially troubled places in that region?

Now, several bitter years later, we all know better. Mediation has many uses, but it cannot solve every problem. It is one among a menu of peacemaking tools – and one which is still not understood everywhere. The first point, therefore, is that what is referred to as mediation, especially mediation in bitter and violent conflict, is very often nothing of the sort. The Dayton agreement that brought the war in Bosnia to an end was not mediation, but arm-twisting, the 'carrot and stick' method of mixing the 'carrot' of rewards and the 'stick' of sanctions or military pressure.

If mediation means anything, it is the action of a third party: on the small scale perhaps an individual; on the large scale a government or great international body such as the UN or one of its regional bodies. In either case the third party tries to help the protagonists to find a way out of the trap of violence. It is essentially a non-violent process; the Dayton negotiation was not.

In this chapter, we shall be concerned primarily with large-scale violence. But the violence of individuals on the one hand and states or guerrilla groups on the other have similarities. I have had experience of violence, both of full-scale war and of the across-the-fence hostilities of neighbours. The essence of both is a pot-pourri of negative emotions such as resentment, anger, hatred, suspicion, selfishness and guilt. The job of mediators, as impartial go-betweens, is to sort this out, to reduce the violence of feelings as well as actions, and to discuss the situation, clarifying any misunderstandings which might prove a stumbling block in negotiations. But there are cases when one side or both really want to go on fighting, and are not prepared to abandon hatred or dreams of total victory. Mediation must then be abandoned and give way to sterner measures.

The main difference between the two is, however, that large-scale violence is much more complex and has many more aspects; and that because people are being killed, the emotions involved are more desperate.

The role of mediators

Patterns of gender role die hard and it is unfortunately true that most large-scale, so-called political mediators are men. This is unfortunate, because experience shows that women do the job better than men. In the modern, if perhaps now moribund, type of patriarchal society, hierarchy is very significant to men. When men meet for the first time, they unconsciously assess each other's dominance: who outranks whom in terms of power, class, education, self-confidence, and so on. The ordinary male mediator immediately feels outranked by the minister, general or guerrilla leader he meets. His response will tend to be inwardly assertive – 'I'll show this guy I'm someone to be taken seriously'; or servile – 'I'll try to make a favourable impression.' Neither approach favours a relaxed relationship in which useful business is carried out.

The ordinary male minister, for his part, will normally be comfortably aware of his own more exalted position. Usually, of course, these prejudicial attitudes are modified by mutual understanding, respect and liking, though perhaps never quite eliminated. However, when women meet prominent men, or even prominent women, they seem to be seldom thus constrained, and are much more able to establish quickly a relationship based on common humanity rather than fancied status.

These issues may sound trivial, but they are not. A mediator must be persuasive, convincing and, above all, demonstrate good judgement and trustworthiness. There must be no barriers of doubt or suspicion. The leader (this word will henceforth be used to indicate the individual with whom the mediator most consistently deals – the president, guerrilla warlord, general, top civil servant, or other prominent person) must have great confidence in him. He must feel sure enough to reveal secrets, or indeed feelings, to the mediator that he would not to a journalist or perhaps a junior official. There must in fact be a measure of friendship between the two.

However, the very nature of the job may make this hard to achieve. A major reason is that the more the leader comes to like the mediator, the more he may become aware of an uncomfortable contradiction: this man for whom he feels warmth also has the same sort of relationship with his opposite number, his enemy. How can this be? Is the mediator's friendship truly genuine? Is it not perhaps a sham? A moment's tactlessness from the mediator may jeopardise the delicate relationship on which any progress towards peace depends.

There is sometimes an equally serious obstacle, but on the side of the mediator rather than the leader. The leader may have been responsible, directly or indirectly, for barbaric acts, or he may be implementing abhorrent policies. How can mediators develop a reasonable relationship with such men?

To start with, they must try to get to know more about them. People who have reached the top in turbulent situations have often had to fight against the oppression of a cruel regime. Perhaps in order to liberate their peoples they have acted brutally; but perhaps their own homes and families have also been destroyed by some tyrannical ruler. An example of this was Jomo Kenyatta, who became president of Kenya and a widely respected leader of the Commonwealth – but a man previously vilified as a drunkard, drug addict and terrorist. And how many of us might not long for vengeance against people who had tortured and killed our family? Even if we cannot identify any redeeming circumstances, we can – and should – consider the deep roots of our common humanity.

But perhaps it is even more important to consider that it is not the job of mediators to react to the morals or policies of leaders, except to the extent that they interfere with the peace process. Rather than becoming alienated from them, they should give up the luxury of moral obloquy and get on with the job of making peace, on which the health, happiness and lives of many thousands may depend.

It is good to remember that those with leadership responsibilities carry a great burden, and the higher the responsibility, the heavier the burden. Part of this burden is loneliness and tension. The strain of ultimate decision making is exacerbated by isolation. Sometimes leaders are surrounded by trusted lieutenants, but just as often there are factions among the followers. The leader himself can seldom be quite sure that one of his staff is not plotting a coup, even an assassination. He becomes tense, wary and suspicious. He may dismiss, imprison or even kill former favourites. He may be uncertain whether his staff or his generals are telling him the truth or lies – either to mislead, confuse so as to supersede him, curry favour or conceal their own blunders and failures.

In this sad isolation the leader may rely on a mediator, as someone completely uninvolved in the charade of disguised motives and hidden plots; someone who will tell the truth and to whom he can talk relatively freely without fearing that his words will be distorted and turned against him. It is a rather strange relationship, half intimate, half formal; the closer the relationship, the greater the mediator's freedom to express his own feelings.

There is one very important rule, however. The mediator must not give advice. To do so is to step dangerously out of the role of an impartial analyst. Even if his opinion is asked about some problem or situation, he must avoid a direct answer. It is not his business to say how a particular government or group should run its own business; that is solely their affair. On the other hand, he cannot just let the question hang in the air.

Probably the best way of coping with this situation is to say that there are (for example) three possible approaches, A, B and C; the implications of following A are D, E and F – and so on. But it is for them to choose which is best suited to their society, culture and present needs. As an outside well-wisher he has no right to express an opinion.

The identity of mediators

The majority of mediators are officials, either of various governments or of international agencies. Obviously only officials of non-involved governments can be mediators, as those from involved governments would be unacceptable to one side or the other. Even mediators from non-involved governments, though often conscientious and able, suffer one great disability. Everyone is aware that, when it comes to the crunch, they must follow the policy dictated by their own government, even though they may feel it is not in the best interests of those between whom they are trying to make peace. This may indeed not apply to the conflict they are mediating. What matters, however, is that people may believe it does – if not today, then perhaps tomorrow. So, however much an individual ambassador or other high official may be personally liked, s/he is likely to be treated, in such delicate situations, with reserve.

The same does not apply so strongly to mediators working for the United Nations (UN) or other international agencies. Nevertheless, even these come under suspicion in certain situations; for example, during the Zimbabwe war the UN was greatly distrusted by the government of what was then Rhodesia, and today it is little respected in Israel or Iraq – however hostile these two are to each other.

These 'official' mediators are probably a little more numerous than the second category of mediators: the unofficial, the citizen or 'second stream' (sometimes called 'Track Two') peacemakers. These generally comprise volunteer representatives of religious bodies, such as the Quakers, Mennonites, or Moral Rearmers; universities or other institutions having a scholarly interest in the study, analysis and resolution of conflict; and individuals who, for a variety of mainly humanitarian reasons, often couple knowledge of and concern for the people and culture of a particular area. Some of these may be particularly involved with some professional activity, such as medicine, but do their mediation, so to speak, on the side.

The advantage of the unofficial mediators is that they are obviously not bound by policies of their government or organisation. They are likely to be more free of timetable pressure (except perhaps academics, who must return to teach during the next term – however, I was given considerable latitude while teaching in universities). In addition, they may be more free to go to places forbidden to officials. For example, in an intra-state conflict, it may well be considered as a hostile act for a foreign official to contact rebels outside the country concerned or to visit the zones they control within it. Paradoxically, however, the regime concerned may be very glad for an impartial foreigner to visit places forbidden to potentially partial ones.

This latitude may pose problems for mediators. On their return from a visit to meet their contacts on the other side, they will be asked eager questions: How's the morale? Are the people well fed or hungry? Are there signs of war weariness? Is there much despondency? Did you see troops at A or B? How were they equipped? Clearly mediators must avoid answering questions on directly military matters, and it should not be hard to make polite excuses. But what should they say about the morale of ordinary citizens, about the mood generally, about food and other shortages, such as medicines? Almost any answer could affect military action. To say that morale seems to be low could be interpreted to mean that a ferocious new push would break it completely. To say that food is short might lead to intensifying the blockade and so to the deaths of many children. But who can predict the response to information? It could always contradict the purpose of mediation, complicating the situation and increasing the violence. It is perhaps safer to politely evade the questions and concentrate on analysing the possibilities for a just settlement.

These pages are obviously written from the point of view of the unofficial mediator. Finally, it must be made clear that the official mediators (who in the nature of things may often be arm-twisters more than mediators) are an essential part of the business of peacemaking. Major official agreements and the implementation of the terms of these agreements cannot be carried out without complex official operations. The unofficial mediators may establish the political and psychological *mise en scène*, but they cannot present it to the world as a fait accompli. Moreover, the officials who carry out their side of the operation often apply the same personal skill and sensitivity that one hopes – sometimes vainly – are possessed by the unofficial mediators. Indeed, the two should always be in close touch and, where possible, co-operate. In fact, in situations of strain and conflict, agencies should and usually do pool their resources in the service of peace. This does not mean that they should abandon their particular specialism, but in consultation with others discover how best to apply it in the particular prevailing circumstances.

How mediation starts

People involved in mediation are often asked how they got involved in what is often thought to be such strange, even exotic activities. If they are official mediators, the answer is of course simple: they were sent by their agency or ministry.

For non-officials, however, the explanation is more complex. Let us take a religious body or perhaps a non-governmental organisation (NGO) involved in development or humanitarian work. Here mediation may begin with one or two people who are concerned over the outbreak of violence in some country, perhaps, where they have worked. They alert their colleagues who may either decide that they cannot possibly get involved – there are no people available or no money or the situation is as yet too unclear; or else that it is worth further investigation. If the latter, local representatives of the groups concerned and the governments or opposition parties are contacted, as are friends who know something about the conflict. As a result, the church or NGO may decide on a more detailed on-the-spot exploration to determine whether an outside intervention might be fruitful; or whether, for example, there appears to be absolutely no toehold in the area concerned, no one who could give local help or useful introductions.

If, however, it is decided to move forwards, the first step is to consult those local representatives they have already met. It is very important to stress that no mention is made at this stage, or indeed at any other, of mediation. This would sound to many both pretentious and interfering: Who are these silly strangers who think they can do anything about our problems? Those problems are our concern and we can cope with them very well ourselves, thank you. No, the approach would be somewhat as follows: 'Our church (organisation or whatever) is worried about the suffering caused to your people by the present situation. We would like to know more about it so that we might be able to do something helpful.'

This is a perfectly sincere statement. Mediation might be out of the question, but not medical or other assistance to refugees or victims of the conflict. This offer will normally be received with gratitude. 'Yes, we would be delighted to welcome you. We think the situation has been unfairly and inaccurately reported in your media, and would be glad for you to see what is really going on, and grateful for your help.'

On arrival in the conflict zone, mediators set about arranging meetings with the main actors. This sounds perhaps difficult, but in practice it is usually accomplished fairly easily. The leaders, when they meet them, say much the same as their representatives in Europe or the USA.

When the mediators tell the leader that they plan to talk to his opposite number, he may approve and ask them, on their return, to report on the visit. He may even send some sort of message, perhaps to a former associate who is now a member of the enemy cabinet, or even a tentative proposal for reducing tension.

The mediators are, of course, eager to do as they are asked. With any luck, the other leader may reciprocate with a counter-proposal. And this may lead to a further round of visits. Eventually, without any mention of such ideas as mediation or negotiation, the mediators will find that they have worked themselves into a job.

Only in one case known to me have mediators of this sort actually been asked to arrange mediation. This was because the leader was aware from personal experience of the character of the organisation concerned.

Dangers for mediators

There is always some danger in working in a war zone. There is, however, a particular risk affecting mediators. In general, as has been suggested, leaders only tolerate the activity of mediators if they are prepared to discuss the possibility of peace. This means that they have in their minds (at least at the back of them) the recognition that they may have to give up one of their proclaimed principles – for example, that they will never, ever, give up a square metre of their sacred soil, even some useless stretch of uninhabitable desert.

But some of their people hold such rhetorical principles very dear. They see the work of the mediators as undermining their leader's resolution. They then decide that, rather than staging a coup and killing the leader, it will be simpler to murder the mediator. Half a dozen people known to me have suffered this fate.

Another danger may be encountered when working in an area such as a large city where both government and rebel spies abound. These tend to keep a constant eye on the comings and goings of people like mediators: Why are they going to this place? Why are they visiting that person? Are they possibly betraying information given them in confidence or acquired by malevolent guile? Are they playing a double game? Perhaps they should be disposed of. In these circumstances the actions of the mediators must be completely transparent. They must explain their motives, if feasible in advance; any failure of frankness, however incidental or forgetful, must be remedied as soon as possible. If not, the mediators' role may be tarnished and their usefulness eroded.

Time scale

Wars tend to drag on for years and because the essence of mediation is in the relationship between the mediator and the minister, the process of mediation may last for years. The popular idea of a mediator is a Kissinger (who was more of an arm-twister than a mediator) swooping from capital to capital until everyone is cajoled or bullied into signing an agreement that nobody really wants.

The facts of mediation, as presented here, are very different. The mediators may be around for years – five years is not unusual – keeping in close touch, watching for any political or military shift that could be exploited for peaceful purposes. Such a shift could be a military stalemate in which both sides, fearing they may lose or at least that they may not be able to win, are more inclined to negotiate than they were. But such lengthy assignments are not always desirable. Mediators may become stale or burn out, or indeed they may make some mistake that reduces others' belief in their integrity. The particular leader with whom they worked may die or be discredited; in the latter case, the mediators may be associated with his fall – in which case they might as well pack their bags. In general, however, mediators may expect a fairly lengthy commitment – interspersed, at times, by occasionally difficult and even dangerous travels between the contestants.

For this reason the work of mediators may become both lonely and tedious. They may wait days in an unappetising hotel for a promised phone call. Why, they wonder, did the leader not get in touch with them when he said he would; has he perhaps lost power, or faith in their integrity? The waiting becomes tense as well as boring. Even if they have a number of local friends, they must be careful how much they say about their work – and their worries. They are aware that they may be being watched by the leader's agents and any indiscretion, however innocent, may be reported to him.

Mediators, in fact, should not work alone. But how large should the team be? Experience tends to show that more than three is too many. If a group of four goes to visit some important personage, s/he feels that a speech must be delivered. Even three may evoke a formal response. Two friends who get on well and understand each other are perhaps ideal. They can together cope with the tedium and difficulties, discuss the meeting they have just had with the leader, assess the significance of what he said, decide on the next steps. They are aware of the importance of their mission. They have experienced the horrors and miseries of the war and are keenly conscious of their part, however minuscule, in trying to bring the suffering to an end.

The practice of mediation

At this stage the reader may think: 'OK, that's fairly interesting' (I hope) 'but what do these mediators actually *do*, what do they *say*?'

Hypothetical meeting of mediator with a leader

There follows a discussion between a mediator or mediators (M) and a leader with or without aides (L). This is a compression of a number of meetings in different places. It is not a transcript of one conversation, but a bringing together of scraps of discussions representing some of the main types of issue that in my personal experience have been of paramount importance.

We might imagine that the leader (L), a president perhaps, is talking to the mediator about his conflict with General X, the military ruler of a neighbouring republic.

L: *You keep telling me that General X is a reasonable man who wants a peaceful settlement to this conflict. But if that's what he wants, why the hell did he start it in the first place?*

M: *Excuse me, but his story is different. His version is that a company of your army invaded a strip of his territory. He says he sent a detachment to warn them to leave and to fire above their heads if they refused. The didn't obey and there was an exchange of fire which somehow got out of hand.*

L: *It was a flagrant act of aggression.*

M: *I really doubt if the Security Council would agree. But can we forget the past for a minute and consider the present? Here is a nasty struggle in which a lot of people have already died. Why not concentrate on stopping the fighting and then, when tempers have cooled down, think about the territorial issue? The UN would surely be able to help at that stage.*

L: *I refuse to have any dealings with X. He is completely untrustworthy. He has picked this quarrel with me because he wants what might seem a legitimate excuse for military action. I can't let him get away with it; there'd be no stopping his demands; he's as ambitious as Hitler, and look what he did.*

[M is well aware that L is very scared of appearing weak and in consequence losing control of his opposition, but he doesn't want to admit this. He wants instead to demonise X and thus increase his own domestic support.]

M: *I have been travelling around the country quite a lot recently. What I have heard convinces me that the people are horrified at what's going on. They hope you will refuse to let the fighting escalate. Several people told me that they would consider this a real show of strength, rather than allowing yourself to be dragged into what they consider a completely unnecessary full-scale war, which will quite probably ruin the country.*

[M and L both remain silent. M is worried that he may have spoken too frankly and strongly; L is torn by conflicting feelings. Eventually L speaks.]

L: *I don't know what to say. Of course my first feelings are for my people. I'm a democratic leader, as you know.*

M: *Of course.*

L: *So I will do my honourable best to bring the conflict to, at least, a temporary halt.*

M: *Are you referring to a ceasefire?*

L: *Well, yes. But I have doubts. I know that bastard and don't trust him farther than I could throw him. We have had rotten relations ever since he took over.*

M: *But if I may say so with all respect, it takes two to tango, and I am not sure that your relationship with him has always been very positive. From my last meeting with him, I gathered he felt much the same about you.*

L: *[Angrily] That's preposterous. Everyone in the world knows that I am a most reasonable and peace-loving man.*

M: *But this really only shows how our feelings become exaggerated under the pressure of conflict. It's what some people call the mirror image — we think about others in the same way as they think about us. It's very understandable, but not logically justifiable, and gets in the way of peace, creating obstacles that really don't exist.*

L: *[Stubbornly] Well, let's see. But going back to the idea of a ceasefire. If it worked, it would be OK, but how can we be sure he wouldn't cheat — use it to bring up more troops, improve his defences, and so on?*

M: *[Placatory] I'm sure you have some ideas about this.*

L: *Well, yes, I have. It could be monitored. [He then gives a list of nations he would not trust to be adequate monitors. He also mentions the UN as being biased in favour of X.]*

M: *Is there no nation you feel could do the job properly?*

L: *Can't think of any. But what about the Commonwealth — Canada, India and Fiji perhaps?*

Did this situation work out satisfactorily? No. After much hesitation and quibbling, L did go ahead with a ceasefire and a monitoring group, but he then did exactly what he feared his enemy would do. He chose as monitors not the Commonwealth or some other impartial body, but a group composed of his allies. This acted in such a manifestly biased fashion that international pressure, angrily aroused by the other side, forced him to withdraw it.

Mediator helps change perceptions

On one occasion the mediator saw a marketplace where 128 market women, mostly with babies on their backs, had been killed by a bomb dropped by a plane. When, after a difficult journey, he reached the capital of the other side, he told the leader, a young military man, of this horrible happening. This leader was shocked, but said: 'Well, some good may come from this terrible happening.'

'How so?'

'Well, the rebels will realise that these things inevitably happen in war, and could happen again and again. And so they will lay down their arms – they know I have offered them amnesty.'

The mediator answered: 'If I may say so, you have quite wrongly assessed their mood. They are now saying that this simply proves that you are waging a genocidal war – why else should your plane attack a group of market women? They are not a military target.'

The leader said that of course it was a complete mistake.

'But they don't realise that,' said the mediator. 'They are only aware of their loss – of their pain and anger. They say this shows you intend to wipe them all out and therefore they might as well go on fighting; then there's always the hope that a miracle will save them.'

He understood, and sent a new set of orders to his front line commanders urging restraint.

Evaluation

So how useful is mediation as described and defined in this chapter? Or, perhaps better, how useful are any combinations of peacemaking measures – negotiation, bullying, 'carrot and stick', arbitration, political pressure, economic sanctions, etc., for they usually become combined in various ways?

Many conflicts drag on interminably. The quarter of a century's duration of the 'Troubles' in Northern Ireland is no record. Perhaps most wars end militarily through defeat of one side by the other, or by exhaustion and collapse by both. But some are said to be beyond the possibility of military solution.

Nevertheless, some conflicts are resolved by a variety of combinations of factors. Compare, for example, the ways in which peace came to two African countries – Zimbabwe and South Africa. In these, violent conflict, political manoeuvring, international involvement and the raising of popular awareness in various ways all played a part, but differently. And so did mediation.

In South Africa very much of the mediation which brought about the amazing shift of consciousness was practised in small quite unofficial groups of people simply meeting and talking and illuminating each other. In Zimbabwe there was certainly arm-twisting, but there was also mediation as we mean it. This was less informal or widespread than in South Africa, but there were a number of individuals and small groups, representing usually religious organisations, moving between the government, the two wings of the Patriotic Front and leaders of neighbouring countries. Some of these were apparently very influential. One mediator received a letter from African leaders saying that he had kept alive the idea that, even in the height of conflict, peace must be continually sought. This, it was said, had helped them to maintain a peacemaking perspective.

In general it can be said that mediators keep at it; they are continually probing and searching for openings – of hearts and minds as well as for negotiable issues. Perhaps their work can be defined as largely educational. They explain the psychology of war and how people become irrational under stress. And that perhaps their enemies are behaving desperately because they are terrified rather than because they are mindless monsters – and indeed that the leaders whom the mediators are talking to are reacting in the same way. And that to threaten is not always a sign of strength, nor conciliation of weakness.

One war in which the mediators had tried to play this part for over three years ended in a miraculous reconciliation. It was feared that the end of the conflict would see a repetition of the massacres with which it had begun. But the victorious soldiers, instead of killing their defeated foes, embraced them, gave them food and money, and took them to hospital if wounded. The mediators were told that their work had helped to bring about this amazingly happy ending.

So, finally, we may be justified in concluding that this type of mediation has its uses. It wears the human face of peacemaking.

The Contributors

Mark Bitel is an evaluator and management consultant with Partners in Evaluation. He has been involved since 1993 in the development of peer mediation programmes, training peer mediators and designing evaluations to assess their impact. Mark is also a lead facilitator for the Alternatives to Violence Project, working mainly in prisons.

Sue Bowers has been involved in mediation since 1981. A founder member of Kingston Friends Workshop Group and of Mediation Dorset, she trained as a mediator in London and New York. She has been a member of the Executive and Accreditation Committees of Mediation UK. Currently a community mediator and trainer, her particular interest is in conflict resolution with young people.

Yvonne Craig is a retired social worker, counsellor and magistrate. She is the founder and co-ordinator of the multicultural Elder Mediation Project and also helped to found Mediation UK. She is author of *Elder Abuse and Mediation* (1997) and editor of *Changes and Challenges in Later Life* (1997) and *Advocacy, Counselling and Mediation in Casework* (1998). She has a doctorate in mediation.

Adam Curle has had a long academic career including chairs in psychology, education and development at the universities of Exeter, Ghana and Harvard, as well as many visiting appointments. He was the first professor of peace studies at Bradford University. He has also worked on problems of poverty and lethal violence, and for the last 30 years as a mediator in Africa, Asia and Europe, recently in ex-Yugoslavia. He is a Fellow of the American Academy of Arts and Sciences and has been nominated for the Nobel Peace Prize.

Hally Ingram is an external affairs adviser at Shell International. Before joining Shell, she was manager of Mediation and Facilitation Services at the Environment Council.

Elizabeth Lawrence taught for over 20 years in the UK, Papua New Guinea and the USA, and was an advisory teacher for multi-ethnic education in London. She currently works as a freelance mediator and consultant/trainer in assertiveness training, conflict resolution skills and mediation, the latter with young people and adults. She has published several articles and teaching packs in these areas. She also works as a volunteer mediator with Edinburgh Community Mediation Service.

Marian Liebmann has worked in education, art therapy, victim support and probation, and has been involved in community, victim–offender and schools mediation. For eight years she worked for Mediation UK, the umbrella organisation for mediation, as director and projects adviser. She has written/edited seven books in the fields of art therapy, mediation and conflict resolution, and contributed chapters to many others. She currently divides her time between freelance mediation training, art therapy, supervision and writing.

Guy Masters is currently part of the Referral Order Evaluation Team based in the Public Policy Research Unit at Goldsmiths College, London. He has provided training and consultancy support to a large number of Youth Offending Teams and compiled the Youth Justice Board's National Guidance on Restorative Justice. From January 2001 he will join the Restorative Justice Working Group at the Australian National University, Canberra.

Paul Newman, MA (Cantab), FCIArb, is a barrister and construction lawyer with Cardiff solicitors, Hugh James Ford Simey. He is a fellow of the Chartered Institute of Arbitrators and an accredited adjudicator and mediator. He has lectured widely on ADR and contributed to several books on the subject as well as on other legal topics.

Francis Noonan has worked for ACAS for many years and is currently director of Operational Policy.

Carl Reynolds is a freelance community, workplace and environmental facilitator and mediator. He was chair of Mediation UK from 1998 to 1999, and in 1999 worked on the establishment of a Joint Mediation Council covering all mediation sectors. Carl has trained hundreds of mediators and worked with a variety of organisations on processes that minimise the destructive effects of conflict and maximise the positive.

Ann Warner Roberts is a researcher and advocate at the Center for Restorative Justice and Peacemaking at the University of Minnesota, USA, working on the development of restorative justice, including victim–offender mediation, group conferencing and circle sentencing. She is also a consultant and practitioner with Dakota County Community Corrections in Minnesota. She spent five years in the UK, working on a cross-national victim–offender mediation research project.

Delia Rolls has worked at Sacred Heart RC Secondary School in Camberwell, London since 1986. For the past eight years she has held the position of school counsellor and co-ordinator of the school's conflict resolution programme.

Roger Sidaway is an independent research and policy consultant, and honorary research fellow at the Institute of Ecology and Resource Management, University of Edinburgh. He specialises in environmental conflict resolution and public participation studies, undertaken for government organisations in Britain and the Netherlands.

Marion Stevenson has mediated for the Oxfordshire Family Mediation Service (affiliated to National Family Mediation) since 1989. She is accredited by the Legal Aid Board. She works as a professional practice consultant for the Family Mediators Association. She helped to found Oxford Community Mediation and was Chair of this service until May 1999. She is also a conciliator for the Oxfordshire Health Authority.

Graham Waddington was co-ordinator of Cardiff Mediation Service from 1996 to 1999. He is now Senior Lecturer in Mediation Studies at Newport College (Gwent), University of Wales, and also works freelance.

Marion Wells has six years' experience as a lay conciliator with Avon Health Authority, and was previously involved with the old complaints procedure and a member of Bristol Community Health Council. She is a practising mediator and a qualified trainer in mediation, advice-giving and counselling skills. She worked for 20 years for the National Citizens Advice Bureaux, and for five years chaired Bristol Mediation, a community mediation service. She currently chairs Mediation UK's accreditation committee.

Jean Wynne has been co-ordinator of the West Yorkshire Probation Service Victim–Offender Unit in Leeds since 1987, and provides training and consultancy for new victim–offender mediators and services across the UK. She has published research on mediation and reconviction rates, and visited the USA to research differences in practice. She is a founder member of Mediation UK's Mediation and Reparation Committee and former vice chair of Mediation UK.

Deborah Boersma Zondervan has a master's degree from Western Michigan University in interpersonal and small group communication. She trained as a mediator in 1987, and was executive director of the Dispute Center of West Michigan from 1991 to 1999. She currently trains, writes and mediates on a freelance basis, providing training in mediation and conflict resolution skills for local businesses, schools and non-profit agencies.

Further reading

General

Acland, A. (1990) *A Sudden Outbreak of Common Sense*. London: Hutchinson.

Acland, A (1995) *Resolving Disputes Without Going to Court: A Consumer's Guide to Alternative Dispute Resolution*. London: Century.

Beer, J.E. (1997) *The Mediator's Handbook*. Philadelphia: Friends Suburban Project. (Available in UK from Jon Carpenter Publishing, The Spendlove Centre, Charlbury, Oxfordshire; Quaker Bookshop, Friends House, 173–177 Euston Road, London NW1 2BJ. Tel: 020-7663 1031.)

Bush, R.A.B. and Folger, J.P. (1994) *The Promise of Mediation*. San Francisco: Jossey-Bass.

Cornelius, H. and Faire, S. (1989) *Everyone Can Win: How to Resolve Conflict*. Sydney: Simon and Schuster.

Liebmann, M. (ed.) (1996) *Arts Approaches to Conflict*. London: Jessica Kingsley Publishers.

Lord Chancellor's Department (1995) *Resolving Disputes Without Going to Court*. London: Lord Chancellor's Department.

Macfarlane, J. (ed.) (1997) *Rethinking Disputes: The Mediation Alternative*. London: Cavendish.

Mediation UK (1998) *Practice Standards (for mediators and management of mediation services)*. Bristol: Mediation UK.

Moore, C. (1986) *The Mediation Process: Practical Strategies for Resolving Conflict*. San Francisco: Jossey-Bass.

Ross, M.R. (1993) *The Management of Conflict*. New Haven CT: Yale University Press.

Stewart, S. (1997) *Conflict Resolution: A Foundation Guide*. Winchester: Waterside Press.

Family Mediation

Ellis, D. and Stuckless, N. (1996) *Mediating and Negotiating Marital Conflicts*. London: Sage.

Fisher, T. (1997) *National Family Mediation Guide to Separation and Divorce: The Complete Handbook for Managing a Fair and Amicable Divorce*. London: Vermilion.

Garlick, H. (1999) *The Which? Guide to Divorce*. London: Consumers' Association and Hodder and Stoughton. (Important to consult the current edition in view of changes in divorce and family law.)

Haynes, J. (1993) *Fundamentals of Family Mediation*. Horsmonden: Old Bailey Press.

National Family Mediation (1994) *Giving Children a Voice in Mediation*. London: National Family Mediation. (for address see page 243.)

Parkinson, L. (1997) *Family Mediation*. London: Sweet and Maxwell.

Roberts, M. (1997) *Mediation in Family Disputes: Principles of Practice*, 2nd edn. Aldershot: Arena.

UK College of Family Mediators (1999) *UK College of Family Mediators Directory and Handbook 1999/2000*. London: Sweet and Maxwell.

Williams, M. (1998) *Mediation – Why People Fight and How to Help Them Stop*. Dublin: Poolbeg Press.

School/Young People Mediation

Broadwood, J. and Carmichael, H. (1996) *Tackling Bullying: Conflict Resolution with Young People*. London: Learning Design. (Available from Leap Confronting Conflict, see p.244.)

Cohen, R. (1995) *Students Resolving Conflict: Peer Mediation in Schools*. Glenview IL: GoodYearBooks. (Available from Quaker Bookshop, Friends House, 173–177 Euston Road, London NW1 2BJ. Tel: 020-7663 1031.)

Fine, N. and Macbeth, F. (1992) *Playing with Fire: Training for the Creative Use of Conflict.* Leicester: Youth Work Press. (Available from Leap Confronting Conflict, see p.244.)

Kingston Friends Mediation (1996) *Ways and Means Today.* Kingston-upon-Thames: Kingston Friends Mediation. (Available from Kingston Friends Mediation, 78 Eden Street, Kingston-upon-Thames, Surrey KT1 1DJ. Tel/fax: 020-8547 1197.)

Kingston Friends Mediation (1996) *Video: Step by Step* (towards resolving bullying). Kingston: Kingston Friends Mediation.

Lampen, J. (1992) *The Peace Kit – Everyday Peacemaking for Young People.* London: Quaker Home Service. (Available from Quaker Bookshop, Friends House, 173–177 Euston Road, London NW1 2BJ. Tel: 020-7663 1031.)

Mediation UK (1998) *Mediation Works! Conflict Resolution and Peer Mediation Manual for Secondary Schools and Colleges.* Bristol: Mediation UK. (for address, see p.244.)

Smith, V., Major, M. and Mnatzaganian, N. (1995) *Peer Mediation Scheme* (for junior and middle schools.) Bristol: Bristol Mediation (Available from Bristol Mediation at Mediation UK address.)

Stacey, H. and Robinson. P. (1997) *Lets Mediate.* Bristol: Lucky Duck.

Tyrrell, J. and Farrell, S. (1995) *Peer Mediation in Primary Schools.* Londonderry: Centre for the Study of Conflict. (Available from the EMU Promoting School Project, Magee College, University of Ulster, Northland Road, Londonderry, Northern Ireland BT48 7JL.Tel: 02871-375225. Fax: 02871-37550.)

Community Mediation

Augsburger, D. (1992) *Conflict Mediation Across Cultures.* Louisville KY: Westminster/John Knox Press.

Dignan, J. and Sorsby, A. (1999) *Resolving Neighbour Disputes through Mediation in Scotland.* Edinburgh: Scottish Office Central Research Unit.

Dignan, J., Sorsby, A. and Hibbert, J. (1996) *Neighbour Disputes: Comparing the Cost-effectiveness of Mediation and Alternative Approaches.* Sheffield: Centre for Criminological and Legal Research, University of Sheffield.

Fitzduff, M. (1989) *Community Conflict Skills: A Handbook for Anti-Sectarian Work in Northern Ireland,* 3rd edn. Belfast: Community Relations Council.

Liebmann, M. (ed.) (1998) *Community and Neighbour Mediation.* London: Cavendish.

Mediation UK (1995) *Training Manual in Community Mediation Skills.* Bristol: Mediation UK. (for address, see p.244.)

Mediation UK (1996) *Community Mediation Video.* Bristol: Mediation UK.

Victim–Offender Mediation

Bazemore, G. and Walgrave, L. (eds) (1999) *Restorative Juvenile Justice: Repairing the Harm of Youth Crime.* Monsey NY: Willow Tree Press.

Consedine, J. (1995) *Restorative Justice: Healing the Effects of Crime.* Lyttleton, New Zealand: Ploughshares Publications.

Galaway, B. and Hudson, J. (eds) (1996) *Restorative Justice: International Perspectives.* Monsey NY: Criminal Justice Press; Amsterdam: Kluger.

Hudson, J., Morris, A., Maxwell, G. and Galaway, B. (1996) *Family Group Conferences: Perspectives on Policy and Practice.* Annandale, NSW: The Federation Press.

Marshall, T. (1999) *Restorative Justice: An Overview.* London: Home Office.

Marshall, T. and Merry, S. (1990) *Crime and Accountability.* London: HMSO.

Roberts, A. and Masters, G. (1998) *Group Conferencing: Restorative Justice in Practice.* Minneapolis: Centre for Restorative Justice and Mediation. (School of Social Work, University of Minnesota, Minneapolis MN, USA. Fax 612-625 8224. E-mail ctr4rjm@che2.che.umn.edu. Also available on web site: http://ssw.che.umn.edu/ctr4rjm)

Mediation UK (1993) *Victim Offender Mediation Guidelines for Starting a Service*. Bristol: Mediation UK. (for address, see p.245.)

Quill, D. and Wynne, J. (1993) *Victim and Offender Mediation Handbook*. London: Save the Children. (Available from Mediation UK, see p.245.)

Standards in Restorative Justice (SINRJ) (1998) *Standards for Restorative Justice*. London: Restorative Justice Consortium. (for address, see p.245.)

Umbreit, M. (1994) *Victim Meets Offender: The Impact of Restorative Justice and Mediation*. Monsey NY: Criminal Justice Press.

Van Ness, D. and Strong, K.H. (1997) *Restoring Justice*. Cincinnati OH: Anderson.

Wright, M. (1996) *Justice for Victims and Offenders*, 2nd edn. Winchester: Waterside Press.

Wright, M. (1999) *Restoring Respect for Justice*. Winchester: Waterside Press.

Youth Justice Board (1999) *Guidance for the Development of Effective Restorative Practice with Young Offenders*. London: Home Office.

Zehr, H. (1990) *Changing Lenses*. Scottsdale PA and Waterloo, Ontario: Herald Press. (Available from London Mennonite Centre, 14 Shepherds Hill, Highgate, London N6 5AQ. Tel: 020-8340 8775. Fax: 020-8341 6807. E-mail: metanoia@menno.org.uk)

Some of the non-UK books in this section are available from Blackstone Press, London.

Employment and Workplace Mediation

ACAS (Library Enquiry Desk: see p.247)

Crawley, J. (1992) *Constructive Conflict Management*. London: Nicholas Brealey.

Findlay, Z. and Reynolds, C. (1997) *The Workplace Mediation Manual*. London: Hill Top Publishing, 207 Waller Road, London SE14 5LX. Tel/fax 0171-652 6467.

Laurance, L. and Radford, A. (1997) *Dealing with Disputes in Voluntary Organisations: An Introduction*. London: National Council for Voluntary Organisations. (for address, see p.246.)

Commercial Mediation

Academy of Experts (1992) *Members Handbook*. London: Academy of Experts.

Brown, H. and Marriott, A. (1993) *ADR – Principles and Practice*. London: Sweet and Maxwell.

Coulson, R. (1984) *Professional Mediation of Civil Disputes*. New York: American Arbitration Association.

Genn, H. (1999) *Mediation in Action*. London: Calouste Gulbenkian Foundation.

Hibberd, P. and Newman, P. (1999) *ADR and Adjudication in Construction Contracts*. Oxford: Blackwell.

Mackie, K.J. (ed.) (1991) *A Handbook of Dispute Resolution – ADR in Action*. London: Routledge.

Mackie, K.J., Miles, D. and Marsh, W. (1995) *Commercial Dispute Resolution – An ADR Practice Guide*. London: Butterworths.

Noone, M. (1996) *Mediation*. London: Cavendish.

Smith, R. (ed.) (1996) *Achieving Civil Justice: Appropriate Dispute Resolution for the 1990s*. London: Legal Action Group.

Stone, M. (1998) *Advising Clients in ADR*. London: Butterworths.

Lord Woolf (1995/1996) *Access to Justice*. Interim and final reports to the Lord Chancellor on the Civil Justice System in England and Wales. London: HMSO.

York, S. (1996) *ADR*. London: FT Law and Training (now LLP).

Medical Mediation

Health Select Committee (1999) *Sixth Report of the Select Committee on Health*. London: The Stationery Office.

NHS Executive (1996) *Complaints Guidance Pack for General Medical/Dental Practitioners*. London: NHS Executive.

Elder Mediation

Craig, Y. (1997) *Elder Abuse and Mediation*. Aldershot: Avebury.

Craig, Y. (ed.) (1997) *Changes and Challenges in Later Life*. London: Third Age Press.

Craig, Y. (ed.) (1998) *Advocacy, Counselling and Mediation in Casework*. London: Jessica Kingsley Publishers.

Environmental Mediation

Acland, A., Hyam, P. and Ingram, H. (1999) *Guidelines for Stakeholder Dialogue – A Joint Venture*. A partnership between the Environment Council and Shell International Ltd. (Available from the Environment Council, see p.249.)

Baines, J. and Ingram, H. (1995) *Beyond Compromise: Building Consensus in Environmental Planning and Decision Making*. London: Environment Council.

Bishop, J. (1999) *Consultation: The How To Guide*. Brighton: National Association of Clean Air, 136 North Street, Brighton BN1 1RG. Tel: 01273-326313. Fax: 01273-735802. E-mail: admin@nsca.org.uk

Healey, P. (1997) *Collaborative Planning*. Basingstoke: Macmillan.

Sidaway, R. (1998) *Good Practice in Rural Development No 5: Consensus Building*. Edinburgh: Scottish Office Central Research Unit. (Available from The Stationery Office Bookshop, 71 Lothian Road, Edinburgh EH3 9AZ. Tel: 0131-622 7050. Fax 0131-622 7017.)

Wilcox, D. (1994) *The Guide to Effective Participation*. Brighton: Partnership Books.

International Mediation

Azar, E. and Burton, J. (1986) *International Conflict Resolution: Theory and Practice*. Brighton: Wheatsheaf Books.

Curle, A. (1990) *Tools for Transformation*. Stroud: Hawthorn Press.

Ignatieff, M. (1993) *Blood and Belonging: Journeys Into the New Nationalism*. London: Chatto and Windus.

Kriesberg, L. (1992) *International Conflict Resolution*. New Haven CT: Yale University Press.

Lederach, J.P. (1995) *Preparing for Peace: Conflict Transformation Across Cultures*. Syracuse: Syracuse University Press.

Miall, H., Ramsbotham, O. and Woodhouse, T. (1999) *Contemporary Conflict Resolution*. Cambridge: Polity Press.

Mitchell, C.R. (1989) *The Structure of International Conflict*. London: Macmillan.

Ross, M.H. (1993) *The Culture of Conflict*. New Haven CT: Yale University Press.

Williams, S. and S. (1994) *Being in the Middle by Being at the Edge: Quaker Experience of Non-official Political Mediation*. London: Quaker Peace & Service. (for address, see p.244.)

Acknowledgements

I would like to acknowledge the help of the following in compiling this book list: Andrew Acland, Jeff Bishop, Centre for Dispute Resolution, Yvonne Craig, Alison Crowther, The Environment Council, Simon Fisher, Mediation UK, National Council for Voluntary Organisations, National Family Mediation, NHS Executive, Paul Newman, Responding to Conflict, Marion Wells and Martin Wright.

National Mediation Organisations in the UK

This list includes some of the main national mediation organisations in the UK.

Family Mediation

Family Mediators Association (FMA)

46 Grosvenor Gardens
London SW1W 0EB
Tel: 020-7881 9400
Fax: 020-7881 9401
E-mail: fmassoc@globalnet.co.uk
Web site: www.familymediators.co.uk
Trains family mediators from legal and counselling backgrounds, and keeps list of mediators working in the independent and legal sectors.

Family Mediation Scotland (FMS)

127 Rose Street South Lane
Edinburgh EH2 4BB
Tel: 0131-220 1610
Fax: 0131-220 6895
E-mail: info@familymediationscotland.org.uk
Web site: www.familymediationscotland.org.uk
Umbrella organisation for local not-for-profit family mediation services in Scotland.

National Family Mediation (NFM)

9 Tavistock Place
London WC1H 9SN
Tel: 020-7383 5993
Fax: 020-7383 5994
E-mail: general@nfm.org.uk
Web site: www.nfm.u-net.com
Umbrella organisation for local not-for-profit family mediation services in England, Wales and Northern Ireland.

UK College of Family Mediators

24–32 Stephenson Way
London NW1 2HX
Tel: 020-7391 9162
Fax: 020-7391 9165
E-mail: ukcfm@btclick.com
Web site: www.ukcfm.co.uk
Sets, promotes and maintains standards of professional conduct and training for those practising family mediation. Has register of qualified family mediators.

School/ Young People Mediation

European Network for Conflict Resolution in Education (ENCORE)
Quaker Peace & Service
Friends House
173–177 Euston Road
London NW1 2BJ
Tel: 020-7663 1087
Fax: 020-7663 1049
E-mail: valeriec@quaker.org.uk
Web site: www.quaker.org.uk
Networking organisation providing information on conflict resolution and mediation in education.

Leap Confronting Conflict
8 Lennox Road
Finsbury Park
London N4 3NW
Tel: 020-7272 5630
Fax: 020-7272 8405
E-mail: info@leaplinx.com
Web site: www.leaplinx.com
Training in conflict resolution and mediation for young people.

Mediation UK
Alexander House
Telephone Avenue
Bristol BS1 4BS
Tel: 0117-904 6661
Fax: 0117-904 3331
E-mail: enquiry@mediationuk.org.uk
Web site: www.mediationuk.org.uk
Umbrella organisation for many of the school mediation projects in the UK.

Young Mediators Network
c/o Leap Confronting Conflict
See address above
Support network for young (13–25) mediators, conflict resolvers and peer educators, designed and led by young people.

Community Mediation

Mediation UK
Alexander House
Telephone Avenue
Bristol BS1 4BS
Tel: 0117-904 6661
Fax: 0117-904 3331
E-mail: enquiry@mediationuk.org.uk
Web site: www.mediationuk.org.uk
Umbrella organisation for most of the community mediation services in England, Scotland and Wales. Provides accreditation scheme for services.

Victim–Offender Mediation

Crime Concern
89 Albert Embankment
London SE1 7TS
Tel: 020-7820 6000
Fax: 020-7587 1617
E-mail: info@crimeconcern-se.org.uk
Web site: www.crimeconcern.org.uk
Provides training and consultancy in restorative practice and manages victim–offender mediation and reparation services.

Mediation UK
Alexander House
Telephone Avenue
Bristol BS1 4BS
Tel: 0117-904 6661
Fax: 0117-904 3331
E-mail: enquiry@mediationuk.org.uk
Web site: www.mediationuk.org.uk
Umbrella organisation for many of the victim–offender mediation services in the UK.

NACRO
169 Clapham Road
London SW9 0PU
Tel: 020-7582 6500
Fax: 020-7735 4666
E-mail: rob.allen@nacro.org.uk
Web site: www.nacro.org.uk
Crime reduction charity, runs and develops restorative justice projects and provides training and consultancy.

Restorative Justice Consortium
c/o Society of Black Lawyers
Room 9, Winchester House
11 Cranmer Road
Kennington Park
London SW9 6EJ
Tel: 020-7735 6592
Fax: 020-7820 1389
Email: national-office@sbl-hq.freeserve.co.uk
Website: www.restorative-justice.co.uk
Has membership of national organisations interested in promoting restorative justice.

Youth Justice Board
11 Carteret Street
London SW1H 9DL
Tel: 020-7271 3011
Fax: 020-7271 3020
E-mail: Helen.Powell@yjb.gsi.gov.uk
Web site: www.youth-justice-board.gov.uk
Provides development funding and guidance to many restorative justice (victim–offender mediation and conferencing) projects involving young offenders.

Employment and Workplace Mediation

ACAS

Library Enquiry Desk
Head Office
Brandon House
180 Borough High Street
London SE1 1LW
Tel: 020-7210 3911
Fax: 020-7210 3615
E-mail: library@libraryacas.demon.co.uk
Web site: www.acas.org.uk
Prevents and resolves employment disputes, and provides information and advice.

Mediation UK

Alexander House
Telephone Avenue
Bristol BS1 4BS
Tel: 0117-904 6661
Fax: 0117-904 3331
E-mail: enquiry@mediationuk.org.uk
Web site: www.mediationuk.org.uk
Many of Mediation UK's member services and individuals provide workplace and organisational mediation.

National Council for Voluntary Organisations (NCVO)

Regent's Wharf
8 All Saints Street
London N1 9RL
Tel: 020-7713 6161
Fax: 020-7713 6300
Helpdesk: 0800 2 798 798
E-mail: judith.moran@ncvo-vol.org.uk
Web site: www.ncvo-vol.org.uk
Provides access to mediation for voluntary organisations in dispute.

Commercial Mediation

Academy of Experts

2 South Square
Gray's Inn
London WC1R 5HP
Tel: 020-7637 0333
Fax: 020-7637 1893
E-mail: admin@academy-experts.org
Web site: www.academy-experts.org
Provides training and mediators for commercial mediation.

ADR Group

Grove House
Grove Road
Redland
Bristol BS6 6UN
Tel: 0117-946 7180
Fax: 0117-946 7181
E-mail: info@adrgroup.co.uk
Web site: www.adrgroup.co.uk
Provides training and lawyer-mediators (drawn from firms of solicitors nationwide) for commercial mediation.

Centre for Dispute Resolution (CEDR)
Princes House
95 Gresham Street
London EC2V 7NA
Tel: 020-7600 0500
Fax: 020-7600 0501
E-mail: mediate@cedr.co.uk
Web site: www.cedr.co.uk
Provides training and mediators for commercial mediation.

Medical Mediation

NHS Executive (National Headquarters)
Quarry House
Quarry Hill
Leeds LS2 7UE
Tel: 0113-254 5000
Fax: 0113-254 6088
Develops and collates policy in the areas of complaints procedures, conciliation and mediation.

Elder Mediation

Elder Mediation Project (EMP)
27 Ridgmount Gardens
London WC1E 7AS
Tel: 020-7580 9706
Provides information, training and mediation for situations involving older people.

Environmental Mediation

The Environment Council
Stakeholder Dialogue Project Team
212 High Holborn
London WC1V 7VW
Tel: 020-7632 0118
Fax: 020-7242 1180
E-mail: stakeholder.dialogue@envcouncil.org.uk
Web site: www.the-environment-council.org.uk
Provides training in stakeholder dialogue, facilitation and mediation around environmental issues.

Institute of Ecology and Resource Management
University of Edinburgh
King's Buildings
Mayfield Road
Edinburgh EH9 3JU
Tel: 0131-650 6439
Fax: 0131-662 0478
E-mail: Vikki.Hilton@ed.ac.uk
Provides training and advice in consensus building and environmental conflict resolution.

International Mediation

Conciliation Resources
173 Upper Street
London N1 1RG
Tel: 020-7359 7728
Fax: 020-7359 4081
E-mail: cr@c-r.org
Web site: www.c-r.org
Supports national and community-based initiatives for the prevention, resolution and transformation of armed conflict around the world.

Conflict, Development and Peace Network (CODEP)
6th Floor, Dean Bradley House
52 Horseferry Road
London SW1P 5AF
Tel: 020-7799 2477
Fax: 020-7799 2458
E-mail: karmstrong@codep.dircon.co.uk
Web site: www.codep.org.uk
Brings together non-governmental organisations, consultants, academics and donors to explore the causes of conflict.

International Alert
1 Glyn Street
London SE11 5HT
Tel: 020-7793 8383
Fax: 020-7793 7975
E-mail: general@international-alert.org
Web site: www.international-alert.org
Works to achieve just and peaceful transformation of violent conflicts worldwide.

Responding to Conflict
1046 Bristol Road
Selly Oak
Birmingham B29 6LJ
Tel: 0121-415 5641
Fax/answerphone: 0121-415 4119
E-mail: enquiries@respond.org
Web site: www.respond.org/
Training and consultancy in working with conflict and peacebuilding for non-governmental organisations worldwide.

Subject Index

Author Index